FIELDING
TRAVEL GUIDES

FIELDING'S
THE BAHAMAS

Fielding Titles

Fielding's Amazon
Fielding's Australia
Fielding's Bahamas
Fielding's Belgium
Fielding's Bermuda
Fielding's Borneo
Fielding's Brazil
Fielding's Britain
Fielding's Budget Europe
Fielding's Caribbean
Fielding's Europe
Fielding's Far East
Fielding's France
Fielding's Guide to the World's Most Dangerous Places
Fielding's Guide to the World's Great Voyages
Fielding's Guide to Kenya's Best Hotels, Lodges & Homestays
Fielding's Guide to the World's Most Romantic Places
Fielding's Hawaii
Fielding's Holland
Fielding's Italy
Fielding's London Agenda
Fielding's Los Angeles Agenda
Fielding's Malaysia and Singapore
Fielding's Mexico
Fielding's New York Agenda
Fielding's New Zealand
Fielding's Paris Agenda
Fielding's Portugal
Fielding's Scandinavia
Fielding's Seychelles
Fielding's Southeast Asia
Fielding's Spain
Fielding's Vacation Places Rated
Fielding's Vietnam
Fielding's Worldwide Cruises

FIELDING'S THE BAHAMAS

The Most In-Depth Guide to the Islands of the Bahamas

Rachel Jackson Christmas & Walter Christmas

Fielding Worldwide, Inc.
308 South Catalina Avenue
Redondo Beach, California 90277 U.S.A.

Fielding's The Bahamas

Published by Fielding Worldwide, Inc.

Text Copyright ©1994 Rachel Jackson Christmas & Walter Christmas

Maps, Icons, Illustrations Copyright ©1994 FWI

FIELDING WORLDWIDE INC.

PUBLISHER AND CEO	Robert Young Pelton
PUBLISHING DIRECTOR	Paul T. Snapp
PUBLISHING DIRECTOR	Larry E. Hart
PROJECT DIRECTOR	Tony E. Hulette
ACCOUNT EXCUTIVE	Beverly Riess
ACCOUNT SERVICES MANAGER	Christy Harp

EDITORS

Linda Charlton   Kathy Knoles

PRODUCTION

Gini Martin   Chris Snyder

Craig South

COVER DESIGNED BY	Digital Artists, Inc.
COVER PHOTOGRAPHERS — Front Cover	Jon Riley/Tony Stone Worldwide
Background Photo, Front Cover	F. Johnson/Sharpshooters
Back Cover	Ron Watts/Westlight
INSIDE PHOTOS	Bahamas Ministry of Tourism (pgs 71 & 111)
	Rachel Jackson Christmas (all others, © 1994)
AUTHORS' PHOTO	Gordon Christmas
MAPS	Geosystems

Inquiries should be addressed to: Fielding Worldwide, Inc., 308 South Catalina Ave., Redondo Beach, California 90277 U.S.A., Telephone (310) 372-4474, Facsimile (310) 376-8064, 8:30 a.m.–5:30 p.m. Pacific Standard Time.

ISBN 1-56952-010-0

Library of Congress Catalog Card Number

94-068343

Printed in the United States of America

Letter from the Publisher

In 1946, Temple Fielding began the first of what would be a remarkable new series of well-written, highly-personalized guidebooks for independent travelers. Temple's opinionated, witty, and oft-imitated books have now guided travelers for almost a half-century. More important to some was Fielding's humorous and direct method of steering travelers away from the dull and the insipid. Today, Fielding Travel Guides are still written by experienced travelers for experienced travelers. Our authors carry on Fielding's reputation for creating travel experiences that deliver insight with a sense of discovery and style.

Rachel Jackson Christmas and Walter Christmas present a unique perspective of this popular resort destination, The Bahamas. They've spent years personally reviewing each and every interesting hotel, restaurant and attraction in these islands to make sure you choose the right places on the right island. Their star rating system for The Bahamas is the standard by which all other guidebooks are judged. Enjoy your next trip.

Today, the concept of independent travel has never been bigger. Our policy of *brutal honesty* and a highly personal point of view has never changed; it just seems the travel world has caught up with us.

Enjoy your Bahamian adventure with the Christmases and Fielding.

RYP

Robert Young Pelton
Publisher and C.E.O.
Fielding Worldwide, Inc.

Fielding Rating Icons

The Fielding Rating Icons are highly personal and awarded to help the besieged traveler choose from among the dizzying array of activities, attractions, hotels, restaurants and sights. The awarding of an icon denotes unusual or exceptional qualities in the relevant category.

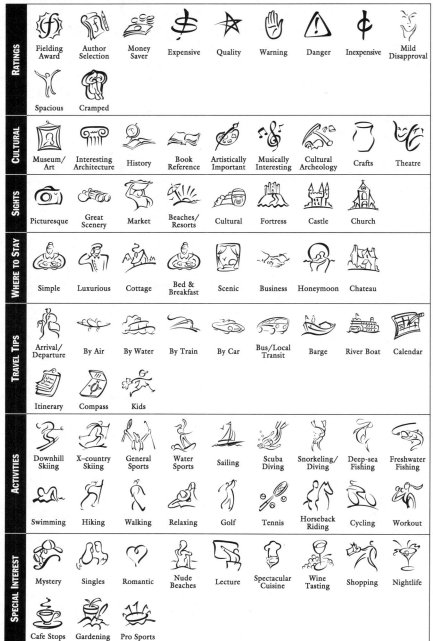

RATINGS: Fielding Award, Author Selection, Money Saver, Expensive, Quality, Warning, Danger, Inexpensive, Mild Disapproval, Spacious, Cramped

CULTURAL: Museum/Art, Interesting Architecture, History, Book Reference, Artistically Important, Musically Interesting, Cultural Archeology, Crafts, Theatre

SIGHTS: Picturesque, Great Scenery, Market, Beaches/Resorts, Cultural, Fortress, Castle, Church

WHERE TO STAY: Simple, Luxurious, Cottage, Bed & Breakfast, Scenic, Business, Honeymoon, Chateau

TRAVEL TIPS: Arrival/Departure, By Air, By Water, By Train, By Car, Bus/Local Transit, Barge, River Boat, Calendar, Itinerary, Compass, Kids

ACTIVITIES: Downhill Skiing, X-country Skiing, General Sports, Water Sports, Sailing, Scuba Diving, Snorkeling/Diving, Deep-sea Fishing, Freshwater Fishing, Swimming, Hiking, Walking, Relaxing, Golf, Tennis, Horseback Riding, Cycling, Workout

SPECIAL INTEREST: Mystery, Singles, Romantic, Nude Beaches, Lecture, Spectacular Cuisine, Wine Tasting, Shopping, Nightlife, Cafe Stops, Gardening, Pro Sports

WHY *THIS* GUIDE TO THE BAHAMAS

When you're on vacation or planning one, you don't have time for missteps. You want to know exactly where to go and what to do to make your trip as enjoyable as possible. You don't need an exhaustive list of everything there is to say about your chosen destination. What you do need is careful evaluations of the best the region has to offer.

Fielding's Bahamas by Rachel Jackson Christmas and Walter Christmas gives you just that. It is written by veteran travelers who share their personal experiences gained over many years of exploring these Atlantic islands. With an emphasis on little-known attractions, this book is designed for travelers who like adventure, new experiences and luscious scenery mixed with a healthy dose of comfort, good food and leisure.

The authors point readers toward the islands' treasures, including the most breathtaking sights, the best accommodations (from intimate inns and charming bed and breakfasts to lavish beach resorts), the least crowded diving and snorkeling spots, the beaches with the pinkest sand, the most colorful festivals and special events, the best local food and the most unexpected places to find serious pampering.

They guide vacationers to nature preserves where flamingoes flourish, natural wonders such as eerie ocean blue holes, dense forests and uninhabited offshore islands with delicious sandy coasts. They note the best golf courses, the most exciting personalized fishing expeditions, the best areas for sailing and the most unusual attractions, such as submarine rides and helmet diving.

For the convenience of readers, the authors rate sights, restaurants and hotels, and they highlight their personal favorites. They provide "Attractions at a Glance" lists as well as descriptions of each area and its sights. So that each annually updated guide can be as accurate as possible, the authors continually revisit the Bahamas.

ABOUT THE AUTHORS

For many years, **Walter Christmas** and **Rachel Jackson Christmas**, father and daughter, have been returning to the Bahamas. Their extensive travels in these Atlantic islands and throughout the world have given them special insights into what vacationers look for when they venture away from home.

Formerly an editor of fiction and general non-fiction at a major New York publisher, Rachel Jackson Christmas is an award-winning free-lance writer. Her articles have appeared in *The New York Times, The Los Angeles Times, The Washington Post, The Boston Globe, Is-*

lands, Travel & Leisure, Essence, Travel Holiday, Diversion and *Newsweek,* among others. Her work has taken her from Hawaii, Bora Bora, Moorea and Australia to Malta, England, Brazil, Costa Rica, Bermuda and the Caribbean, in addition to the Bahamas. She has lived in both Mexico and Spain.

A retired corporate public relations director, Walter Christmas has advised many Fortune 500 companies. He has also served as consultant to the Ghana Information and Trade Center, where he helped develop investment opportunities and tourism for that African nation. On business trips and vacations, he has traveled to Asia, Africa, South America, the Caribbean and most of Europe, and he has lived in Belgium.

The Christmases bring a two-generational perspective to *FIELDING'S BAHAMAS,* now in its twelfth edition. They pay particular attention to the lesser known hideaways, including natural wonders above and below the Atlantic. Their thorough knowledge of people, places and activities guides readers to unforgettable Bahamian adventures.

ACKNOWLEDGMENTS

Special thanks go to the Bahamas Ministry of Tourism.

The assistance and knowledge of the following people made an invaluable contribution to the book: Eileen Fielder, Erma Grant–Smith, Bert Deveaux and Nelson and Brenda Reynolds.

TABLE OF CONTENTS

LIST OF MAPS

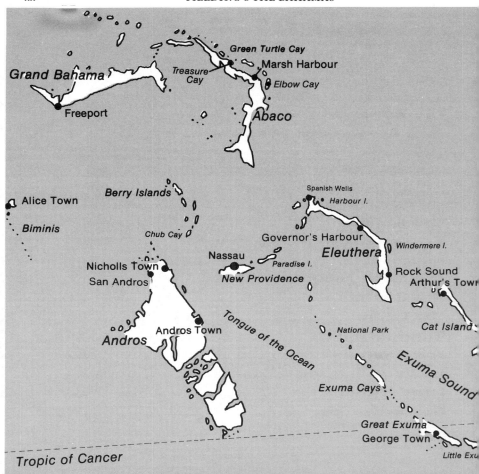

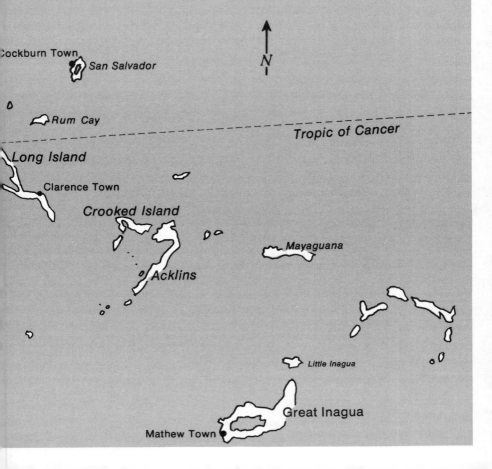

The Bahamas

ATLANTIC OCEAN

N

Cockburn Town
San Salvador

Rum Cay

Tropic of Cancer

Long Island

Clarence Town

Crooked Island

Mayaguana

Acklins

Little Inagua

Great Inagua

Mathew Town

WHAT'S INSIDE

RATINGS FOR SIGHTS AND RESTAURANTS

★ ★ ★   Excellent
★ ★   Very good
★   Good

HOTEL RATINGS

We have used a star-rating system to give you more information about hotels. These ratings are based on our own opinions as well as those of guests and residents of the islands.

☆ Hollow stars indicate comfort, variety and quality of facilities

★ In addition to all of the above, filled stars indicate charm, atmosphere, impressive decor and/or exceptional service

★ ★ ★ ★ ★   Top of the line
★ ★ ★ ★   Excellent
★ ★ ★   Very good
★ ★   Good
★   Plain or modest

No Stars: Guest houses or housekeeping units; low-budget hotels that have limited facilities and/or services; or accommodations undergoing major renovations or other changes at press time.

The **Accommodations Chart** at the back of the book includes basic information about the accommodations we describe and highly recommend as well as about other accommodations.

HOTEL PRICES

Unless otherwise indicated, the daily EP (no meals) rates of standard double rooms in season are categorized as follows:

Expensive:	More than $160
Moderate:	$90 to $160
Inexpensive:	Below $90

RESTAURANT PRICES

The following prices are based on the approximate cost, per person, of a full dinner. Lunch and breakfast will be about 15 to 25 percent less.

Expensive:	More than $40
Moderate:	$20 to $40
Inexpensive:	Less than $20

UPDATES

During our frequent trips to the Bahamas, we gather the most accurate and up-to-date information possible. However, hotels, restaurants and their menus, sights, airlines and cruise line schedules do change during the course of the year. We welcome any comments or suggestions about things that may have changed since our most recent visit or about the guide in general. Write to us c/o Fielding Worldwide, Inc., 308 South Catalina Ave., Redondo Beach, CA 90277.

Note that all prices quoted are approximate.

WHY THE BAHAMAS?

Bahamian waters offer divers spectacular vistas.

Beginning forty miles off the tip of Florida and sprawling across 100,000 square miles of water, the Bahamas chain—contrary to popular belief—is in the Atlantic Ocean, not the Caribbean Sea. It ends just north of Hispaniola, the island of Haiti and the Dominican Republic. However, since it shares much of its heritage and beauty with its southern neighbors, it is often referred to as part of the Caribbean. Independent from Britain since 1973, this archipelago is comprised of more than 700 large islands, smaller low-lying land-masses called cays ("keys") and landfalls hardly larger than boulders.

The nation's population of nearly 255,000 lives on only about two dozen of these mainly flat, coral islands.

The variety of vistas, breathtaking coastlines and different lifestyles is what makes the Bahamas special. From the international city of Freeport and its neighboring Lucaya resort to the pink sand beaches of tiny Harbour Island, the Bahamas offers a wide choice of vacation opportunities. With its many islands and cays, this country could take months of exploration. In the old days, mail boats often spent weeks completing the circuit of inhabited islands. Before the arrival of airplanes, these boats served as the local inter-island transportation for people as well as correspondence. Even today, some Bahamians and adventurous visitors still choose this leisurely, rough-and-tumble mode of travel.

Nineteen-ninety-two marked the 500th anniversary of Christopher Columbus' arrival in the "New" World. Bahamians are proud that this is where it all began. While historians disagree on exactly which island his first landfall was, most point to San Salvador, which today remains one of the least developed parts of the country.

Visitors looking for the excitement and conviviality of casinos, a vibrant nightlife and varied dining have Nassau and the adjoining Paradise Island, as well as Freeport. Some of the larger resorts here are quite self-contained and cater to guests not interested in exploring much beyond their hotels. Vacationers who do wish to get to know Nassau and Freeport during their stay can begin with bus or taxi tours available through hotels and the tourist bureau. Those with a more adventurous spirit can take tours on their own by using the local jitneys, or mini vans. Doing so can be fun and gives the flavor of what life is like for residents.

Vacationers seeking a slower pace, fewer fellow tourists and more serene surroundings should definitely consider visiting one of the Out Islands. Formerly called the Family Islands, these more reclusive spots are often striking in their beauty. They bring visitors closer to the natural wonders of the islands' land and sea and introduce them to people not jaded by the tourist trade that booms in Nassau, Paradise Island and Freeport.

DIVERSIONS

Attractions throughout the Bahamas include swimming, sailing, fishing (such as big game and bonefishing), diving, snorkeling, windsurfing and tennis. The best golf courses are in Nassau, Freeport, Eleuthera and Treasure Cay in the Abacos. Parasailing can be set up through hotels in Nassau and Freeport. Travelers whose idea of a vacation is to sit lazily on a terrace, read, sunbathe or beachcomb can find plenty of desirable hideaways for these quieter pursuits. Through some hotels and resorts, you can even arrange to spend a day "marooned" on a deserted island beach; you and a friend, well provisioned, can be left alone all day. If you like even more seclusion, consider staying on one of the private islands of the Exumas.

When you're ready to explore, the Bahamas can introduce you to countless empty beaches, old churches, mysterious ocean holes, plantation ruins, early Bahamian architecture, undersea caves and wrecks, spectacular marine life, lacy gingerbread manor houses, bird sanctuaries, salt flats, eerie pine forests, time-worn fortresses, international research centers, sun-drenched lighthouses, wild boars and much more. None of these sights is ever too far from the incredibly colored and ever-changing sea.

Through its popular People-to-People Program, the Bahamian government sponsors a means of getting acquainted with its citizens. This free program enables visitors to meet Bahamians, go to their homes and take part in local activities that would otherwise be missed by most tourists.

NASSAU AND PARADISE ISLAND

The best-known city in the Bahamas is Nassau, the capital. It is located on the island of New Providence, where more than 171,000 Bahamians live. In the past it was a playground for the international rich. Just before World War II, the Duke and Duchess of Windsor were in residence while the Duke served as Governor General. Their royal presence helped to attract the world's affluent, especially Americans. International conferences and meetings are frequently held in Nassau and foreign jet-setters, entertainers and politicians still find their way here to enjoy the beaches, posh hotels, secluded hideaways and casinos.

Nassau is also full of the nation's history. Visitors can explore the sites of both intact and crumbling fortresses and see legendary homes and monuments. They can wander through settlements such as Grant's Town, Carmichael, Adelaide and Fox Hill, founded by or for people who had been freed from slavery. Vacationers can bask on beaches where buccaneers once strolled and see rocky coasts where ships were deliberately wrecked for plunder. Around Christmastime and on New Year's Day, Junkanoo (an elaborate festival with roots reaching back to slavery) erupts throughout the islands. But nowhere is it as sizzling as in Nassau.

The shore makes a scenic locale for braiding hair.

For shoppers, Bay Street and some of its tributaries in downtown Nassau are full of stores with bargains in linens, woolens, china, crystal, perfumes, cameras and watches. The Straw Market offers a wide variety of "native" crafts. Bahamians often surprise visitors by their use of the word "native" to describe their food, crafts, music and some traditions. Visitors are cautioned not to use the word themselves in describing Bahamians, as some people consider it demeaning.

Nassau has enough restaurants to satisfy the dining whims of any visitor. The cuisine ranges from Continental to local, and from elegant to inexpensive and homelike. Settings run the gamut from seaside to the dining rooms of elegant former homes.

Connected to Nassau by an arched toll bridge, Paradise Island is a long, narrow sand bar dotted with hotels and restaurants, a casino and a variety of nightspots. Communities of condominiums and private homes also share the island. The beaches attract visitors from the island's hotels and condos as well as from Nassau.

FREEPORT/LUCAYA

Freeport, the second city of the Bahamas, has fewer hotels than Nassau and is less compact. It is located on the island of Grand Bahama, which has a population of about 41,000. Built during the sixties, Freeport lives in its dazzling present, making its history *now* since, unlike Nassau, it boasts very little evidence of its past. Carefully planned and landscaped, the city adjoins Lucaya, the beach area, merging as Freeport/Lucaya, with wide, palm-lined boulevards and gleaming white buildings. The island's main attractions are the casinos, one of which is entered through a domed, Moorish archway; the two shopping and dining plazas (the 10-acre International Bazaar and the waterfront Port Lucaya); and the Dolphin Experience, a program through which visitors can learn about and stroke Flipper's cousins.

Outside the central Mall and Lucaya beach area, there are some good restaurants appealingly set at the water's edge. Toward the West End you'll find settlements of local Bahamians whose families have lived on the island since long before an American, Wallace Groves, began its development. Wealthy individuals with a financial stake in the area have created tourist attractions such as the Garden of Groves, named for Groves and his wife, and the Rand Memorial Nature Centre. Oil refineries, pharmaceutical factories and other manufacturing plants give a glimpse of the day-to-day life of Bahamians not associated with tourism.

THE OUT ISLANDS

It's easy to find a Bahamian beach of one's own; Little San Salvador.

Except for some game fishermen, confirmed sailors and dedicated divers, most visitors know little of the Bahamas beyond Nassau, Paradise Island and Freeport. But away from those bustling tourist centers are the serenity, calm, and beauty of the Out Islands, where 42,000 Bahamians live and work in more sparsely settled communities. Some residents, young and old, have never been to Nassau, the country's capital. Still sometimes called the Family Islands, the Out Islands are largely undeveloped. Only a handful have tourist accommodations. Many are breathtaking reminders of Winslow Homer watercolors. They make no demands for activity, and you can organize your day or let it go to pot with no pangs of guilt.

Most of the islands have few large trees. The thick vegetation that stretches for miles between towns consists mainly of shrubs and bushes. The flat terrain of many of the smaller islands encourages walking when venturing out to explore and see the sights. You may come upon unexpected settlements, discover a small fishing colony or be awed by a natural wonder peculiar to the islands such as a cave, unusual flora or an inland pool teeming with sea creatures. You'll see chickens, donkeys, sheep and goats wandering freely through yards and on roads. Should you find nature too intimate, you can always flee to one of the islands' more up-to-date resorts with comfortable, often luxurious appointments and services for the less rugged.

Because Out Island settlements are small, it is easy to meet and socialize with locals, most of whom are farmers, fishermen, craftspeople, or service workers at resorts. With tourism a seasonal business, many islanders combine resort service with one or more other occupations. Some of the older people will say "God bless you" instead of good-bye. The numerous churches (there is at least one in even the tiniest of towns) are another indication of the importance of religion here. While the majority of people adhere to Christianity, on the more remote islands some still practice obeah, rooted in their African ancestry.

The buildings in the islands' settlements, formerly constructed of wood, limestone and coral, are now mainly of concrete block. You may see some that appear abandoned, with weeds, grass and shrubs growing within the windowless, roofless walls. These are homes in progress, which grow as their owners can afford building materials. When the house is finally finished, the owner is secure in an unmortgaged home.

Striking examples of colonial manor houses and native thatched-roof stone homes remain in some Out Island settlements. Others seem transported from New England, such as Dunmore Town on Harbour Island, Hope Town on Elbow Cay and New Plymouth on Green Turtle Cay. You can see outdoor ovens for baking bread in Gregory Town in northern Eleuthera. There are blue holes, caves and reefs to attract divers, including one of the longest reefs in the world. Many divers and snorkelers are stunned by the drama and beauty of Thunderball Grotto, off Staniel Cay in the Exumas.

GOVERNMENT

Now a member of the British Commonwealth of Nations, the Bahamas is a parliamentary democracy with a two-chamber parliament, an independent judiciary and a government headed by a prime minister. The British queen appoints the governor general. The first Bahamian-born governor general was appointed in 1977. In 1979, the government of the Bahamas celebrated its 250th year of uninterrupted parliamentary democracy.

ECONOMY

Tourism accounts for the greatest part of the Bahamian gross national product, about 70 percent. Oil and pharmaceuticals, based on Grand Bahama, are also important contributors to the GNP. Other significant areas supporting the economy are finance, based primarily in Nassau, and, to a lesser degree, fishing and agriculture. Bahamians pay no sales tax or income tax.

MUSIC AND FESTIVALS

Most of the music you will hear on the radio and in discos and night clubs will be calypso (sometimes called merengue), reggae and American pop or rock. One type of indigenous Bahamian music, played with goatskin drums and West African rhythms, is called "goombay." (The Bermudian version is "gombey.") The name has been adopted for the July and August "Goombay"festival, with its street dancing, music and other activities to attract tourists during the off season.

The biggest and most popular of the Bahamian festivals is Junkanoo, celebrated on Boxing Day (December 26), and on New Year's Day. As in pre-Lenten carnivals in the Caribbean, celebrants dance through the streets in colorful and fantastic costumes, masks and intricate and creative headdresses, blowing whistles and jangling bells, creating Junkanoo music. In Nassau, Bay Street truly comes alive during Junkanoo celebrations. The parade begins at 4 a.m., followed by a "boil fish" and johnny cake breakfast at 9 a.m. The origin of Junkanoo remains in dispute, but it was celebrated with a vengeance by enslaved Bahamians, whose only day off all year was the day after Christmas. It clearly has roots in West Africa, indigenous Indian culture and the American South, among other sources. Some say the name comes from a West African called "Jananin Canno," others, the American folk hero "Johnny Canoe," and still others, someone called *l'inconnu*, meaning "the unknown" in French. Whether this figure was a god, a slave, a Mayan Indian or an African prince, there is a move to develop Junkanoo into the primary Bahamian music. To see the range of costumes and floats that celebrate Junkanoo, visit the Junkanoo Expo on Prince George Dock in Nassau.

EATING AND DRINKING

"Jaws" bursts in on diners at a Grand Bahama restaurant.

The surrounding sea is the main source of Bahamian food. Chief among the varieties of fare available is conch, pronounced "conk" and said to be an aphrodisiac. High mounds of discarded conch shells indicate that the meat has gone into delicacies such as cracked conch (beaten and fried), conch salad (raw, with vegetables and lime juice) and conch fritters. You can watch fishermen on docks prepare scorched conch, eaten raw from the shell after being spiced with salt, hot pepper and lime.

Fish, especially grouper, which turns up for dinner, lunch and even breakfast, is also a staple, along with varieties of shellfish. Lobster is usually what Americans call crayfish. Minced lobster, a favorite, is made of shredded crayfish cooked with tomatoes, green peppers and onions, then served in the shell. Among other local specialties are crab and rice, okra soup, chicken and dough (dumplings), mutton, turtle steak, wild boar and souse (pig's feet, chicken, sheep's tongue or other meat in a savory sauce). By the way, if you see men eating souse or conch salad in the morning, chances are they're trying to kill hangovers; they say it's the hot peppers that do the trick. Lunch and dinner come with heaping portions of peas and rice, potato salad or cole slaw—sometimes all three. Mildly sweet johnny cake is often served on the side.

Don't let the various ways of preparing seafood confuse you. "Boil fish" (a popular breakfast item served with hominy grits) is cooked with salt pork, onions, green peppers and spices. Also eaten as the day's first meal, stewed fish is in a rich brown gravy. Steamed fish (which may sound bland, but is far from it) isn't eaten before noon and is cooked with a tomato base. Of course, you'll also find beef, lamb and pork, but they are imported and somewhat more expensive.

Guava duff, a rich and delicious dessert, is to Bahamians what apple pie is to people in the U.S.A. It is made by spreading guava jelly on dough, rolling it, boiling it for about 90 minutes, then topping the warm slices with a white sauce. Benny (sesame) cake is another popular local treat (the benny seeds are boiled with sugar). Coconut jimmy is chewy dumplings in coconut sauce.

Because most food is imported, it tends to be expensive. Restaurants serving Bahamian specialties can save you money and introduce new and interesting tastes. Salads and greens are not much in evidence, but you'll also discover such dishes as roti, curried chicken and plantain, inspired by Caribbean neighbors. For serious home cooking, stop by one of the fundraising cookouts and parties thrown for various causes on beaches and in the churches of Nassau and Freeport. Ask staff at your hotel or check local papers for details.

While local restaurants, especially in the Out Islands, stress traditional Bahamian fare, American and continental cuisines are available almost everywhere. Thirst is quenched with beer, beer and more beer, some of it imported directly from Germany and the Netherlands. The Bahamas now brews its own (high quality) brew, called Kalik (which is the sound cowbells make in Bahamian Junkanoo music). Fruity concoctions such as Goombay Smashes, Bahama Mamas and Yellowbirds, all with a rum base, are also popular drinks.

BUSH MEDICINE

Particularly on the Out Islands, many Bahamians are well versed in healing ailments naturally. The leaves, bark, stems, roots and sap of various plants are boiled for tea, injested raw, ground to make salves or slathered on as ointments.

Kermit Rolle, a taxi driver-restaurateur-farmer in the Exumas, learned about herbal medicine from his great-grandmother, a midwife. Though born into slavery, she lived to be 108. She would tell him horrible stories of her childhood encounters with the slavemaster. Her mother was very beautiful, and the master would beat her when she refused his advances or those of the overseers. Kermit Rolle's great-grandmother remembered a day when she clung to her mother's skirt in terror while the master whipped her mother all the way from Rolleville to Richmond Hill, two distant settlements. Sometimes the whip would catch the child as she tried to hide in the folds of her mother's clothing.

Enslaved men and women were forbidden to pick up anything that looked readable, and they had to be their own doctors. Thus, they carried on the tradition of bush medicine that their forebears had brought with them from Africa. Here are a few of the plants Kermit Rolle recommends for various problems:

- jack-me-dark bush for colds and fever
- cerasee for flu and coughs
- aloe for burns
- rooster comb bush for burns or sores
- love vine for "loss of sex power"
- breadfruit leaves for high blood pressure
- hard bark leaves for a severe headache

ILLEGAL DRUGS

You may hear some rumors about illegal drug traffic in the Bahamas. However, unless you make a point of searching out drug dealers, you are unlikely to be affected by whatever behind-the-scenes action there might be. During the late 1980s and early '90s, the Bahamian government came under attack by the United States (which certainly has its own drug problem) for not doing enough to control its borders. The Bahamas responded that, with so many uninhabited islands and so much coastline, putting an end to the drug trade here was a mammoth task for any government. The Bahamas has joined forces with the U.S. and the problem appears to be lessening.

DAYS GONE BY

IN THE BEGINNING

The earliest known Bahamians were Lucayan Indians (who named the island chain after themselves) along with Caribs and Arawaks. During his 1492 voyage to the "New" World, Christopher Columbus landed on either Guanahani (now San Salvador) or a smaller, more southerly island called Samana Cay. Eventually, the island group came to be known as Bahama, derived from "baja mar," meaning shallow sea in Spanish.

Caribs and Arawaks were the first people to be enslaved by the newly arrived Europeans. However, they proved too intractable. Not long after Europe became aware that these islands existed, the outsiders had succeeded in wiping out virtually all of the original inhabitants.

NEWCOMERS AND THE SLAVE TRADE

White settlers wanted another source of free labor, so in 1503 they began enslaving Africans who had been controlled by the Portuguese. Fifteen years later, Africans were being purchased directly from Africa's Guinea Coast and imported to the "New" World. Sir John Hawkins—a wealthy merchant from Plymouth, Massachusetts, who, ironically, was known for his strong religious beliefs—became the first recognized English slave trader.

By dribs and drabs, more Europeans settled in the Bahamas. In 1649, Captain William Sayle and 70 other Englishmen came to these islands from Bermuda in search of religious freedom. They brought a group of enslaved Africans with them and made new homes for themselves on the island known as Cigatoo among the resident Arawaks. Calling themselves the Eleutherian Adventurers, these settlers were later joined by Puritans from New England and they renamed the island Eleutheria, based on the Greek word for freedom. (Today this link in the Bahamian chain is known as Eleuthera.)

New Providence Island was settled in 1666 by a group of Britons, some of whom also came from Bermuda looking for a better way of life. The new colony was supposedly ruled from the Carolinas on the North American mainland, but supervision was lax and the remote Bahamas were pretty much left on their own. Near the busy shipping lanes connecting Europe with the "New" World, the Bahamas had become a lucrative haven for pirates seeking treasure. They found endless hiding places, entrapment areas and points of attack among the many islands and cays.

PROFITEERING PIRATES

Spain, in an effort to end these incessant and irksome raids on ships, took over the New Providence settlement called Charles Town, named for Britain's Charles II. However, Spain's occupation of the town was short-lived because with the aid of France, the new king of England soon expelled the Spanish. The settlement was renamed Nassau, after William III of Orange-Nassau, and later became the capital of the Bahamas.

Fierce pirates sailing Caribbean and Bahamian waters continued to keep settlers and their governors in turmoil. Chief among the marauders were Edward Teach, alias Blackbeard, and his cohorts, "Calico" Jack Rackham, Major Bonnet (a Frenchman) and the notorious women pirates, Mary Reed (who was eventually hung) and Anne Bonney, Rackham's mistress. The marauders were not driven out until the ruthless Captain Woodes Rogers was appointed Royal Governor of the Bahamas in 1718. In tribute to his feat, a statue of him stands before Nassau's imposing British Colonial hotel, and a waterfront road in this capital city bears his name.

LOYALISTS AND UPRISINGS

As the American Revolution came to a close, many of those loyal to the British king (called Loyalists) also left with people they had enslaved and settled in the Bahamas. Seeking a better life as well, Americans who had freed themselves from slavery found these shores. Between 1783 and 1789, the islands' black population tripled. Loyalists brought about such legislation as "An act for regulating and policing the town of Nassau and the suburbs thereof," which decreed that people of African descent were to live outside the city of Nassau and could not enter the town after sundown.

The only surviving journal from the Bahamas' days of human bondage was kept by Charles Farquharson, a large plantation owner on San Salvador. His chief crop was corn and his commercial crop, although in decline, was cotton. He also raised cattle, most of which was marketed to Nassau. The largest absentee slave owner in the Bahamas was Lord John Rolle. His father had emigrated from England to Florida in 1783, shortly after that southern U.S. region was acquired from Spain. When the American Revolution ended, Rolle gathered his slaves and moved to the Bahamian island of Exuma, settling in an area that is now Rolleville and Steventon. Once his holdings were no longer profitable, Lord Rolle deeded his land in Rolleville, Rolle Town, Mount Thompson and Ramsey to his slaves and their descendants, who then numbered over ten thousand.

About 1800, Vendue House was erected in Nassau as a convenient place for public auctions and sales of Africans. When enslaved people were not being sold, cattle and a variety of imported products were offered in the same fashion. Vendue House became a gathering place where merchants and farmers came for news, notices of sales (including sales of loot from wreckers) and to inspect the new arrivals. Now refurbished and transformed into the Pompey Museum and art gallery, two-storied Vendue House stands on Bay Street, a few paces from the British Colonial Hotel.

As in the United States, slave resistance and rebellions became a thorn in the system of servitude. Recorded slave uprisings took place in Abaco in 1789, Exuma in 1828 and 1834, Cat Island in 1831, and Watlings Island (now San Salvador) in 1832. Individual enslaved Africans defied their self-dubbed masters by feigning illness, refusing to work, being deliberately inefficient and absconding every chance they got.

EMANCIPATION

When Emancipation arrived in August 1834, newly liberated Africans in Nassau moved "over the hill" to establish settlements that remain today in Grant's Town, Adelaide, Gambier and Carmichael. They also went to Highbourne Cay, a tiny islet in the northern Exuma cays. Other settlements for freed Africans were built in such Out Islands as Long Island, Rum Cay, San Salvador and Ragged Island. However, they were unused to their new environment and were not prepared for farming in such shallow soil. Divided by diverse African cultures and languages, and not experienced in the overriding European governance, the residents of these settlements did not prosper.

MILLIONAIRES AND ROYALTY

Bahamians of African descent had become the country's majority population. Yet over the years, economic and political power remained in the hands of the minority of white residents. Beginning in the 1930s, millionaire developers such as Axel Wenner-Gren from Sweden, Sir Harry Oakes and Sir Stafford Sands from England, and Wallace Groves and Huntington Hartford from the United States all began to make their marks. The gap between the rich and the poor grew ever wider.

With the coming of World War II, through U.S. bases and growing defense production, the Bahamian economy began to boom. Britain's Duke of Windsor had abdicated the throne to wed Wallis Simpson, a divorcee from Baltimore. Despite his scandalous marriage, the business community was delighted when this member of the Royal Family was appointed Governor General of the Bahamas.

LABOR UNIONS AND THE BIRTH OF A NATION

U.S. workers were among those brought in as managers and laborers for the burgeoning economy. Although a minimum wage had been established, local workers were paid less. This led to unrest by black Bahamians who, in June 1942, expressed their displeasure through a civil disturbance in which businesses along Nassau's Bay Street were destroyed. The black population was no longer seen as a subservient group that would take whatever was doled out. This new view of Bahamians of African descent strengthened their political power. Bent on majority rule, black leaders formed the Progressive Liberal Party (PLP) in 1953.

When the new International Airport opened in 1957, taxi drivers were furious over the government's plan to provide low-cost buses to take tourists to hotels. Drivers parked their cars on roads leading to and from the airport, closing it down for several days. But the drivers' demands were not met and trade union leaders called a general strike. After three weeks, the unionists won. Bolstered by the surge in the power of workers, Bahamians joined black political parties in droves. You'll note that there is still no public bus service to and from the airport.

In 1961 men who did not own property were finally granted the right to vote, and women won the right to vote for the first time. Eight years later, the islands became a commonwealth nation and PLP leader Lynden Pindling became the country's first prime minister. Despite reluctance on the part of Her Majesty's government and resistance by the "Bay Street Boys" (the white businessmen who, in effect, ran the Bahamas), independence from Britain was gained in 1973.

After spending more than two decades at the helm, Prime Minister Lynden Pindling was defeated by Hubert A. Ingraham, of the Free National Movement (FNM) party, on August 19, 1992.

BAHAMIANS

Friendly schoolchildren "say cheese" in South Andros.

Today in the Bahamas, the British heritage persists, along with African, Caribbean and American influences, as well as traces of the cultures of Amerindians, the original inhabitants. In a country that is more than 80 percent black, it was not until 1956 that black Bahamians could legally patronize theaters, hotels and restaurants. The populations of several islands (Spanish Wells, Man-O-War Cay, and Elbow Cay among them) are still exclusively or predominantly white. However, it can now be said that Bahamians of all colors like to regard themselves simply as Bahamians. Some will assure you that animosities and prejudices based on race are behind them and that,

as a nation, they are moving confidently forward to a more enlight-
ened time.

With tourism the major industry, black people, historically the
poorest members of the nation, were once restricted to service jobs.
Since independence from Britain in 1973, increasing numbers of
black people have found their way into hotel administration and
management. Some have opened their own small hotels and guest
houses. Young Bahamians continue to leave the Out Islands, attracted to Nassau and Freeport by employment opportunities in the nation's largest industry.

CONVERSATING

When spoken by Bahamians, English, the national language, may
sound West Indian to some ears. But it actually has its own lilt, into-
nation, syntax and idiom. You'll hear accents ranging from somewhat British to those where the letters v and w are interchanged. "So
you wisitin', ay?" translates into "So you're visiting, are you?" Some
words even sound as if they were imported from Brooklyn: "woik" is
what you do "fuh" a living and a waiter will "soive" you.

If a Bahamian tells you he's going "spilligatin'," he means that he
is planning to "carry on bad." In short, he intends to "party," "paint
the town red," or have an all-out good time. If he says he'd like to
"conversate" with you a while, he wants to chat. Some Bahamians—
Harbour Islanders and people from Abaco, for example—add or
drop h's. Harbor becomes "'arbor" and the name Anderson becomes "Handerson."

OLD TIME RELIGION

The church plays a major role throughout the Bahamas. Representing the leading religions and their denominations, houses of
worship are very visible. Structures run the gamut from almost cathedral in size to one-room shacks. Great numbers of the smaller
churches are scattered throughout the poorer residential neighborhoods (and, ironically, there are often just as many bars). On the Out
Islands, no village or settlement is complete without at least one
church. Itinerant preachers travel from island to island for local services as well as large revival meetings. As in small towns of the American South, Sunday mornings bring the comforting sounds of hymns
and gospel. Some services are even held in the shade of trees by the
edge of the sea.

GAMBLING TABOOS

It is against the law for Bahamian citizens to gamble in the country's casinos. Some visitors have suggested that this restriction is paternalistic, that adults should be able to decide for themselves whether or not to risk their own money. However, most Bahamians seem to agree that the law is good, especially since the purpose of casinos is to bring in new money, not to recirculate Bahamian money. Besides, they add, Bahamians who want to gamble find other means: witness the many domino games, regattas and other sporting events where more than a few bets are placed.

MEETING THE PEOPLE

The free People-to-People Program, sponsored by the government through the Bahamas Tourist Bureau and with hundreds of volunteers, gives visitors unique opportunities to meet, socialize with, and get to know Bahamian families and individuals. As well as meeting Bahamians in their homes, visitors can participate in an array of local social and cultural events.

Visitors might be invited to activities such as performances of the local theater group, civic and sporting events, monthly teas at Government House and receptions not generally open to tourists. On several occasions, visitors have gained access to behind-the-scenes political events. What you do and see depends on you and your host.

Information about the People-to-People Program is available at the Bahamas Tourist offices on Market Square in downtown Nassau and at Prince George Dock. Other offices are on Rawson Square, just west of the fountain, and at the arrival and departure points of Nassau International Airport. In the Freeport/Lucaya area, you can make arrangements to participate at the International Bazaar tourist office. For Eleuthera, Abaco and Exuma, contact the Bahamas Tourist Office on those islands. People-to-People encounters on other Out Islands can be set up through the Bahamas Ministry of Tourism in Nassau. Especially for the Out Islands, it is best to make arrangements prior to your arrival.

PASSING FOR BAHAMIAN

If you're the kind of person who returns home to Kansas from a vacation in England speaking with a British accent, or who comes back from Sweden craving pickled fish and dying to lay out a smorgasbord, then you're a prime candidate for passing for Bahamian. You won't be able to resist trying the colorful, gregarious, proud, outspoken Bahamian personality on for size. It doesn't matter whether your ancestors were born in Africa, Europe or Asia—these islands are home to all kinds of folk.

A Bahamian will tell you that the country's three main ethnic groups are

- Black (of obvious African descent),
- Conchy ("conky") Joe (mostly of European heritage, but some may have blood relatives with African ancestors), and
- Long Island or Eleuthera Red (they might have freckles, reddish hair and blue or green eyes, but there's definitely some coffee in their cream).

No matter what you look like, follow these tips, and someone just might come up to you saying, "Who your people is? Wait—you're a Bethel, ain't you? Yeah! The second cousin of Miss Knowles' brother-in-law aunty that lives over by Veronica's store down the road. Sure, you the one that went to school in Miami."

- First you'll have to get the lingo straight. Trade your w's for v's (and "wice wersa") and you're off to a good start. When being formal with friends named Bill, call them "Villiam."

Give a tourist directions to your favorite "fishenin'" (fishing) spot. Let him know that the "onliest" people you share it with are folks you really like. When you see him later, ask, "Ya reach?" (You got there?)

- However, no matter how friendly you are, be sure to look off to the left or the right while you're talking to people, especially if they're strangers. Making too much eye contact is a dead giveaway that you're not really Bahamian.

- When you're angry at someone, be sure to make a show of not speaking to him or her whenever your paths cross. And don't forget to suck your teeth and cut your eyes with great ceremony.

- Wear clothing and carry bags with as many visible "designer" logos as you can muster. If you're a woman, be sure that your jeans are good and tight, no matter how ample your lower quarters.

- If you drive a car, do it on the lefthand side of the road. And be sure to pump up the volume of the reggae on the radio at least loud enough for you to feel the bass line from your toenails to your teeth.

- Don't do anything or go anywhere at a pace any faster than that of scuba divers beneath the Bahamas' translucent waters—unless, of course, you're driving. If it looks like you're in jeopardy of arriving someplace on time, be sure to stop off to "conversate" with a few friends along the way so that you arrive on BT (Bahamian Time—known in the United States as CPT, "Colored People's Time" or "fashionably late" among Caucasians).

- When you hear of someone who has "Brown Curtis" (bronchitis), "amonia" (pneumonia) or some other ailment, be sure to suggest that he or she try some bush medicine that has worked for you or someone you know.

- Don't act surprised if the way you learn of the death of a friend or relative is through a radio announcement. In the Bahamas, it's common for long lists of the dearly departed to be read over the airwaves so that people on even the most remote islands can get the sad news.

- If someone offers you fish and grits for breakfast, don't ask if he or she has just returned from Mississippi. Real Bahamians know that grits (ground corn) are a local staple, like conch.

- Speaking of conch, if you want to introduce a new food to the Bahamas (sushi, perhaps?), convince people that it gives men "strong back" (heightens male sexual prowess) and it could be all the rage—just like conch.

- You may not be able to make it to the Bahamas for Christmas, but be sure to show up in George Town, Exuma, in April for the annual Out Island Regatta.

- When you're low on funds—say you're trying to send your son away to school or your daughter needs her tonsils out—don't hesitate to throw a fund-raising "cookout" or host a cruise. As long as there is plenty of chicken, fish, macaroni and cheese, conch fritters, peas and rice, cole slaw—and music thundering from speakers— everyone will be happy.

PHOTO OPS

We're told of a man who went to a photo store to pick up several rolls of film he'd shot during a vacation spent sailing in the Exumas. He was among many who found these islands to be some of the most beautiful in the Bahamas. So he was disturbed when the clerk greeted him with a distressed look and began stuttering that he was terribly sorry, but that something had gone wrong, that the color in the pictures was way off, that perhaps the processing chemicals were bad or the customer had gotten hold of some damaged film. "I mean, look at that water," the clerk exclaimed as he showed the man his photographs. "A real ocean doesn't look like that!" But to the clerk's surprise, the customer burst out laughing with relief. The electric turquoise, navy, teal and peacock aquatic swirls were exactly as the vacationer remembered.

And it's not just the many hues of the ocean that look surreal in the Bahamas. Somehow, the fuchsia, lavender, orange and yellow flowers seem more intense than they should, the sky appears bluer, the fluffy clouds whiter. The sand comes in both chablis and blush, depending on what beach you're on. Varying shades of rich brown skin are set off by bright red t-shirts, white dresses and beige straw hats. From handsome cottages and serene waterways through mangrove marshes to weathered churches and eerie bat-filled caves, there are all kinds of photographic opportunities in the Bahamas.

A 12th-century French cloister stands in Versailles Gardens, Paradise Island.

You don't have to own a fancy camera or study photography to bring home some exceptional vacation mementos. Here are a few tips that can help amateur shutterbugs preserve those special moments:

- First of all, prepare before you leave: If your camera is new or has just been repaired, take a practice roll and have it developed before your trip. Be familiar with how your camera works so you don't miss great shots while fiddling with it. It's a good idea to bring your instruction booklet along.

- Pack more film than you think you'll need. It can be expensive in the Bahamas, and especially if you're shooting slides, the type of film you want may not be available (particularly on the Out Islands). Carry fresh spare batteries with you as well.

- Much of the Bahamas' beauty is all wet. If you don't have an underwater camera, consider buying or renting one, or purchasing one of the inexpensive disposable kind. They can come in handy while you're snorkeling or diving in shallow water.

- Before photographing residents, it's courteous to ask permission, unless you're shooting from a discreet distance. The problem with asking permission, though, is that you no longer have a candid shot. When we want a close and candid shot of a stranger, a trick we sometimes use is to have a companion stand near the intended subject. We pretend to shoot the friend, then we move the camera slightly and photograph our true target. Zoom or telephoto lenses can also be quite useful. You'll notice that children tend to be the most willing subjects. They often *insist* that you take their pictures.

- If you tell people you'll send them copies of the photos you shoot of them, don't forget to do so. Many Bahamians complain that visitors always take their addresses and promise to mail them pictures that never arrive.

- Whether you photograph people, animals or objects, make sure that your subject is framed properly and is close enough to be interesting. Many a person has ended up with a pole or a palm tree growing out of his or her head because a photographer didn't notice that the subject was in that unfortunate spot. And many a shot is wasted because the subject is too far away to be clearly seen. Also, before shooting, look around to make sure there will be no stray soda cans or other pieces of trash in the photo.

• Remember that your subject need not always be in the dead center of the shot. Play around with framing by putting the subject off to the side, if your camera will focus properly when you do so. (Some auto-focus cameras will focus only on what is in the center of the frame.)

• In the Bahamas, light is at its best and colors will be richest before about 10 a.m. and after about 4 p.m. However, shadows are long at these times of day, so be sure that the photographer's shadow isn't in the photo—unless you want it there.

• Except when going for silhouettes or an overexposed effect, the photographer should always shoot with his or her back to the sun.

• Above all, be sure to take the time to observe and digest your surroundings when not looking through your camera's lens. Many vacationers spend their trips clicking away, then can't remember exactly where some of the photos were shot once they get home.

CHOOSING YOUR ATLANTIC ISLE

A COUNTRY OF CONTRASTS

The Bahamas has the mellowed colonial charm of old Nassau contrasted with the young, modern city of Freeport, and the quiet natural beauty of the Out Islands, also called the Family Islands. In Nassau, you'll see flower-bedecked villas with walls overgrown with lush tropical foliage. Busy Bay Street, lined with stores, boutiques and restaurants, is the city's main thoroughfare. Cruise ships dock at Prince George Wharf, a stone's throw from bustling Rawson Square, where taxis and horse-drawn carriages await passengers. Historic sights, such as Government House and the gardens of the nineteenth-century Royal Victoria Hotel, are within walking distance of the square. A short public bus ride or a stroll from downtown Nassau takes you to the bridge to Paradise Island, the home of some of the more glittery hotels.

Freeport, developed in the 1960s, sports broad, palm-lined avenues and high-rise, balconied hotels and condominiums. It was designed to attract visitors as well as to become the center of industrial development. Here you can find everything from casinos and gourmet restaurants to the International Bazaar, the Port Lucaya waterfront esplanade and exciting night club revues.

Most of the Out Islands are sparsely settled and as windswept as a Winslow Homer watercolor. They present a less hectic way of life than Nassau or Freeport and attract the dedicated fisherman as well as the devoted yachtsman. On many of these islands, chickens, goats and sheep roam through yards and across winding dirt roads. New England-like villages are set against the sea and tropical foliage. Sun worshippers can find stretches of empty palm-shaded, pink sand beaches where they can spend the day undisturbed. Divers and snorkelers find undersea wrecks, aquatic caves, and vivid marine life. Sailors have a field day exploring deserted beach-fringed islands.

The atmosphere of the Out Islands encourages living close to nature, usually without the formalities of attention to dress and rigid schedules. You could book a room at a resort where guests dress up for dinner and meet for cocktails on elegant terraces, or you could stay at a rustic hotel at which vacationers are rarely out of their bathing suits.

In Nassau and Freeport, there is a variety of restaurants, including Italian, French and Chinese, as well as those specializing in local cuisine. Particularly on the Out Islands, menus revolve around treats from the sea, but dishes for landlubbers are also available. Depending on where you go, you can have a steak or lobster dinner or sample local specialities such as cracked conch or boiled fish and grits.

THE HUMAN FACTOR

For nearly four centuries, the cultures of Amerindians, Europeans, Africans, Americans and West Indians have been melding to form the colorful ways of life unique to the Bahamas. While you can have afternoon tea and climb the Queen's Staircase, you can also enjoy the influences of the African and Caribbean ancestors of islanders. At Christmastime, for instance, when the streets fill with Junkanoo music and masked dancers dressed in bright, elaborate costumes, you can witness an old tradition with roots in Africa.

Whether you are on your honeymoon, addicted to beaches or just looking for a change of pace, you will do yourself an injustice if you do not make an effort to get to know some local people and learn something about the way they live and see the world.

As you travel around the islands, you will find that Bahamians are very friendly and helpful. However, as is too often the case in countries that rely heavily on tourism, some residents have felt slighted or taken for granted by visitors. Many locals have expressed resentment of vacationers who act as if residents exist solely to accommodate tourists. But if you treat people as you would like to be treated, talk to clerks and cab drivers and visit beaches, restaurants and night spots frequented by locals, your stay will be enhanced tremendously.

Meeting residents can be simple. Locals often strike up conversations with visitors in bars, night clubs or at the beach. Feeling too shy for such informal encounters? Then consider taking part in the celebrated People-to-People program, in which, for example, you can spend an evening at the theater with a Bahamian couple, be a guest at their home for a meal or have tea at Nassau's Government House.

At many restaurants, resorts, and shops in the Bahamas, life moves at a slower, more relaxed pace and service is more casual than what most Americans, Canadians and Europeans are used to. For example, foreigners can find it infuriating to wait for what seems like ages for a waiter to notice them, then wait just as long for the meal to be brought. However, you'll enjoy yourself most if you simply relax and go with the flow.

No matter what you do or where you go in the Bahamas—whether you choose the faster pace of Nassau or the seclusion of a drowsy Out Island cay—you're in for a memorable visit.

The following chart will help you zero in on the best Bahamian island or islands for the kind of vacation you have in mind.

THE BEST PLACES FOR...

ADVENTURE

Staniel Cay, Exuma: Snorkel or scuba dive in Thunderball Grotto

The Exumas: Take a kayak/camping trip

The Abacos: Take a kayak trip (and stay at hotels)

Travel between islands by mailboat

Long Island and Nassau: Explore caves

Long Island: Dive (safely) with sharks

The Exuma Cays Land and Sea Park: Volunteer

ANIMAL ENCOUNTERS

Freeport or Nassau: Swim with dolphins

The Exuma Cays Land and Sea Park: See iguanas

Inagua: Watch the flamingos

BEACHES

Long Island

San Salvador

The Abacos

Harbour Island, off Eleuthera

The northern Exuma cays

CHILDREN

Club Med Eleuthera

Nassau

Atlantis, Paradise Island

CULTURE AND HISTORY

George Town, Exuma (April): The Out Island Regatta

Nassau (December 26 and January 1): Junkanoo Parades

Nassau: The Junkanoo Expo museum

Nassau: The Public Library and the Pompey Museum (Vendue House)

ESCAPE

The private islands of the Exumas

Great Guana Cay, the Abacos

Inagua

Andros

FISHING

Bimini

Walker's Cay

Deep Water Cay Club, Grand Bahama (where Freeport is located)

Andros

The Exumas

GOLF

Freeport

Nassau

The Cotton Bay Club, Eleuthera

Treasure Cay, Abaco

LUXURY

The private islands of the Exumas

Le Meridien Royal Bahamian hotel, Nassau

Graycliff hotel, Nassau

The Ocean Club hotel, Paradise Island

Deep Water Cay Club hotel, Grand Bahama (where Freeport is located)

The Cotton Bay Club hotel, Eleuthera

Columbus Isle Club Med, San Salvador

MINGLING WITH RESIDENTS

The Out Islands

NATURAL AND HUMAN-MADE BEAUTY

The Exumas

Great Guana, Elbow, and Green Turtle cays in the Abacos

Harbour Island, off Eleuthera

Nassau

NIGHTLIFE

Nassau

Paradise Island

Freeport

ROMANCE

Paradise Island, off Nassau

Elbow, Green Turtle, and Great Guana cays in the Abacos

Southern or central Andros

Harbour Island, off Eleuthera

George Town area, Exuma

San Salvador

SAILING

The Exumas

The Abacos

SCUBA DIVING AND SNORKELING

Andros

The Abacos

The Exumas

Long Island

San Salvador

SHOPPING

Nassau

SINGLES

Nassau

Freeport

Paradise Island

TENNIS

Nassau

Freeport

Eleuthera

The Abacos

WALKING TOURS

Nassau

THINGS TO KNOW

COSTS

In high season, from December through April or May, double-room rates range from about $50 per night at a small guest house to $200 or more at a resort. Off-season rates are appreciably lower. Meal plans offered by hotels are FAP (room and three meals), MAP (room, breakfast and dinner), FB (room and full American breakfast), CP (room and light breakfast) and EP (room only). If you plan to stay at an accommodation where you can prepare your own meals, you should be aware that although supermarkets may be nearby (in Nassau and Freeport), food prices may be quite high because many foods are imported.

Travel agents can advise you on economic package deals. Many packages have specific requirements for day and time of departure and return, and a limited choice of hotels and locations. However, particularly if you plan a trip to the more remote Out Islands, you may want to design your own vacation. The accommodations charts in the back of the book will help you make your own reservations should you choose to do so.

Hotels charge an 8 percent to 10 percent service/government tax on rooms and many also add an energy surcharge. There is no sales tax. Most restaurants and hotels add a 15 percent service charge to cover gratuities for food and drink. The smaller, locally operated restaurants specializing in homestyle cuisine are the least expensive and often serve better food than hotel dining rooms. Taxi drivers and tour guides are also given tips of at least 15 percent. Bellmen and porters are tipped about $1 for each bag. Some hotels and restaurants add a surcharge if you pay with "Traveler's cheques" or an American Express card.

It is best to arrive with enough film and reading material to last the duration of your stay. Film and imported books and magazines are sold at inflated prices compared to those back home.

TRAVEL FOR THE PHYSICALLY CHALLENGED

With rising concern for improving and extending leisure-time facilities and services for the physically challenged, many cruise ships and hotels in the Bahamas, including some resorts in the Out Islands, have made their accommodations more accessible to this group of visitors. Nassau's Crystal Palace Hotel, for instance, has set aside a number of specially designed rooms for people confined to wheelchairs. The Bahamas Paraplegic Association, based in Nassau, has made a survey of hotels and resorts throughout the Bahamas where ramps, elevators, dining areas, baths and other facilities can also serve those with limited mobility. Contact the association at ☎ *(809) 322-2393 or (809) 323-1392*. Renal House, a dialysis facility, recently opened in Nassau. Visitors needing dialysis may make arrangements with this modern professional clinic by calling Princess Margaret Hospital at ☎ *(809) 322-2861*.

SPECIAL SERVICES

Members of **Weight Watchers** need not postpone or forgo a trip for fear of interrupted regimens. For the latest information on Weight Watchers programs in the Bahamas, ☎ *(809) 322-1432*.

Chapters of **Alcoholics Anonymous** meet in the Bahamas in the following areas: Nassau; Freeport; George Town, Exuma; Hope Town, Abaco; and Moxey Town, Andros. For specific information, contact Alcoholics Anonymous at *468 Park Avenue South, New York, NY, 10016*; ☎ *(212) 686-1100*.

WHEN TO GO

WEATHER

Although many people consider the weather ideal at any time of year, the Bahamas' most popular (and most expensive) tourist season is during the winter and spring (from December through April). Daytime temperatures are generally in the 70s and low 80s. Swimming is often comfortable in January and February, but some days and most evenings may be quite cool, making a jacket or heavy sweater necessary.

While there is more rain at times during the summer and fall, rates are lower. Showers are usually brief and the temperature averages in the 80s. Hurricanes, which often hit the Caribbean in late summer, seldom strike the Bahamas. In recent years, August has become a prime month for visitors. Before Hurricane Andrew arrived in August, 1992, a serious storm hadn't hit the Bahamas since 1965.

Note that if you plan to go sailing, it is best to travel during the spring or summer when the water is calmest. In the winter, the Atlantic is rougher and days and nights can be cool and windy.

The Tropic of Cancer cuts through the Bahamas at Exuma, bringing the warmest weather to the southernmost islands and cooler Gulf Stream temperatures to the northern islands, which include Nassau and Freeport.

Most hotels have air conditioning, but trade winds make it unnecessary at some. On the Out Islands, many visitors prefer the ceiling fans that stir the already refreshing air.

AVERAGE TEMPERATURES AND RAINFALL

Month	Average Temperature Fahrenheit/Centigrade		Average Rainfall Inches
January	70°	21°	1.9
February	70°	21°	1.6
March	72°	22°	1.4
April	75°	24°	1.9
May	77°	25°	4.8
June	80°	27°	9.2
July	81°	27°	6.1
August	82°	28°	6.3
September	81°	27°	7.5
October	78°	26°	8.3
November	74°	23°	2.3
December	71°	22°	1.5

HOLIDAYS AND SPECIAL EVENTS

Junkanoo and Goombay are two festivals that may help you to determine when to visit the Bahamas. Junkanoo is a festival that occurs during the Christmas/New Year's season. Goombay is an annual series of special events to attract visitors during the summer season, when the weather is hotter and somewhat wetter. Other special events such as those for boaters, sports fishermen and divers will also help you decide when and where to go.

Event	Month	Location
Junkanoo Parade*	Jan. 1	All Islands
Supreme Court Opening	2nd Wed. in Jan.	Nassau
Annual Miami-Nassau Boat Race	Feb.	Nassau
Annual Nassau Yacht Cup Race	Feb.	Nassau
International 5.5 Metre World Championships	Mar.	Nassau
Annual Bacardi Snipe Winter Championship	Mar.	Nassau
George Town Cruising Regatta	Mar.	George Town, Exuma
Annual Abaco Fishing Tournament	Apr.	Abaco
Family Island Regatta	Apr.	George Town, Exumas
Supreme Court Opening	1st Wed. in Apr.	Nassau
Annual Walker's Cay Billfish Tournament	May	Walker's Cay Abaco
Penny Turtle Billfish Tournament	May	Marsh Harbour, Abaco
Long Island Sailing Regatta	June	Long Island
Cat Cay Billfish Tournament	June	Cat Cay
Bimini Big Game Blue Marlin Tournament	June	Bimini
Labour Day Parade	1st Fri. in June	Nassau & Freeport
Supreme Court Opening	1st Wed. in July	Nassau
Abaco Regatta	July	Abacos
Independence Day	July 10	All Islands
Pepsi-Cola Independence Open Golf Tournament	July	Nassau
Commonwealth Exhibition and Fair	July	Nassau
Chub Cay Blue Marlin Fishing Tournament	July	Chub Cay Berry Islands

Event	Month	Location
Emancipation Day	1st Mon. in Aug.	All Islands
Bimini Local Fishing Tournament	Aug.	Bimini
Cat Island Regatta	Aug.	Arthur's Town Cat Island
Jazz Festival	Sept.	Nassau
Fox Hill Day Celebration	2nd Tues. in Aug.	Nassau
Supreme Court Opening	1st Wed. in Oct.	Nassau
Discovery Day Regatta	Oct.	Nassau
Discovery Day	Oct.	Nassau & San Salvador
Remembrance Day	Nov.	Nassau
Abaco Week Festival	Nov.	Abaco
Annual Bahamas Bonefish Bonanza	Oct./Nov.	George Town Exumas
Annual International Pro-Am Golf Championship	Nov.	Nassau
Boxing Day Junkanoo Parade*	Dec. 26	All Islands
Adam Clayton Powell, Jr. Memorial Fishing Tournament	Dec.	Bimini

*Visitors may join in the Junkanoo Parades by applying before Dec. to the Bahamas Tourist Office.

GETTING THERE BY AIR

Airlines fly to the Bahamas from the U.S.A., Canada, the Caribbean, Great Britain and Europe. Bahamasair, the national airline, has daily flights from Nassau to the Abacos, Andros, Eleuthera and Exuma. Flights to other Out Islands leave from Nassau several days a week. Some small airlines, in addition to those listed below, fly from Florida to Freeport, Abaco, Eleuthera, and Exuma.

Airline	From	To
Air Jamaica	Jamaica	Nassau
American	New York Miami	Nassau Freeport
American Eagle	Miami	Marsh Harbour, Treasure Cay, Great Exuma, Eleuthera

Airline	From	To
Bahamasair	Newark	Nassau, Freeport, All Out Islands (except Bimini, Berry Islands, Walker's Cay)
British Airways	London, Bermuda, Jamaica	Nassau, Freeport
Chalk's International	Miami, Ft. Lauderdale, Nassau	Bimini
Island Express	Ft. Lauderdale	Marsh Harbour, Treasure Cay, Great Exuma
Gulfstream Airlines	Miami, Ft. Lauderdale	Marsh Harbour, Treasure Cay, Great Exuma
Major Air	Freeport	Bimini, Walker's Cay
Paradise Island Airlines	Miami, Ft. Lauderdale, West Palm Beach	Paradise Island

Commuter Airlines

Various commuter airlines fly into the Bahamas from Florida. Before booking a flight, check with the hotel where you'll be staying about the reliability of the company. We've received bad reports about Airways International, for example, which sometimes changes routes without letting passengers know.

Charter Planes

Charter flights are frequently used to reach Out Island resorts from Nassau or Florida. You can make arrangements through the hotel where you plan to stay. Following are some Bahamian inter-island charter services:

CHARTER AIRLINES		
	Phone Number	FAX Number
Air Link	800-882-LINK	407-283-1303
Aerojet	305-772-5070	
Cleareair	809-377-0341	
Congo Air	809-327-5382 (to or from Nassau only)	809-393-5802
Miami Air Charter	305-251-9649	
Island Air Charters	800-444-9904 305-763-8811	

HOTEL CHARTERS		
	Phone Number	**FAX Number**
Fernandez Bay Village, Cat Island	800-940-1905 305-792-1905	305-792-7860
Small Hope Bay Lodge, Andros	800-223-6961 305-359-8240	305-359-8238
Stella Maris Resort, Long Island	800-426-0466 305-359-8236	305-359-8238
Greenwood Inn, Cat Island	809-342-3053	

Private Planes

Private planes are free to enter and leave the Bahamas at their own convenience. Aircraft pilots, however, should contact the Bahamas Tourist Office for the Air Navigation Chart or Flight Planner Chart.

Private plane pilots must also file declaration forms with customs officials. A copy is retained by the pilot as a cruising permit when visiting other islands. U.S. Airmen's Certificates are recognized flying credentials in the Bahamas, but an extension of the aircraft's insurance may be needed to include the islands. Declaration forms are obtainable from Fixed Base Operators at points of departure, or at Bahamian ports of entry.

GETTING THERE BY SEA

Boaters are free to sail in and out of the Bahamas, and many do so from Florida. Another popular way of traveling is by cruise ship. To encourage bookings, many lines offer incentives for potenial passengers. For those who don't live near a departure point, some lines include bus or air transport to the port as part of the package. A few cruises even include stopovers at Florida's Disney World. Small children are often put up in their parents' stateroom without additional cost. Some ships offer baby-sitters, special activities and recreational areas for youngsters. An increasing number are adding facilities for the physically challenged, including wheelchair accessibility to cabins and corridors and the installation of ramps.

Low fares are obtainable for those who book far in advance. Sometimes, if all cabins are not filled close to the sailing date, fares can be even lower for last minute bookings. Another possibility for a lower fare comes when a passenger has already booked and a lower promotional rate is advertised before the sailing. The passenger is then refunded the difference.

A scuba lesson is conducted aboard a cruise ship.

WHAT'S ON BOARD

The well-appointed ships that cruise to the Bahamas have so many amenities that travelers need never leave the vessel. In response to the current physical fitness vogue, exercise rooms, jogging areas and spas have burgeoned. Now more than ever, sumptuous and almost continual dining, formal as well as in snack bars and soda fountains, is a feature of shipboard life. Young people can dance until all hours in discos, and many ships put on lavish nightclub extravaganzas. Passengers with the itch can visit the ships' casinos. Those who prefer a more relaxed trip have the choice of libraries, lounges, in-cabin television, sun decks and indoor and outdoor pools.

Ships carry from several hundred to more than 1000 passengers. Some voyages tend to be sedate, while others are marked with continual activity. Carnival Cruise Lines, for example, calls its vessels "Fun Ships" and tends to attract a younger and more budget-conscious crowd. However, on the same ships, Carnival also offers posh suites with private decks. For all lines, extras usually include bar service, sightseeing tours ashore and on-board tipping.

Some cruise lines have added Cashphones, so that passengers may call the United States as well as other countries. On most lines, calls to the U.S.A. range from $11 to $15.50 per minute, with calls to other countries costing more. A hallmark of ships of the Royal Caribbean Line, Viking Crown Lounges are glass-enclosed public rooms circling the ships' funnels, to give a 360-degree, panoramic view of the sea and the decks below.

SeaEscape, Ltd. *(1080 Port Blvd., Miami, FL 33132;* ☎ *(800) 327-7400)*, offers a one-day cruise from Miami or Fort Lauderdale to Freeport for a day of shopping, gambling or hitting the beach.

Celebrity Cruises suffered a setback in July 1994 when there was an outbreak of Legionnaire's disease on the *Horizon's* trip to Bermuda. Under the adverse publicity, the line offered free flights back to New York, the embarkation point. The source of the problem was found to be a faulty hot tub filter. After a thorough cleaning down of the *Horizon*, it was put back into service.

One line, American Canadian, departs from Nassau in the Bahamas for a seven-day cruise to cays in the Out Islands. Because most Bahamian cays do not have landing docks, the line's 72-passenger *New Shoreham II* has a landing ramp in its bow permitting direct access to the cays and their beaches. *The Sea Fever,* a 90-foot, air-conditioned, aluminum boat, departs Miami for diving cruises that visit Andros and the Berry Islands. Dive equipment is provided and dress when not in bathing suits is extremely casual. Cruises range from four to six nights. For information on sailings and costs, ☎ *(305) 531-3483 or (800) 443-3873.*

CRUISING DETAILS

The U.S. Immigration and Naturalization Service has imposed a $5 inspection fee for all U.S. cruise passengers (except military personnel) arriving in the U.S. on ships that have stopped at foreign ports. In most cases, the fee is collected from the cruise line, which adds it to the passenger fare.

Embarkation points for The Bahamas are primarily Miami, Fort Lauderdale, and Port Canaveral.

The following chart gives an overview of the various choices available. However, because schedules, ships and prices change from season to season, it is advisable to confirm the itinerary with the ship line or your travel agent when planning a trip.

CRUISE LINES THAT PROVIDE SERVICE TO THE BAHAMAS

Cruise Line	Destination	Passengers	Facilities	From
IP	Indoor Pool	YC	Youth Center	
OP	Outdoor Pool	T	Theatre	
C	Casino	W	Whirlpool	
CPh	Cashphone	TK	Track	
S	Spa or Exercise Facilities			
Admiral Cruises **1220 Biscayne Boulevard** **Miami, FL 33132; ☎ (305) 374-1611**				
Emerald Seas	Nassau, Freeport	980	OP, C	Ft. Lauderdale
American Canadian Lines **P.O. Box 368** **Warren, RI 02885; ☎ (401) 247-0955, (800) 556-7450**				
New Shoreham II	Nassau	72		Caicos
Carnival Cruise Line **522 N.W. 87th Avenue** **Miami, FL 33166; ☎ (305) 599-2600**				
Fantasy	Nassau, Freeport	2044	3 OP, S, C, TK	Miami
Mardi Gras	Freeport, Nassau	906	2 OP, IP, C	Port Canaveral
Celebrity Cruises **5200 Blue Lagoon Drive** **Miami, FL 33126; ☎ (305) 262-8322, (800) 437-3111**				
Meridian	Nassau	1106	OP, TK, S, C	Ft. Lauderdale

CRUISE LINES THAT PROVIDE SERVICE TO THE BAHAMAS

Cruise Line	Destination	Passengers	Facilities	From
Chandris Fantasy Cruises **900 Third Avenue** **New York, NY 10022; ☎ (800) 621-3446**				
Britanis	Nassau	960	OP, C	Miami
Costa Cruises **1 Biscayne Tower** **Miami, FL 33131; ☎ (305) 358-7330, (800) 447-6877**				
Costa Riviera	Nassau	1000	OP, C	Ft. Lauderdale
Crown Cruise Lines **2790 N. Federal Highway** **Boca Raton, FL 33431; ☎ (800) 841-7447**				
Crown del Mar	Nassau	486	OP, C	Palm Beach
Dolphin Cruise Line **1007 North American Way** **Miami, FL 33132; ☎ (305) 358-2111**				
Dolphin IV	Nassau	588	OP, C	Miami
Seabreeze	Nassau	840	OP, C	Miami
Fantasy Cruises **5200 Blue Lagoon Drive** **Miami, FL 33126; ☎ (305) 262-5411, (800) 423-2100**				
Britanis	Nassau	926	OP, C	Miami
Holland America Lines, Westours **300 Elliott Avenue West** **Seattle, WA 98119; ☎ (206) 281-3535, (800) 426-0327**				
Westerdam	Nassau	1494	2 OP, S, C	Ft. Lauderdale
Noordam	Nassau	1214	2 OP, S, C	Ft. Lauderdale
Majesty Cruise Line **901 South American Way** **Miami, FL 33132; ☎ (305) 536-0000, (800) 532-7788**				
Royal Majesty	Nassau	1056	OP, S, C	Miami
Norwegian Caribbean Lines **1 Biscayne Tower (Suite 3000)** **Miami, FL 33131; ☎ (305) 358-6670, (800) 327-7030**				
Norway	Pleasure Isle	1864	1P, 2 OP, C, CPh	Miami
Seaward	Pleasure Isle	1534	2 OP, C	Miami
Sunward	Nassau, Pleasure Isle	804	2 OP, C, S	Miami

CRUISE LINES THAT PROVIDE SERVICE TO THE BAHAMAS

Cruise Line	Destination	Passengers	Facilities	From
Odessa America Cruise Company 250 Old Country Road Mineola, NY 11501; ☎ (516) 747-8880, (800) 221-3254				
Columbus Caravelle	Freeport, Nassau	250	P	Boston, New York
Princess Cruises 2029 Century Park East Los Angeles, CA 90067; ☎ (213) 553-7000				
Sky Princess	Nassau	1212	3 OP, C	Ft. Lauderdale
Premier Cruise Lines P.O. Box 573 Cape Canaveral, FL 32920 or 101 George King Blvd., Port Canaveral, FL; ☎ (305) 783-5061, (800) 327-7113				
Star/Ship Atlantic	Nassau	1600	2 IP, C	Port Canaveral
Star/Ship Majestic	Treasure Cay, Green Turtle Cay (Abaco)	950	C, W	Port Canaveral
Star/Ship Oceanic	Nassau, Salt Cay	1500	2 OP, C	Port Canaveral
Princess Cruises 10100 Santa Monica Blvd. Los Angeles, CA 90067; ☎ (310) 553-1770				
Crown Princess	Nassau	1500	2 OP, S, C	Ft. Lauderdale
Regal Princess	Nassau	1596	2 OP, S, C	Ft. Lauderdale
Sky Princess	Nassau	1200	3 OP, S, C	Ft. Lauderdale
Royal Caribbean Cruise Line 903 South America Way Miami, FL 33132; ☎ (305) 379-2601				
Nordic Empress	Nassau	1610	2 OP, C, S	Miami
Nordic Prince	Nassau	1038	OP, C	Miami
Royal Cruise Line 1 Maritime Plaza, Suite 1400 San Francisco, CA 94111; ☎ (415) 956-7200				
Star Odyssey	Nassau	750	2P, S, C	New York
SeaEscape, Ltd. 1080 Port Blvd. Miami, FL 33132; ☎ (800) 327-7400				
1-day cruises Miami, Fort Lauderdale				Freeport

CRUISE LINES THAT PROVIDE SERVICE TO THE BAHAMAS

Cruise Line	Destination	Passengers	Facilities	From
Sitmar Cruises **10100 Santa Monica Blvd.** **Los Angeles, CA 90067; ☎ (213) 553-1666**				
Fairsky	Nassau	1212	2 OP, S, YC, C	Ft. Lauderdale
Fairwind	Nassau	925	2 OP, YC, C	Ft. Lauderdale

ENTRY AND DEPARTURE REQUIREMENTS

TRAVEL DOCUMENTS

To enter the Bahamas, you must have proof of citizenship and an on-ward-bound ticket. A valid passport is preferred. However, a passport expired less than five years or a birth or Baptismal certificate with photo I.D., is also accepted.

Citizens of Canada and the United Kingdom visiting for three weeks or less may enter upon showing a passport or the same items required for U.S. citizens. Citizens of Commonwealth countries do not need visas for entry.

All visitors must fill out and sign immigration cards. Vaccination certificates for smallpox and cholera are needed only for people coming from areas where such diseases still occur.

DEPARTURE TAX

Upon departure by air, travelers are required to pay a $15 tax from Nassau (on New Providence) or the Out Islands, and $18 from Freeport (on Grand Bahama).

CUSTOMS

Although no written declaration is required, baggage is subject to customs inspection. For dutiable items such as furniture, china, and linens, a declaration is necessary. New items should be accompanied by sales slips. Any used household items are subject to assessment by the Customs Officer.

Each adult visitor is permitted 50 cigars or 200 cigarettes or one pound of tobacco and one quart of alcohol duty free, in addition to personal effects. Purchases of up to $25 are allowed all incoming passengers.

DUTY-FREE ALLOWANCES

United States residents, including children, may take home duty-free purchases up to $600 in value if they have been out of the United States for more than 48 hours, and have not taken such an exemption within 30 days. The exemption includes up to 32 ounces of alcohol per person over 21, and families may pool their exemptions.

Canadians absent from their country for at least a week may take home up to $300 (Canadian) worth of duty-free merchandise, which must accompany the passenger.

Residents of the U.K. may take home duty-free purchases up to a value of £32.

Personal items such as jewelry, cameras and sports equipment may be brought in duty-free.

PETS

The Bahamian Ministry of Agriculture and Fisheries, with headquarters in Nassau, requires a permit for all animals entering the country. Written applications for permits should be submitted to the Ministry of Agriculture and Fisheries, *P.O. Box N-3208, Nassau,* ☎ *(809) 32-21277.* Forms are available at the Bahamas Tourist Offices. Although most hotels exclude pets, several accept them when arrangements are made in advance and a permit has been obtained.

DRUGS, ALCOHOL AND FIREARMS

Possession of marijuana, cocaine or other such drugs is an extremely serious and punishable offense. If you indulge here or attempt to bring narcotics into the country, you are looking for trouble, especially since the government has been cracking down on drugs more than ever lately. The minimum drinking age is 21.

Under no circumstances may firearms be brought in without a Bahamian gun license.

LANGUAGE

The language of the Bahamas is English, accented with West Indian, Scottish and Irish influences. Like Bermudians, Bahamians often substitute *w*'s for *v*'s. This is thought to date back to 18th-century English.

DRESS

In the Bahamas, dress is generally casual although, in season, most hotels and restaurants request that men wear jackets and ties for evening meals. Off-season dress is more relaxed. At some of the larger hotels and posher resorts, long skirts or cocktail attire are preferred for women in the evening. Out in the Out Islands, dress is much more casual, except in one or two resorts. Beachwear is discouraged in the public rooms of hotels, and wearing short shorts in town is frowned upon for both men and women.

BUSINESS HOURS

In Nassau, banks are open 9:30 a.m. to 3 p.m. Monday through Thursday, and on Friday from 9:30 a.m. to 5 p.m. Note that international ATMs are located in strategic spots (such as casinos!). Stores are open 9 a.m. to 5 p.m. every day except Sunday and holidays.

Banks in Freeport are also open 9:30 a.m. to 3 p.m. Monday through Thursday and from 9:30 to 5 p.m. on Friday. Most stores are open 9 a.m. to 6 p.m. except Sundays and holidays. Many shops in the International Bazaar and Port Lucaya stay open until 9 p.m. on Saturdays during the winter season. Some banks on the Out Islands are open only several days a week, with limited hours. Many stores close for an hour or two for lunch.

ACCOMMODATIONS

The large hotels and resorts have daily activities and many facilities such as shops, restaurants, large dining rooms, cycle rental stations and watersports equipment. Most also have nightly entertainment. When not located on a beach, many provide complimentary transportation. Most establishments that have few or no sports facilities will arrange sporting activities for their guests elsewhere. All large accommodations are fully air-conditioned. Smaller hotels and guest houses have fewer facilities and many are partially air-conditioned, if at all. Particularly in the Out Islands, many establishments rely on fans and trade winds. Some of the smaller guest houses are in former private homes and have shared baths. In the Out Islands, with power generators in wide use at hotels, visitors may sometimes find themselves without electricity for short periods of time. It is therefore a good idea to note the location of candles that are put in most guest rooms.

Hotels add an 8 percent to 10 percent service charge/government tax to room rates. High season runs from about December through April. During the summer (or "Goombay") season, rates are about 20 to 50 percent lower.

In the **Accommodations Chart** at the back of this book, you'll find more information about the accommodations described in each island section as well as details about other establishments.

RENTING PRIVATE HOMES, VILLAS, CONDOS AND ISLANDS

Vacation Home Rentals, Worldwide *(235 Kensington Ave., Norwood, NJ 07648,* ☎ *(800) 633-3284 or* ☎ *(201) 767-9393, FAX (201) 767-5510)* personally inspects all of the villas, condos and suites in its rental pool. This company has properties in Nassau, Freeport and the Out Islands. Following are some local real estate agencies that also handle private homes throughout the Bahamas:

- **Caribbean Management, Ltd.**, *P.O. Box N-1132, Nassau, The Bahamas;* ☎ *(809) 322-8618/1356.*

- **Ingraham's Real Estate**, *Hospital Lane North, P.O. Box N-1062, Nassau, The Bahamas;* ☎ *(809) 325-2222/3433/8930.*

- **Jack Isaacs Real Estate Co., Ltd.**, *25 Cumberland St., Nassau, The Bahamas;* ☎ *(809) 322-1069/325-6326.*

- **Plot Realty Co., Ltd.**, *P.O. Box N-1492, Nassau, The Bahamas;* ☎ *(809) 322-2460.*

If you and some friends or relatives would like to have an island virtually all to yourselves—and if you can afford it—consider renting the luxurious villas on Cistern Cay *(*☎ *809/326-7875)* in the peaceful Exuma Cays Land and Sea Park. The hefty $38,000 per week price tag covers three gourmet

meals a day, liquor, a fishing guide, watersports equipment and more for
up to 10 adults (and a couple of children).

MONEY

Bahamian money is pegged to the American dollar, with the same desig-
nations for bills and coins and exchanged at the same rate. Visitors are likely to receive change in mixed American and Bahamian dollars and coins.
"Traveler's cheques" are accepted throughout the islands and are cashable
at banks and hotels. However, banks and some restaurants will add a service charge. Credit cards are widely accepted, but you may have to pay a
service charge if you use American Express.

In Nassau and Freeport, commercial banks are open from 9:30 a.m. to 3
p.m., Monday through Thursday, and until 5 p.m. on Friday. Most banks
will cash verifiable personal checks. Nassau's American Express office for
check cashing and cash advances is conveniently located downtown at the
Playtours office, upstairs at the intersection of Shirley and Parliament
streets. In Freeport, American Express is located in the Kipling Building,
off Kipling Lane in Churchill Square. International ATMs can be found in
various locations—including some hotels and casinos.

TIPPING

A 10 or 15 percent service charge is often automatically added to restaurant checks. Ask if you're not sure. Hotels also add an 8 to 10 percent service charge/government tax to their rates (so there is no need to leave a tip
for the housekeeper). Taxi drivers usually receive 10 or 15 percent. Tour
guides expect to be tipped a few dollars, depending on the cost of the excursion.

TAXIS

Taxis are available in New Providence, Grand Bahama and most of the
Out Islands. In Nassau and Freeport, as well as the Out Islands where there
are no tour buses, drivers will serve as island guides. The rates, often negotiable, are about $16 an hour. Some Out Island roads are not in the best
of repair. A bumpy ride with a friendly driver can be an adventure in itself.

In Nassau and Freeport, taxis, which are metered, wait for passengers at
airports and hotels. If drivers don't turn on their meters, be sure to ask
them to do so, even if they insist they know the fare. Otherwise, you're
likely to be overcharged. From Nassau International Airport to a hotel on
Cable Beach, two people should expect to pay about $10 and about $15 to
Rawson Square; from the airport to Paradise Island, the ride will be about
$20, including the $2 bridge toll. From Freeport's International Airport to
the hotel districts, the fare will range from about $6 to $10. Taxis in the
Out Islands are not metered and tend to be more expensive than in Nassau
or Freeport. On most Out Islands, taxis (sometimes simply the cars or vans
of local residents) meet planes. However, to be on the safe side, check with
your accommodation about land transportation before arrival. Some Out
Island resorts meet planes with their own vehicles. Ask how much you

should expect to pay for a taxi from the airport to the hotel. Rides can vary anywhere from $10 to $50, so be prepared.

RENTAL CARS

Visitors with valid U.S. or Canadian driver's licenses can rent cars in the Bahamas. *Note that driving is on the left.* Daily rates range from about $70 to $80. You'll save renting by the week. Rental agencies in Nassau and Freeport are at airports, hotels and downtown locations. During high season, a reservation is suggested before leaving home. In addition to local companies, **Avis**, **Budget**, **Dollar Rent-A-Car**, and **National** have offices at the Nassau airport. An Avis agency is in back of Nassau's British Colonial Beach Resort and National agencies are on nearby Marlborough Street and at the Crystal Palace Hotel. You'll also find an Avis office in Freeport's International Bazaar. You can rent cars in the Out Islands (sometimes from taxi drivers), but many of the models are battle scarred by years of use on bumpy roads. Be sure to check your car's condition before pulling off. You can import your own car for touring, duty-free, for up to six months. A deposit of up to 70 percent of the vehicle's value is required, but it is refunded if the car is shipped out within six months. The value is assessed by Customs upon arrival.

CYCLES

Cycles are a popular mode of travel in the Bahamas and visitors take to them with a passion. At most hotels and resorts, you can rent mopeds on the premises or at nearby cycle shops if you are 16 or older. No driver's license is necessary. Wearing a helmet, which you are given with the moped, is required by law. Until you become accustomed to motorized bikes, it is best to practice driving in a low-traffic area. Renting a moped ranges from about $16 a day, $8 a half day to about $30 a day, $18 a half day, including insurance. You'll be asked to leave a deposit of about $30. Bicycles are about $15 a day. *Remember, Bahamians drive on the left.*

BUSES

Visitors can take advantage of public transportation in getting around Nassau and Freeport. Bahamians will come to the rescue with directions if you seem uncertain. Nassau has buses and minivans (about 75¢) you can pick up at bus stops, and they go to Cable Beach, downtown Nassau, public beaches and other points in the city. To go east, toward the Paradise Island bridge, pick up these public buses downtown at Frederick Street at the corner of Bay Street; to go west to Cable Beach, pick up buses and minivans in front of the British Colonial at Bay Street. Some hotels run complimentary buses to downtown Nassau and to the casino on Cable Beach. Buses on Grand Bahama (about $1) connect Freeport with Lucaya and all hotels with beaches, the International Bazaar and Port Lucaya. Vacationers traveling on package deals generally get prepaid vouchers for bus transportation between the airport and hotels.

FERRIES

Ferries run between downtown Nassau and Paradise Island from Prince George Dock. These "water taxis" also operate in the Out Islands to various offshore cays.

MAILBOATS

Inter-island mail boats travel between Nassau and the Out Islands. The mail boats depart for the outer islands from Potter's Cay, next to the Paradise Island bridge, off East Bay Street in Nassau. Boats leave once a week, stopping at one or two islands, in a trip that takes almost a day and is usually made overnight.

Mail boats are an economical way of traveling, if only for the more adventurous visitor. Decks are crowded with local commuters, freight, varieties of cargo, produce and livestock. Schedules are constantly revised and there are often postponements. Passage cannot be arranged in advance. Bookings can only be made after arrival in the Bahamas.

Information on mail boats may be obtained at the Dock Master's office on Potter's Cay in Nassau ☎ *(809) 323-1064.*

CASINOS

Gambling at the casinos of the Bahamas is legal for all visitors over the age of 21. Bahamian citizens, however, are not permitted to play. Two casinos are located in Nassau: one on Paradise Island, and the other on the mainland between Carnival's Crystal Palace and Radisson Cable Beach resort. Two more are found in Freeport, Grand Bahama—one between the Princess Tower Hotel and the International Bazaar, the other at the Lucayan Beach Resort and Casino.

TIME

Eastern Standard Time is in use throughout the Bahamas. Eastern Daylight Saving Time is used during the summer months coinciding with the U.S. When it is noon in New York, it is noon in the Bahamas, year round.

ELECTRICITY

American electrical appliances can be used in the Bahamas without adapters.

INSECT REPELLENT

Don't forget to pack some. Many people find that fragrant Avon Skin So Soft, a bath oil, works very well as a bug repellent when smoothed on skin like lotion.

MEDICAL CONCERNS

There are excellent medical services in the Bahamas. Hospital, public and private medical facilities, and personnel are available in Nassau and Freeport. There are also health centers and clinics in the Out Islands. In medical emergencies, patients are brought to Princess Margaret Hospital, a government-operated institution in downtown Nassau. The government also operates the 58-bed Rand Memorial Hospital in Freeport.

The water throughout the Bahamas is potable. However, on most Out Islands it is best to drink bottled or filtered water, if only because tap water can be quite salty.

TAR ALERT

Unfortunately, tar from oil leaking from ships is hidden on some beaches. Where this problem exists, hotels have "tar stations" or provide packets of "Tar Off" in rooms. You can also remove tar with Lestoil, vegetable oil, and Avon Skin So Soft (a bath oil that many have discovered works as a mosquito repellent as well).

COMMUNICATIONS

Nassau's two newspapers are the *Nassau Guardian*, published Monday through Saturday, and the *Tribune*, an afternoon paper. Freeport's paper, the *Freeport News,* is published afternoons, Monday through Friday. *The New York Times,* the *London Times,* the *Daily Telegraph* and the *Wall Street Journal* are available at most of the larger hotels and newstands, but sometimes a day late. Radio Bahamas operates two radio stations in New Providence, ZNS1 and ZNS2, and ZNS3 in Grand Bahama. Its television station, TV-13 ZNS, operates out of New Providence.

VISITOR INFORMATION

The address of The Bahamas Ministry of Tourism is *P.O. Box N-3701, Nassau, The Bahamas.* Contact the Out Islands Promotion Board at *1100 Lee Wagener Boulevard, Suite 206, Fort Lauderdale, FL 33315,* ☎ *(305) 359-8099 or (800) 688-4752,* or The Grand Bahama Promotion Board, *P.O. Box F650, Freeport, Grand Bahama.* Following are the locations and phone numbers of the Bahamas Tourist Offices in the United States and Canada:

Atlanta
2957 Clairmont Rd., Suite 150
Atlanta, GA 30345
☎ (404) 633-1793

New York
150 E. 52 St.
New York, NY 10022
☎ (212) 758-2777

Miami Area
19495 Biscayne Blvd., 8th Fl.
Aventura, FL 33132
☎ (305) 932-0051

Boston
1027 Statler Office Building
Boston, MA 02116
☎ (617) 426-3144

Chicago
875 North Michigan Avenue
Chicago, IL 60611
☎ (312) 787-8203

Philadelphia
437 Chestnut St.
Philadelphia, PA 19106
☎ (215) 925-0871

Dallas
2050 Stemmons Freeway
Dallas, TX 75201
☎ (214) 742-1886

District of Columbia
2220 Massachusetts Ave.
Washington, DC 20008
☎ (202) 319-0004

Los Angeles
3450 Wilshire Boulevard
Los Angeles, CA 90010
☎ (213) 385-0033

Montreal
1255 Phillips Square
Montreal, Quebec H3B3G1
☎ (514) 861-6797

Toronto
85 Richmond Street West
Toronto, Ontario M5H2C9
☎ (416) 363-4441

The United States Embassy is located in Nassau in the Mosmar building on Queen St. (☎ *322-1181).* **The Canadian Consulate** is in the Out Island Traders building on East Bay St. in Nassau (☎ *323-2124);* and the **British High Commission** is in the Bitco building on East St. in Nassau (☎ *325-7471).*

WHAT TO DO AND WHERE TO DO IT

A tug of war happens on the shore on Little San Salvador.

For most visitors, having a good time in the Bahamas revolves around watersports and just being outdoors. Because the islands are surrounded by some of the clearest, most beautiful and game-stocked waters in the world, fishing, boating and undersea exploration are very popular. Nassau, the adjoining Paradise Island and Freeport offer lively nightlife, including their casinos, and the Out Islands are paradise for those looking for real escape. For more specific information on sports, nightlife, shopping, tours or dining, refer to the individual island chapters.

SPORTS

You can get further information about exactly where and when various sports are available before leaving home. Contact The Bahamas Sports Information Center at ☎ *(800) 32-SPORT* for answers to any sports related question.

BOATING

The marinas, ports and harbors of almost every island are thronged with pleasure boats making use of the extensive Bahamian boating facilities. Those sailing have a wide choice of marinas throughout the Out Islands as well as in New Providence and Grand Bahama, where Nassau and Freeport are located. Dotted with picturesque cays, the Abacos, Bimini and the Exumas are excellent for sailing. Visitors without boats can charter bare boats or, if needed, a captain and crew. Provisions, fuel and instruction are all at hand on the islands. You can make arrangements through many accommodations.

GAME FISHING

Scores of world-record catches have been made in the Bahamas. Fishing tournaments are held throughout the islands at various times of the year and attract fishing enthusiasts from around the world. Even those not wishing to take part in tournaments can be bitten by the fishing bug on almost any island. Arrangements can be made through your accommodation. Bimini is known as the fishing capital of the world, and locals as well as visitors are addicted to this pastime. Andros is loved for its bonefishing. Walker's Cay in the Abacos and Chub Cay in the Berry Islands are both excellent for deep-sea and shore fishing.

Here are some of the Bahamas' most plentiful game fish and the best times of year to catch them:

Fish	Best Month(s)	Other Good Month(s)
Blue Marlin	May, June	March, April, July
Bluefin Tuna	May	April, June
Dolphin	April	March, May
King Mackerel	March, April	January, February
Wahoo	January, February, March	April
White Marlin	May	March, April, June

GOLF

Most courses are in and around the cities of Nassau and Freeport/Lucaya. Courses designed by such luminaries as Robert Trent Jones and Dick Wilson are also at the Cotton Bay Club in Eleuthera and Treasure Cay in the Abacos. Grand Bahama's Lucayan Park Golf and Country Club is the oldest in the country. The newest is at the Crystal Palace Hotel & Casino in Nassau. The one at the Ramada South Ocean Golf & Beach Resort is considered among the best. The Emerald Course in Grand Bahama is considered less challenging than the Ruby Course. Bahamian courses play host to several tournaments, including an annual Pro-Am and an Open to celebrate Independence Day.

HORSEBACK RIDING

In Freeport you can go horseback riding at Pine Tree Stables and in Nassau, at the Paradise Island Riding Stables.

JOGGING

For some barefoot joggers, the hard-packed sand near the waterline of beaches throughout the Bahamas can be sufficient. Those who run in shoes, however, prefer places like the wide, tree-lined, traffic-free esplanade of Nassau's Cable Beach area. There is also the cool, tree-vaulted Casuarina Walk on Paradise Island that leads to the dock and to the heliport. In Grand Bahama's Freeport/Lucaya area, there is a choice of streets in a broad, landscaped, well-paved network. The Bahamas Princess Resort & Casino has a 10km (6.2 mile) jogging course, dedicated to world marathon champion Grete Waitz. On the Out Islands, most joggers blaze their own paths, using either the beaches or the paved roads.

PARASAILING

If you've ever had the urge to be strapped to a brightly colored parachute that is tied to a boat, then gently lifted into the air as the boat takes off, parasailing is for you. In Nassau, you can enjoy this sport at the Crystal Palace Hotel & Casino, the Ambassador Beach Hotel, and the Forte Nassau Beach Hotel; on Paradise Island, at the Radisson Grand Hotel and at Atlantis Paradise Island, and in Freeport, at the Atlantik Beach Hotel, the Radisson Resort on Lucaya Beach and the Lucaya Beach Resort.

SAILING

See "Boating."

SCUBA DIVING AND SNORKELING

The Bahamas' magnificent undersea attractions have helped to encourage the growth of scuba and snorkeling. Centers such as the Underwater Explorers Society (UNEXSO) in Freeport have sprung up for certified divers as well as beginners. The centers give instruction and lead expeditions to the undersea wrecks, special marine life and coral formations. UNEXSO offers a week-long course in underwater photography. It also hosts The Dolphin Experience (in Freeport), a program that allows people to swim with several of those friendly mammals.

Most hotels will make arrangements for snorkeling and diving if facilities are not on the premises. The Out Islands are major attractions for those fascinated by underwater spectacles such as Thunderball Grotto off Staniel Cay in the Exumas. One of the largest barrier reefs in the world is just off the coast of Andros. Excellent scuba programs are run by Small Hope Bay Lodge in Andros, the Green Turtle Club in the Abacos, Riding Rock Inn on San Salvador and Stella Maris Inn on Long Island (which some veterans say offers the best dive sites in the Bahamas).

By merely donning a helmet, novice divers of any age can take an undersea walk to see fish, coral and other marine life through Hartley's at the Nassau Yacht Haven.

TENNIS

Nassau and Freeport have many courts and you can also play on a number of Out Islands, such as the Abacos, the Berry Islands, Eleuthera, Long Island and Exuma. The larger resorts have pro shops for players. The first-class tennis facility shared by the Crystal Palace Hotel & Casino and the Radisson Cable Beach Casino & Golf Resort has 10 courts, five of them lighted, as well as a stadium for tournament and exhibition games. Next door is an indoor complex with three courts each for **squash** and **racquetball**. A junior national tennis championship for youngsters 10–18 years old is sponsored annually in Nassau to encourage the sport among young Bahamians.

WATER-SKIING

This sport is available at most large beach hotels throughout the Bahamas.

WINDSURFING

Seeing several windsurfers at once is as thrilling as watching one of the Bahamas' popular regattas. In addition to Nassau and Freeport, windsurfing is available in Walker's Cay, Marsh Harbour and Elbow Cay in the Abacos; and Harbour Island and Rock Sound in Eleuthera.

NIGHTLIFE

Nassau and Freeport/Lucaya are the places to see and enjoy Bahamian nightlife in its most elaborate and sophisticated form. Entertainment tends to run to what Bahamians refer to as "native." Native shows include some elements common to countries in the Caribbean like calypso, limbo dancing and steel drums. A difference is that goombay and Junkanoo beats alter these rhythms, transforming them into Bahamian music. The Bahamas' casinos are located in Nassau's Cable Beach, Paradise Island and Freeport/Lucaya. They are open to the small hours.

The larger hotels have discos and present revues and single acts in their night clubs, lounges, and sometimes in dining-room areas. Performances can be loud, lavish, and brassy at the casino theaters, or smooth, refined, or intimate as when a single player strums a guitar and softly croons songs of the tropics. Discos and nightclubs are also found away from the hotels in places such as the Bay Street area in Nassau and the International Bazaar and Port Lucaya area in Freeport. Visitors should venture out for Bahamian entertainment away from their hotels and resorts for another aspect and flavor of life in the islands. On the Out Islands, entertainment is on a smaller scale. Some performances by local musicians are so understated that they gain even more in overall effect.

SHOPPING

The Bahamas is a duty free territory. Bargain hunters can find the best deals along Nassau's Bay Street, in some Paradise Island shops, and in Freeport. Prices can be 25 to 50 percent lower than in the U.S. for things such as crystal, china, woolens, linens, perfumes, watches, clocks, leather goods, cameras and liquor. You don't even have to leave the larger hotels to dip into your purse or wallet. Many have arcades filled with tempting shops and boutiques. Most visitors agree, however, that it's more fun (and usually less expensive) to venture out and rub elbows with resident shoppers.

Seeming to jostle for attention, shops line Bay Street and Bank Lane, two of Nassau's main thoroughfares, and several tributary streets on both sides. Arcades such as the International Bazaar, Beaumont House and Colony Place run from Bay Street out to Woodes Rogers Walk. For Seiko and Rolex watches, clocks, jewelry; English, Meissen and Limoges porcelain and much more, stop in at **John Bull**, between East Street and Elizabeth Avenue. The **Brass and Leather Shop**, on Charlotte Street off Bay, sells wallets, belts, Bottega Veneta luggage and the like. French, American and local perfumes are available at the **Bahamas Fragrance and Cosmetic Factory** on Charlotte Street, which makes its own, and at **Lightbourn's** on Bay Street. **Marlborough Antiques**, across from the British Colonial Beach Resort on the street of the same name, has beautifully displayed antique items, and **Balman Antiques** specializes in old maps.

In Freeport, many shops, boutiques and restaurants are clustered in the **International Bazaar. Midnight Sun** is where you'll find a wide selection of Scandinavian bargains, and the **Discount Bazaar** is worth checking out. The multimillion dollar **Port Lucaya** is an appealing shopping, dining and entertainment complex, across from the Lucaya hotels and casino.

Handmade straw goods are sold on most Bahamian islands, but the greatest variety is found in Nassau and Freeport. The largest straw market in the Bahamas is on Bay Street in Nassau. On Nassau's Cable Beach, a straw market is located across from the Ambassador Beach and Crystal Palace hotels. Shoppers can pick up straw hats to keep the sun off, or straw bags and baskets for overflow on the way home. Don't be shy about bargaining—no one expects you to pay the first price quoted.

Throughout the Bahamas you'll find bright resort wear made of **Androsia batiks**. These colorful bathing suits, shirts, shorts, shifts, head ties and dresses come from the factory begun by the owners of Small Hope Bay Lodge on Andros.

TOURS

In Nassau and Freeport, bus, taxi and boat tours can be arranged at hotel tour desks, or at Bahamas tourist offices. From Rawson Square in Nassau, you can also take 30-minute horse-drawn carriage tours for about $9 per person. Horses rest from 1 p.m. to 3 p.m. from May to October and from 1 p.m. to 2 p.m. November through April. In the Out Islands, taxi tours can be arranged through resorts or guest houses. Bus, boat and horse-drawn carriage tours run most frequently during the winter season. In Nassau, avoid guided nightclub tours, which usually aren't much fun.

DINING OUT

Especially in Nassau and Freeport, restaurant reservations are generally required for dinner during the winter season. Men are expected to wear jackets at night at the more expensive restaurants. Off season, these requirements are relaxed at most places. While Nassau and Freeport have many restaurants, those in the Out Islands are mainly limited to hotel and resort dining rooms and small locally operated restaurants.

On some islands, such as Abaco, there are individuals who prepare elaborate Bahamian feasts for visitors who call ahead. Hotel staff members and other residents can tell you how to find these chefs. (Also see section on "Eating and Drinking.")

ATTRACTIONS AT A GLANCE

NASSAU

ATTRACTION	PLACE
FORTS	
Fort Charlotte	Off West Bay Street
Fort Fincastle	Bennett's Hill
Fort Montagu	East Bay Street
GARDENS, PARKS & NATURE RESERVES	
Ardastra Gardens	Near Fort Charlotte
Royal Victoria Gardens	Near Government House
Versailles Gardens	Paradise Island
Botanical Gardens	Near Fort Charlotte
GOVERNMENT BUILDINGS	
Government House	Blue Hill Road
Public Library	Shirley Street
HISTORICAL SIGHTS	
Blackbeard's Tower	Fox Hill Road
Queen's Staircase	Shirley Street
Gregory Arch	Near Government House
Pompey Museum (Vendue House)	Bay Street
MUSEUMS & ANIMALS	
Roselawn Museum	East Street & Bank Lane
Sea Gardens	East End of Nassau Harbor
Coral Island	Coral Island
Hartley's Undersea Walk	East Bay Street
Junkanoo Expo	Prince George Dock
Nautilus Submarine	Marina
LOCAL SIGHTS	
Hair Braiding Pavilion	Prince George Dock

NASSAU

ATTRACTION	PLACE
Water Tower	Bennett's Hll
Potters Cay	Under Paradise Island Bridge
Straw Market	Market & Bay Streets

FREEPORT

ATTRACTION	PLACE
SHOPPING & DINING PLAZAS	
International Bazaar	Torii gate at West Sunrise Highway
Port Lucaya Marketplace and Marina	Lucaya
LOCAL INDUSTRIES	
Straw Market	Next to International Bazaar
Perfume Factory	Near International Bazaar
Bahamas Artsand Crafts Market	Near International Bazaar
GARDENS, PARKS & NATURE RESERVES	
Rand Memorial Nature Center	Settlers Way East
Garden of the Groves	Off Midshipman Road
Lucayan National Park	Eastern End
Hydroflora Garden	East Beach Drive
MUSEUMS & ANIMALS	
Grand Bahama Museum	Garden of the Groves
The Dolphin Experience	UNEXSO Dock, Lucaya

THE BAHAMAS OUT ISLANDS

ATTRACTION	PLACE

ABACOS

Manjack Cay	North of Green Turtle Cay
Albert Lowe Museum	New Plymouth,Green Turtle Cay
Memorial Sculpture Garden	New Plymouth,Green Turtle Cay
Hope Town Lighthouse	Elbow Cay
Wyannie Malone Museum and Garden	Elbow Cay
Tahiti Beach	Elbow Cay
Local Shipbuilding	Man-O-War Cay
Sea and Land Park Preserve	Fowl Cay
Tilloo and Pelican Cays	South of Elbow Cay
Art Colony at Little Harbour	South of Marsh Harbour

ACKLINS/CROOKED ISLAND

Bird Rock Lighthouse	Crooked Island Passage
Crooked Island Caves	Crooked Island
Marine Farm	North End of Crooked Island
Southwestern Beaches	Crooked Island
French Wells	Crooked Island

ANDROS

Andros Barrier Reef	Parallel to the East Coast of Andros
Ocean and Inland Blue Holes	Throughout the Island
Morgan's Bluff	North Andros
Androsia Batik Works	Fresh Creek
Turnbull's Gut	Off Small Hope Bay Lodge

THE BAHAMAS OUT ISLANDS

ATTRACTION	PLACE
The Barge	Small Hope Bay Lodge

THE BIMINIS

Hemingway Memorabilia	Compleat Angler Hotel,Alice Town
Hall of Fame	Anchors Aweigh Guest House, Alice Town
The Sapona	Between South Bimini and Cat Cay

CAT ISLAND

The Hermitage	Town of New Bight
Deveaux Plantation	Town of Port Howe
Armbrister Plantation	Near Port Howe

ELEUTHERA

Gregory Town Plantation	Gregory Town
Ocean Hole	Tarpum Bay
Preacher's Cave	Bridge Point
Glass Window	Upper Bogue
Hatchet Bay Plantation	Hatchet Bay
Hatchet Bay Cave	Hatchet Bay
Historic Churches	Harbour Island

THE EXUMAS

The Exuma Cays Land and Sea Park	Northern Cays
Stocking Island	Exuma Sound,Off George Town
St. Andrew's Church	George Town
The Hermitage	Near George Town
Thunderball Grotto	Staniel Cay

THE BAHAMAS OUT ISLANDS

ATTRACTION	PLACE
Rolle Town Tomb	Rolle Town
Williams Town Salt Marsh	Williams Town
Patience House	Little Exuma
Out Island Regatta	George Town

INAGUA

Inagua National Park	Island interior
Morton Bahamas Salt Company	Near Matthew Town

LONG ISLAND

Dunmore's Cave	Deadman's Cay
Dunmore Plantation	Deadman's Cay
Father Jerome's Churches	Clarence Town
Spanish Church	The Bight
Conception Island	Off Stella Maris
Deadman's Cay Caves	Deadman's Cay
Adderley Plantation	Cape Santa Maria
Columbus Point	North of Stella Maris

SAN SALVADOR

Observation Platform	Near Riding Rock Inn
San Salvador Museum	Cockburn Town
New World Museum	North Victoria Hill
Columbus Monuments	Long Bay, Fernandez Bay, Crab Cay
Grahams Harbour	Northern San Salvador
Father Schreiner's Grave	Grahams Harbour area

THE BAHAMAS OUT ISLANDS

ATTRACTION	PLACE
Fortune Hill Plantation	Eastern San Salvador
East Beach	Northeast Cost
Dixon Hill Lighthouse	Dixon Hill
Watling's Castle	Sandy Point Estate
Farquharson's Plantation	Pigeon Creek
Big Well	Sandy Point Estate
Dripping Rock	Sandy Point

Nassau

NASSAU

Queen's Staircase, in Nassau, was named for Victoria.

FIRST IMPRESSIONS

One of the first places most visitors see upon arrival in the Bahamas is the 7-by-21-mile island of New Providence, where Nassau, the capital, is located. The island has an international airport, and gleaming white cruise ships dock at its busy harbor. Some of the largest and most luxurious hotels and restaurants serve its visitors, and the city is rich in Bahamian beauty and history. If you arrive at the International Airport, your taxi takes you along a scenic drive, with glimpses of surf, exotic blossoms, ancient trees and leafy, overhung roads dappled with sunlight. You see pastel-colored, shuttered hous-

71

es with balconies, some from colonial times, with flowers and shrubs spilling in abundance over their walls and fences. Among the greenery are elderly ficus trees, flowering oleander and islands of palms. As you turn onto Bay Street, you'll see two low, gaping caves on the right side of the road. Historians believe that they were once inhabited by Indians, but the government doesn't have the money to conduct an archaeological study. Aptly named Caves Beach is across the way, not far from Orange Hill Beach. Nearby Sandy Point is a community of attractive villas. The condominiums and hotels along Cable Beach are followed by historic downtown Nassau. If you're bound for one of the Paradise Island hotels, your taxi turns off Bay Street and takes you over the toll bridge.

Unfortunately, too few visitors venture much beyond Cable Beach, downtown Nassau or Paradise Island. To see more of New Providence you can take part in the popular free **People-to-People Program**, where Bahamians will be your hosts. You might be taken on a personalized sightseeing tour. Your host might also give you the opportunity to join in some local event to which visitors are seldom privy, such as a church picnic or local beach party. In any case, you will learn about the Bahamas from people who know the islands intimately. Arrangements can be made through one of the Bahamas Tourist Bureau offices.

Some Bahamians and visitors get to know each other in another way: it's been *de rigueur* in the last few years for visiting women (and even some men) to have all or part of their **hair cornrowed** and beaded by Bahamian women on the beach or in the straw markets. Depending on the number of braids, this can take anywhere from a few minutes to over an hour. The price, which varies greatly from braider to braider, is negotiable. Be forewarned: If you don't have much melanin in your skin, put some sunscreen on the exposed scalp between braids!

On Prince George Dock, just outside the Junkanoo Expo, an open-air hair-braiding pavilion opened in December, 1993. Until then, the beach and the Straw Market were the most common locales for visitors to have their hair cornrowed. Now uniformed braiders are certified and supervised as they turn out attractive, often intricate hairstyles. Sinks, mirrors and benches for those waiting are all provided in this convivial tropical beauty parlor.

While taxis are available for traveling between Cable Beach, downtown Nassau and the foot of the Paradise Island bridge, and some of the larger hotels provide complimentary bus service, riding jitneys is

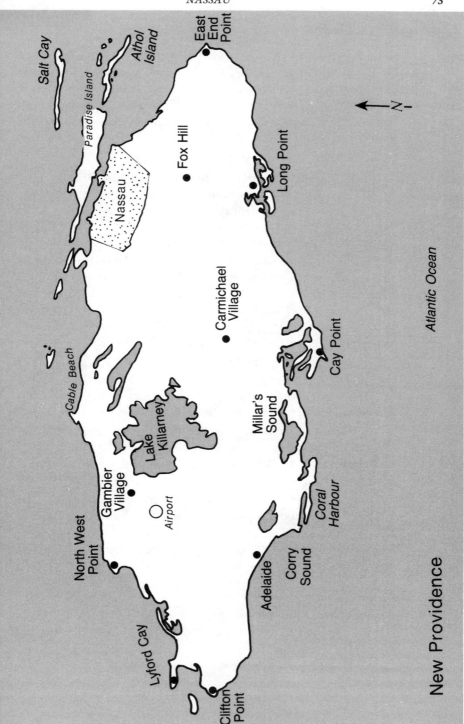

New Providence

much more fun. For about 75¢, with the radio playing loud reggae or calypso, you'll pass sights most visitors miss—tiny churches, homes with lush banana trees growing in their front yards, local stores and bars, wide-trunked silk cotton trees, a bakery decorated with huge red polka dots, a row of tiny clapboard houses painted bright blue or yellow with pink and green or orange shutters. If you call out "Bus stop!" as you approach your destination, you might even pass for Bahamian.

A BIT OF HISTORY

New Providence was settled in 1656 by a colony of Britons, some of whom came from Bermuda, looking for a better way of life. The new colony was supposedly ruled from the Carolinas on the North American mainland, but supervision was lax and the new and remote Bahamians were pretty much on their own.

Spain, in an effort to end the incessant and irksome raids on its ships by pirates based in the Bahamas, attacked the settlement called Charles Town, named for Britain's Charles II. Spain's occupation of the town was short lived and she left almost immediately, because there was a new king in England. The settlement was renamed Nassau, after William III, of Orange-Nassau.

The pirates, notably Blackbeard, alias Edward Teach, remained there along with his cohorts, "Calico" Jack Rackham, Major Bonnet (a Frenchman) and the notorious women pirates, Mary Reed (who was eventually hung) and Anne Bonney, Rackham's mistress.

The marauders were not driven out until the ruthless Captain Woodes Rogers was appointed governor. In tribute to his feat, a statue stands before the British Colonial Hotel, and a waterfront road bears his name.

Nassau was once an acknowledged playground for the rich. The height of that period was probably during the tenure of the Duke of Windsor, the abdicated king of England, just before World War II. The wealthy still come to Nassau, many finding their way to Lyford Cay, a private resort where foreign notables often stay.

CABLE BEACH

Jet skiing is a thrill at Cable Beach, Nassau.

With one of the most beautiful (but busy) strips of beach in the Bahamas, this area was named in 1892 after the laying of a telegraph cable from Jupiter, Florida, to the Bahamas. For the first time, messages could be sent directly from the Bahamas to the United States and England. Horse racing, all the rage with officers of the British West India Regiment stationed in Nassau, was once Cable Beach's prime attraction. In 1933 an annual racing season began, lasting until 1975 when the track closed. In the past, pineapples to be exported to the United States were grown in much of the Cable Beach area.

New Providence's first luxury beach resorts began springing up here after World War II. Meridien's Royal Bahamian Hotel, formerly the Emerald Beach, was one of the first in the area to be restored. Then the lavish 700-room Cable Beach Hotel & Casino was built. Now called The Radisson Cable Beach Casino & Golf Resort, it adjoins Carnival Cruise Line's Crystal Palace Resort & Casino, which dominates the area with its painted Pompidou Center-like exterior pipes and eye-catching colors. With the smaller Cable Beach hotels joining in, the area is being touted as the Bahamian Riviera. Actually between downtown and Cable Beach, Villas on Silver Cay is included among Riviera resorts. Stalls selling straw goods, jewelry and t-shirts are right across the road from the Crystal Palace, the Radisson, Forte Nassau Beach and Wyndham Ambassador Beach hotels, clustered in the busiest section of Cable Beach.

Along the luscious sandy shore itself, calypso music floats down from hotel pool areas where guests are playing musical chairs and doing the limbo. Vendors wend their way between glistening sunbathers. Many sell shell jewelry, t-shirts, beach cover-ups and fresh coconuts (for drinking coconut water). Others offer to braid or cornrow vacationers' hair or sign them up for party cruises to Discovery Island (one of several beach-rimmed cays just offshore), or parasailing, jet ski and banana boat rides, water-skiing and other aqua action. However, the hotels here recommend that guests use only their authorized watersports agents, whom you'll find at the marked kiosks along the beach. Independent vendors may or may not follow proper safety requirements.

Runners jog along tree- and flower-lined West Bay Street in front of the hotels. **Delaporte Beach**, at the western end of the area, is never crowded. **Goodman's Bay** and **Saunders Beach**, on the way to downtown Nassau, are other pleasant beaches, and are popular with locals for fundraising beach parties (with food and music) as well as swimming.

DOWNTOWN NASSAU

Bay Street, full of all sorts of shops and restaurants, is in the heart of Nassau. The annual Junkanoo Parade, rivaling Caribbean carnivals and New Orleans' Mardi Gras, passes rhythmically along this thoroughfare. Here you'll find bargains in a variety of items from china and crystal to liquor and cameras, and you can visit Nassau Art Gallery By the Waterfront. At one end of the street is the dignified British Colonial Beach Resort. The busy straw market in the open-air Ministry of Tourism building sells t-shirts and jewelry in addition to countless straw products. Off the waterfront, from Cumberland east to Church Street, Bay Street brings back memories of the "Bay Street...Boys." This notorious group of businessmen ruled The Bahamas from Nassau, and are alleged to have divided the spoils among themselves and their enterprises. The Duke of Windsor was tainted by their scheming during his tenure as wartime governor general.

Nearby palm-shaded Rawson Square is full of bright flowers where horse-drawn carriages wait to give tours. It sits between Prince George Dock and the government buildings across Bay Street. Visitors from cruise ships pour out into the square heading for restaurants and bargains on Bay Street. Tourists from hotels in town compete with the cruise passengers for the taxis and surreys that line up at the square. The 45-minute surrey trips are about $8 per person.

Prince George Dock is the busiest point in Nassau. Cruise ships dock here. Freighters, tugs, charter boats, sightseeing boats, pleasure boats, fishing craft and mail boats to the Family Islands all use this wharf. It teems with pedestrians and vendors coming and going, mirroring the activity of the harbor. Facing the water is a statue by Randolph W. Johnston of Little Harbour, Abaco, in tribute to the Bahamian woman. It was dedicated in 1974 by the prime minister, and the inscription begins, "In grateful tribute to the Bahamian woman whose steadfast love and devotion sustained our nation through countless years of adversity."

Woodes Rogers Walk, bordering the waterfront, is a colorful place for a stroll. Near the Straw Market, across from the towering cruise ships, women sell home-cooked meals from pots in the trunks of their cars. You might see a man hawking conch salad from a jar and someone else trying to attract customers to a shopping cart full of ripe bananas. Near Parliament St., ferries depart for Paradise Island and Coral World marine park. Off Bay Street by the British Colonial Hotel you can catch local jitneys or minibuses to Cable Beach. Buses depart for the Paradise Island bridge and elsewhere from nearby Frederick Street, off Bay. Young men with sacks slung over their shoulders will sell you peanuts through the window of your bus as you wait for it to take off.

In Parliament Square, with its statue of a slim, young queen Victoria, visitors can watch ceremonial parades or attend the solemn opening of the nation's Supreme Court. Also housed in the colonial government buildings here are the House of Assembly, the Supreme Court, the office of the Colonial Secretary, the Central Police Station and the octagonal public library, formerly a prison. Spend some time at the garden of Remembrance, where a monument honors the war dead. As well as being the capital and the seat of government, Nassau is the financial center. It is also the hub of air and boat traffic to the outer islands.

The Paradise Island bridge is about a mile east on Bay Street from the heart of downtown Nassau. Although you can take a jitney to the Nassau side of the bridge, the walk makes a pleasant stroll. You'll pass some handsome old wooden gingerbread houses with covered front porches. Children often play soccer in the park by Eastern Cemetery, with its above-ground tombs, in front of St. Matthew's Anglican Church, at East Bay and Dowdeswell Streets. This large,

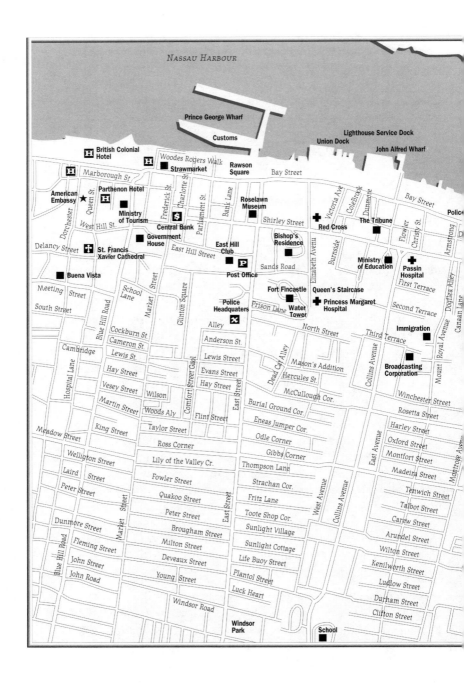

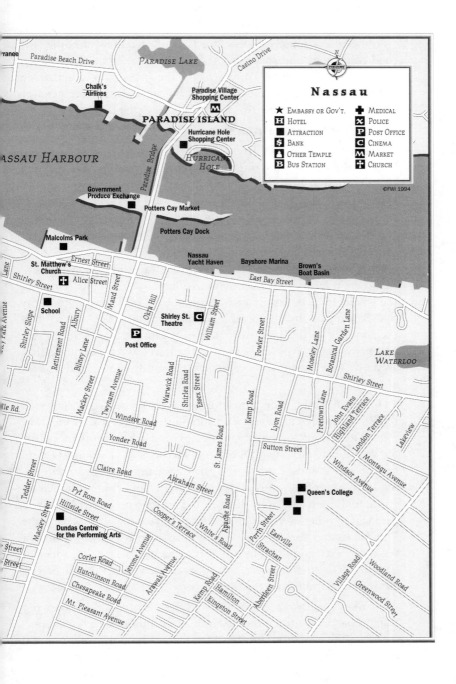

Paradise Beach Drive
PARADISE LAKE
Casino Drive
Chalk's Airlines
Paradise Village Shopping Center
PARADISE ISLAND
Hurricane Hole Shopping Center
HURRICANE HOLE
Paradise Bridge
NASSAU HARBOUR
Government Produce Exchange
Potters Cay Market
Potters Cay Dock
Malcoms Park
St. Matthew's Church
Ernest Street
Alice Street
Shirley Street
Nassau Yacht Haven
Bayshore Marina
Brown's Boat Basin
East Bay Street
School
Shirley Slope
Retirement Road
Albury
Bilney Lane
Maud Street
Otra Hill
Shirley St. Theatre
William Street
Fowler Street
Moseley Lane
Botanical Garden Lane
LAKE WATERLOO
Post Office
Mackey Street
Twynam Avenue
Warwick Road
Shirlea Road
Essex Street
Kemp Road
Lyon Road
Freetown Lane
John Evans
Shirley Street
Windsor Road
Yonder Road
St. James Road
Sutton Street
Highland Terrace
London Terrace
Lakeview
Claire Road
Abraham Street
Windsor Avenue
Montagu Avenue
Tedder Street
Pyf Rom Road
Hillside Street
Cooper's Terrace
Apache Road
White's Road
Perth Street
Eastville
Queen's College
Mackey Street
Dundas Centre for the Performing Arts
Jerome Avenue
Arawak Avenue
Strachan
Village Road
Woodland Road
Corlet Road
Hutchinson Road
Chesapeake Road
Kemp Road
Hamilton
Aberdeen Street
Greenwood Street
Mt. Pleasant Avenue
Kingston Street

Nassau

★ EMBASSY OR GOV'T.   ✚ MEDICAL
H HOTEL   ✗ POLICE
■ ATTRACTION   P POST OFFICE
$ BANK   C CINEMA
▲ OTHER TEMPLE   M MARKET
B BUS STATION   ✝ CHURCH

©FWI 1994

impressive stone church is one of the oldest in the Bahamas. It is set back on a great lawn dotted with stately palms.

Public buses or minivans leave for Cable Beach in front of the fast-food restaurants and shops across from the foot of the Paradise Island bridge. The masted boats filling the harbor make a striking sight. Here at East Bay Yacht Haven, you can make arrangements to scuba dive, or try helmet diving with Hartley's Undersea Walk.

BEYOND NASSAU'S RESORTS

To get the scoop on current social issues, stop by the Bahamian Forum, the weekly gathering that is a cross between a town meeting and a cultural happening. You might hear a historian spinning tales about the African roots of Junkanoo, a local playwright discussing his craft, or a debate about whether the Bahamas should institute a national lottery. The forum meets every Wednesday at 5:30 p.m. at the Roman Catholic Sisters Convent on West Hill St. in Nassau.

As far as a Bahamian lottery goes, by the way, some people believe that there is far too much gambling in these islands as it is. They rue the day in 1920 when the first casino opened in Nassau. Others say that Bahamians already spend a great deal on lotteries—by sending their money to the U.S. so that friends can purchase state lottery tickets for them. Why allow so much cash to leave the country, they argue. With a Bahamian sweepstakes, these tidy sums could be kept at home.

On Watch Night, otherwise known as New Year's Eve, you'd think the Zion Baptist Church on East and Shirley streets was giving away money instead of conducting services. Hundreds of people, no matter what their denomination, begin to fill the pews at around 11 p.m. for the exhilarating sermon and the energetic countdown to midnight. As in Freeport, most folks go straight from church to their favorite nightclub and from there to the frenetic pre-dawn Junkanoo parade. On other evenings throughout the year the stage is set at the Dundas Center for the Performing Arts for plays, instrumental or vocal concerts, and other local entertainment. Check newspapers for details. Pick up tickets at Nassau Stationers, on Rosetta Street, around the corner from the theater.

On Western Esplanade beach, across from Fort Charlotte between Cable Beach and downtown Nassau, local fundraising "cookouts" are often held on Saturdays. The food is actually cooked at home and brought to be sold to raise money for schools, churches, medical expenses of individuals and other causes. People go from table to table, deciding whose version of fish, ribs, chicken, conch fritters, peas and rice, macaroni and cheese and johnny cake looks the most irresistible. Children splash in the water while teenagers and adults dance to the music blasting from loudspeakers.

Some neighborhoods outside downtown Nassau and Cable Beach are poor and studded with ramshackle buildings. Yet the ghosts of their rich history creep out between the weathered wooden or cinderblock houses, churches, bars and mom-and-pop shops. In addition to the dominos and checkers played religiously in many front yards, you'll see people deeply involved in *warri*, a game brought over by enslaved Africans.

One area seldom visited by tourists begins just beyond the most frequented streets of the capital. Gregory Arch, on Market St. and visible from downtown Bay St., is one of the gateways to this populous region. Locally known as Over-the-Hill, this area contains settlements such as Grant's Town and Bain Town. A 19th-century Black Bahamian businessman, Charles H. Bain, purchased a land grant to found the town bearing his name.

South of here, Fox Hill was once divided into four villages. In the beginning, three of these had populations consisting of freed people who had been born in Africa. The other was settled by Bahamian-born people of African descent. Every year in Freedom Park and on the Village Green, in the center of Fox Hill, residents celebrate Emancipation Day (the first Monday in August) and Fox Hill Day (the second Tuesday in August) with food, music and other festivities.

Carmichael Village, farther southwest, was one of the earliest settlements of freed slaves. At a farm near the Carmichael Chicken Farm, about a 15-minute drive from the Ramada South Ocean Golf & Beach Resort, you can pick your own vegetables, juicy grapefruit and other citrus. Another place to gather your own goodies is Claridge Farm, on Harold Road, about five miles from downtown Nassau, near the Bacardi distillery. This fresh produce is especially welcome for those staying in time-share units, condos and housekeeping apartments.

Down on the southwestern coast, the settlement called Adelaide was named for Queen Adelaide, consort of William IV of England. Its first settlers were Africans captured by the Portuguese in the early 1800s and headed for enslavement. Their vessel, the *Rosa*, was taken by the British, and the 150 or so Africans landed in Nassau as free people since slavery had already been abolished in the British colonies. As late as the 1960s, more than a few thatched-roof houses remained in this town, which was reminiscent of 19-century African villages.

Gambier Village sits on the northern coast, west of Cable Beach. Its original settlers were freed Africans who arrived in 1807 with the British Royal Navy. One of its best known residents was Elizah Morris, a former slave, who helped bring about the 1841 Creole Mutiny off the coast of Abaco.

Visitors can see some of these areas by taxi or in inexpensive jitneys. These minibuses take circular routes, so you'll have no trouble returning to your point of departure.

CRUISING INTO NASSAU

Visitors arriving in New Providence for the first time, by cruise ship, are likely to be moved by the sense of adventure and anticipation as the vessel approaches Nassau. From a distance, the island begins to take form. As the ship nears shore, trees, buildings and a bulbous hill come into view. The vessel slips slowly and majestically between Nassau and Paradise Island, offering a look at the handsome bulk of the historic pink British Colonial Hotel. Ahead is the graceful arch of the Paradise Island bridge with the tangle of fish, fruit, and vegetable vendors along Potters Cay dock below. On the rise just in front is the Water Tower and, farther west, the stone pile that is Fort Charlotte.

The ship pulls alongside the dock. Stories below, dockworkers are scurrying around and a line of taxis and ancient limousines wait to waft passengers into town. But for most cruisers, wheels are unnecessary since town, with its many restaurants and economical shops, is a short walk beyond the pier.

A CRUISER'S STROLL INTO TOWN

Amble across Prince George Dock and you might stop to look in on the Junkanoo Expo (which honors the Bahamas' major festival). Nearby, you'll see the hair-braiding pavilion where you can get your tresses cornrowed. At the Tourist Information office, you can arrange for one of the guided walking tours or sign up to socialize with Bahamians through the People-to-People program (ask about tea at Government House, hosted once a month).

Passing a line of horse-drawn carriages under a thatched canopy, you see Rawson Square, where a statue of a young Queen Victoria sits in welcome before the cluster of pink and white government buildings. Bisecting the square is Bay Street. Turning left to the east or right to the west will lead you to restaurants, both elegant and no-frills shopping, and to sights such as the Straw Market.

Should you want to see Cable Beach and its casino, hailing a taxi or catching a mini bus (at Bay and Frederick Streets) is your best bet. A taxi or your feet will take you to the beach, restaurants, shops or casino across the bridge on Paradise Island.

PARADISE ISLAND

This lacy gazebo makes a romantic spot in Versailles Gardens, Paradise Island.

Paradise Island is connected to New Providence Island by a dramatic arching bridge that gives a spectacular view of the harbor. Ferries (water taxis) run between downtown Nassau and Paradise Island (about $2 each way). Paradise Island Airlines links the island with Florida, as well as with Marsh Harbour and Treasure Cay in the Abacos. As you cross the bridge (25¢ by foot, 75¢ by bike or moped,

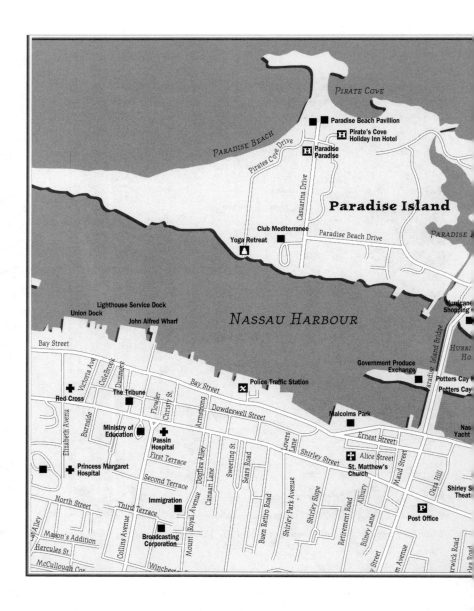

PIRATE COVE

Paradise Beach Pavillion

Pirate's Cove
Holiday Inn Hotel

Paradise
Paradise

PARADISE BEACH

Pirates Cove Drive

Casuarina Drive

Paradise Island

Club Mediterranee

Paradise Beach Drive

PARADISE I

Yoga Retreat

NASSAU HARBOUR

Hurricane
Shopping

Lighthouse Service Dock
Union Dock

John Alfred Wharf

Paradise Island Bridge

HURRI
Ho

Bay Street

Government Produce
Exchange

Potters Cay
Potters Cay

Victoria Avenu
ColeBrook
Dunmore

Bay Street

Police Traffic Station

Red Cross

The Tribune

Flower
Christ St.

Dowdeswell Street

Malcolms Park

Nas
Yacht

Elizabeth Avenu
Burnside

Ministry of
Education

Passin
Hospital

First Terrace

Armstrong

Sweeting St.

Sears Road

Lovers
Lane

Shirley Street

Ernest Street

St. Matthew's
Church

Alice Street

Maud Street

Och Hill

Princess Margaret
Hospital

Second Terrace

Doglea Alley

Canaan Lane

Royal Avenue

Shirley Park Avenue

Buen Retiro Road

Shirley Slope

Retirement Road

Albury

Bilney Lane

Shirley S
Theat

North Street

Third Terrace

Immigration

Collins Avenue

Mount

Post Office

y Alley
Mason's Addition

Hercules St.

McCullough Cor.

Broadcasting
Corporation

Winchester

m Avenue
y Street

rwick Road
lpa Road

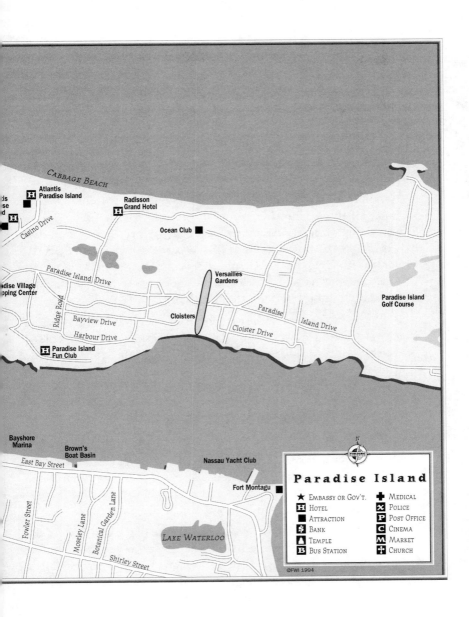

Paradise Island

$2.00 by car, round trip), you will see colorful fruit and vegetable stands at Potters Cay Dock on the Nassau side next to piles of conch shells. The sprawling pink and white waterfront complex on the Paradise Island side is Hurricane Hole Marina and Portside Condominiums, one of the many condos you'll find on the island. The multi-level two- and three-bedroom apartments here are for sale and rent.

Now lavishly landscaped and stocked with a casino, an 18-hole golf course, bridle path, tennis courts, deluxe hotels, condominiums, time shares, restaurants and a transplanted ruin, Paradise Island went by the unglamorous name of Hog Island when it was farmland. The original concept to develop Hog Island came from a Swedish millionaire, Axel Wenner-Gren. He purchased the old Lynch estate on the island and set about digging canals to connect a lake with the Nassau harbor. He then proceeded to rebuild the estate, the former home of the Edmund C. Lynch of Merrill, Lynch fame. During World War II, it was discovered that Mr. Wenner-Gren's munitions works in Sweden were allied with and partially owned by the Nazi-controlled Krupp works. Despite a boycott, the war made him even wealthier, but he sold his Hog Island holdings to another millionaire, Huntington Hartford, the A&P heir.

After a few false starts, the island's serious development was begun again by Hartford, who planned to make it a showplace. A medieval cloister had been dismantled earlier and brought stone by stone from France by William Randolph Hearst and stored with the rest of his Old World treasures. Hartford took it off Hearst's hands and had it reassembled in Versailles Gardens, where it now stands, an ancient attraction for the new Paradise Island.

The island continued its ascent toward prestige and glamour even after the departure of Hartford. Other hotels sprang up to take advantage of the new space and its attractive beaches. World renowned statesmen, politicians, jet setters and European royalty came to sample the enticements of this fashionable new playground.

The busiest section of the broad, stark white beach is in front of the sprawling Atlantis, Paradise Island resort, with its aquarium, waterscape, Folies-Bergère-like Cabaret Theatre and an array of shops, restaurants, bars, and boutiques. Women walk up and down the shore selling t-shirts and offering to cornrow hair. Men carry boxes of coconuts on their heads, inviting you to drink fresh coconut water straight from the shell. Windsurfers, Sunfish and parasailers splash the turquoise water with the bright colors of their sails and parachutes. Banana boats, bright yellow tube-like rafts pulled by motor boats, bounce across the waves. Watch out for the rocks hidden at the water's edge in some places. The best swimming in this area is in front of the Britiannia Towers section of Atlantis, Paradise Island. However, don't go in the water if you see the red flags (which warn that the current is too strong or the waves too rough).

Guests from nearby hotels and condos as well as from more remote island locations find their way to the casino, including those at the island's self-contained Club Med. The only visitors who seem to shun the casino are patrons of the Yoga Retreat, who prefer contemplation, vegetarianism and exercise. Shuttle buses connect the island's hotels, restaurants and casino. The Ocean Club & Tennis Resort, one of the small luxury hotels in a quiet part of the island, began as a vacation home for Hartford. It remains one of the preferred hostelries for those with deep pockets. Romantics who have dreamed of going horseback riding along a beach can have that fantasy come true at the stables nearby.

In addition to hotel boutiques and dining rooms, shops and restaurants are found in Paradise Village shopping center and the newer Hurricane Hole Plaza. Along with the usual t-shirt, resort wear, jewelry, and perfume shops, there are grocery and liquor stores, and places to buy fishing gear, ice chests and other supplies.

At the docks near Club Med and the Paradise Island Bridge, you can catch ferries to Nassau as well as glass bottom boat cruises, and boats to offshore islands for diving and snorkeling. With beautiful beaches and hammocks strung between palms, nearby **Blue Lagoon Island** is popular for snorkeling cruises. Lunch at the pavilion, live music, and use of snorkeling gear are included in the rates. (See "Sports," or make arrangements through your hotel.)

Also known as Salt Cay, this island was once frequented by pirates. For decades afterwards, it was privately owned by an American family who entertained royalty, politicians and socialites here. During the 1970s, Bahamians began bringing tourists to and around the island. To discourage these visits, the family who owned the island would sometimes appear stark naked, and the embarrassed outsiders would scurry off.

WHAT TO SEE AND DO

PERSONAL FAVORITES

Hartley's Undersea Walk, for its spectacular views of marine life.

Versailles Gardens, for its terraced landscaping, 12th-century cloister, and harbor view.

SIGHTS AND ATTRACTIONS

New Providence is one of the Bahamian islands that was settled early and has a number of points of historical interest, most of which can be reached in a day's tour. Nassau, as the seat of government, has reminders of former British rule, and remnants of slavery.

Ardastra Gardens and Zoo

Near Fort Charlotte off Columbus Avenue and Chippingham Road, Nassau; ☎ *323-5806* • The national bird of The Bahamas, the flamingo, is used to put on a show for visitors to the gardens. Among the attractions is a precision parade of the pink birds to the command of their trainer. Visitors are invited to pose for photographs with the birds.
Open 9 a.m.to 4:30 p.m. Admission $8.

Atlantis Submarine

Charlotte Street, Prince George Dock, Nassau; ☎ *356-3842* • This undersea tour in an air-conditioned submarine accompanied by an informative narration reveals some of the Bahamas' dramatic marine life. The complete trip, including transport out to the sub, takes 2-1/ 2 hours.   *Cost: $70 for adults; half price for children.*

Blackbeard's Tower

East of Fox Hill Road, Nassau • The climb to Blackbeard's Tower is worth the trip if only to view the sweep of the Nassau harbor and the city stretching east and west. However, what remains of the tower itself is not as spectacular. The structure was supposedly used as a lookout point by the pirate Edward Teach, alias Blackbeard, to watch for approaching ships during the period when he was a marauder in Bahamian waters.

Botanical Gardens

Near Fort Charlotte, off Columbus Avenue, Nassau • This protected area has 18 acres of 600 species of tropical flowers and plants. There is a lily pond, a cactus garden and a children's playground.
Open daily 9 a.m. to 4 p.m. Admission: $1.

Coral Island

Coral Island, between Cable Beach and downtown Nassau: ☎ *328-1036 or 800/328-8814* • At least a couple of hours are needed to take in this marine park not far from Fort Charlotte. Built around a natural reef by the developers of Coral World in the U.S. Virgin Islands, the Bahamian version also has a natural undersea observatory. At the Pearl Bar, select an oyster guaranteed to contain a pearl. Flamingos, macaws and other rare birds flutter about the grounds. Sharks, in their tank, can be seen from above and below. There are morays, rays, parrot fish, huge sea turtles and many other creatures. A crow's nest, 85 feet above sea level, gives photographers a breathtaking panorama of Nassau. A souvenir shop, snack bar and a restaurant are on the grounds. There's a touch tank for children. Groups of giggling Bahamian schoolchildren on education excursions are admitted without charge.

Open daily from 9 a.m. to 6 p.m., with extended hours during Daylight Saving Time (April–October); Admission $16. A round-trip boat departs from Woodes Rogers Walk every half hour, $19 including admission. Free shuttle bus service from Cable Beach hotels, 9 a.m. to 5 p.m.; and free boats from Paradise Island hotels, 9:15 a.m. to 3:30 p.m.

Dolphin Encounters ★★★

(809)

9/4/95

Blue Lagoon Island, off Nassau; ☎ *363-1653 or 363-1003* • On a cay a 20-minute sail from Nassau, several programs allow people to become intimately acquainted with dolphins. After learning about these irresistible mammals, you can meet them from the edge of the water, plunge in and swim with them or spend a day with them (including lunch and snorkeling gear). *Prices range from $30 to $115.*

Fort Charlotte ★★

Off West Bay Street overlooking Nassau harbor • This is the largest fort in The Bahamas. Built in 1788, it guards the entrance to Nassau's harbor. Like Blackbeard's Tower, it also affords a panoramic view of the harbor. Of special interest are its moat, dungeon and gun emplacements. The guide often waits to collect a group and expects a tip at the tour's end. The tourist office in Nassau has information on the frequency of tours, since they are not regularly scheduled; ☎ *322-7500.*

Fort Fincastle ★

On Bennett's Hill overlooking Nassau harbor • The "bow" of this 18th century fort (which is shaped like a paddle wheel steamer) points toward the nearby Water Tower and top of Queen's Staircase. Climb to the top of the fort to check out the cannons and the stunning view of the harbor, with Fort Charlotte in the distance. This fort was named for Lord Dunmore, the Royal Governor who had it built in 1793 and whose second title was Viscount Fincastle. History gave it little opportunity to do its job—protecting Nassau from invaders. So it became a lighthouse until 1816, and then was turned into a signal tower. The young men who wait to give tours in exchange for tips can be quite persistent, so if you'd rather explore on your own, be polite but firm when declining. By the entrance to the fort, browse among the t-shirts, straw goods, refreshments and other wares of vendors.

Fort Montagu ★

Off East Bay Street, Nassau • Fort Montagu is the oldest of Nassau's remaining forts. Facing the eastern entrance to the harbor, it was built in 1741 to ward off an attack by Spaniards that never came. The fort, however, was occupied for a short time by Americans during the Revolutionary War. The nearby park, with lawns, shade and vendors, is a pleasant place to stop.

Government House ★

Off Blue Hill Road, Nassau • The official residence of the British-appointed governor general stands on one of the island's highest points. In front of the colonial mansion is a statue of Christopher Columbus wearing a broadbrimmed hat, draped in a cloak and carrying a staff. Every other Saturday morning, the changing of the guard takes place here. The mansion's grounds are thick with lush tropical foliage and plants. Visitors can sign the guest book in a small guardhouse located near the exit gate.

Gregory Arch ★

East of Government House at Market Street, Nassau • This arch marks the entrance to Grant's Town, just over the ridge from the Nassau harbor. The town was established at Emancipation on land given to ex-slaves to build homes and set up farms.

Hairbraider's Centre ★★

Prince George Dock, Nassau • At this government-sponsored open-air pavilion, visitors and residents may have their hair braided or cornrowed in a variety of styles by expert and certified hairdressers at prices ranging from $2 to $75.

Harbour Island ★★★

Sandpiper 4-Way Charter; ☎ *809/377-5602 or 809/377-5751* • No, this wonderful cay is not in Nassau—it's off the northern coast of Eleuthera—but you can fly over from the capital city to visit it for a day. With gingerbread cottages enclosed by white picket fences and a mostly empty pink sand beach, its beauty is legendary. Ask about the excursion that includes roundtrip flights, time for swimming and exploring and lunch at one of the beach hotels as well as use of its facilities. **Cost: about $100 to $130 per person.**

Hartley's Undersea Walk ★★★

Nassau Yacht Haven, East Bay St., Nassau; ☎ *325-3369* • This 3-1/2-hour cruise on the yacht Pied Piper includes an escorted undersea walk to see varieties of tropical fish, coral formations and other undersea life. Even kids, the elderly and non-swimmers can enjoy the experience. The trick is the helmet you wear with air pumped in through a tube.
The yacht leaves at 9:30 a.m. and 1:30 p.m. daily. Check-in time is a half hour before departure. About $36 per person.

Helicopter Tours ★★

Paradise Island; ☎ *363-1040* • Air-conditioned whirlybirds fly from the old Chalk's seaplane aiport on Paradise Island. You'll gaze down on that island as well as the city of Nassau and some of the nearby surrounding isles and cays. On good days, the varied hues of the water are incredible. All pilots are certified and the helicopters are inspected and maintained by the Federal Aeronautics Administration.

Cost: $10, $25 and $50, depending on length of flight.

Junkanoo Expo

Prince George Dock, Nassau • In a vast former customs shed, an array of bright floats and costumes used in annual Junkanoo parades and celebrations are on display. If you miss the real deal (on Boxing Day—December 26, and on New Year's Day), wandering among the colorful glittering exhibits is the next best thing to seeing the festival live.

Admission: $2.

Nautilus

Bay and Deveaux Streets, Nassau; ☎ *325-2876 or 325-2871* • This glass-bottomed surface submarine lets you stay dry while getting a glimpse of the underworld. You'll see purplish-midnight blue parrotfish darting in and out of an old shipwreck near Paradise Island. Tiger-striped sergeant majors, angelfish and four-eyed butterfly fish swarm around the spectacular coral reef that resembles an underwater jungle. You'll also take in the sights of Nassau Harbour.

Potters Cay

Under Paradise Island Bridge, Nassau • At this colorful market, you can buy fresh fish, fruit, and vegetables, and watch fishermen shell conch.

Powerboat Adventure

Nassau; ☎ *327-5385* • This day trip in a 900-horsepower speed boat takes passengers from Nassau out into the waters and government-protected reefs of the Exuma cays, some of the most beautiful islands in the Bahamas. Drinks and lunch are provided, as well as snorkeling gear and opportunities to see colorful marine life.

Cost: $150 for adults; $100 for children under age 12.

Public Library

Parliament and Shirley Streets, Nassau • This octagonal building was once a prison. Now a library, it has facilities and materials for research on a variety of subjects related to the Bahamas. History buffs looking for more in-depth information should head to the Bahamian Archives.

Queen's Staircase

Across Shirley Street, toward the rise away from the harbor and near Princess Margaret Hospital, Nassau • These 65 steps-of-stone have come to represent the number of years Victoria ruled the British Empire. One hundred and two feet high, the staircase is said to have been hewn by slaves from solid limestone, and leads to the remains of Fort Fincastle and the Water Tower at the top. When the weather and/or water supply permit, a cascade spills down next to the staircase, causing an iridescent mist when the sun hits the enclosure. The high stone walls of the cut that leads to the bottom of the steps are bordered by lush trees and hung with vines. In this jungled, shady passage, vendors sell straw goods and t-shirts. At the top and bottom of the stairs, boys wait to give you the well-memorized history of the staircase in exchange for tips. You can walk from the top to neighboring Fort Fincastle and the Water Tower, both of which have sweeping views. If you'd rather walk *down* the Queen's Staircase, then hit the fort and tower first. Go up East Street, turn left onto Sands Road, then take the next right, and a quick left up to the fort.

Roselawn Museum

East Street and Bank Lane, Nassau • In a house built in 1820, The Rose-lawn museum displays memorabilia from Nassau and the Out Islands, including Bahamian coins, maps, stamps, parts of shipwrecks, old bottles salvaged from the sea and Junkanoo costumes.

Open 9 a.m. to 5 p.m. Free admission.

Royal Victoria Gardens

Across Shirley Street and up toward Government House, Nassau • The sprawling Royal Victoria Hotel was built during the American Civil War and was used as the headquarters of Bahamians who ran arms for the Confederacy. Part of the building was later used for government offices. In its time, the hotel was the showplace of the Bahamas, and its gardens reflected its grandeur and opulence. The gardens contain about 300 kinds of tropical plants. Although the grand old hotel was closed in 1971, then destroyed by fire, the gardens survived and remain open to the public. With blackened pillars and gaping window openings, the shell of the hotel now resembles Roman ruins.

Sea Gardens

Eastern end of Nassau harbor • This fantastic underwater attraction covers 40 acres of coral, fern and all the colorful marine life found in tropical waters. **$15 from Prince George Dock**

Straw Market

Bay and Market Streets, Nassau • Everything that can be rendered in straw—plus much more—is on sale here. Market women may beckon you to examine their handicrafts. They may quickly slip a necklace over your head in an attempt to convince you to buy. The wares include hats and baskets, which are much in evidence, along with objects of shell, bead jewelry, wood sculpture and t-shirts. Many items are fashioned on the spot. The merchants are aggressive and bargaining is spirited. In addition to the beach, this is the place to go to get your hair cornrowed and beaded.

The Pompey Museum (Vendue House)

Dating from about 1800, this striking building was erected as a market for auctions and sales of enslaved Africans. Goods from wreckers could also be purchased here. The house is presently a museum of Bahamian history and has an art gallery on its second floor.

Free admission.

Versailles Gardens   ★★★

At the Ocean Club, Paradise Island • Even if you're not on your honeymoon, be sure to spend some time in this romantic oasis. Walk down from the swimming pool at the Ocean Club, and you'll enter a garden studded with bronze and marble statues. In a tree-shaded corner, a huge likeness of Roosevelt stands wearing a cape. Across the way, gaze up at David Livingstone (1813–1873), the Scottish explorer of Africa. In a pond with a surface covered with tiny, bright green plants, turtles poke their heads out of the water. Follow the central path that leads to the 12th century cloister that is dramatically perched on a rise. Built by the Augustinian order in France, it was reassembled here, stone by stone, in 1962 for Huntington Hartford, who developed Paradise Island. With its aging columns, this structure is particularly stunning at night when it is illuminated. Overlooking the boatfilled harbor, the nearby lacy gazebo seems a perfect place to exchange or renew wedding vows.

Walking Tour of Downtown Nassau   ★★

Tourist Bureau, Rawson Square; ☎ *326-9781 or 326-9772* • Those who'd like to learn more than they would by strolling on their own should consider this guided tour. The walk permits amblers to have close-up looks at and learn the history of sights including Fort Fincastle, the Water Tower, the Queen's Staircase, Bay Street, Government House, Princess Margaret Hospital and the Bahamas Historical Society. ***Cost: $2 for adults; 50¢ for children.***

Water Tower   ★

On Bennett Hill near Fort Fincastle, Nassau • Near Fort Fincastle and the top of Queens Staircase, the Water Tower is the highest point on New Providence, 216 feet above sea level. An elevator takes you to the observation deck for an unusual view of Nassau and points beyond. ***Open 9 a.m. to 5 p.m. Admission: 50¢.***

SPORTS

Although plenty of independent vendors walk along Cable Beach signing people up for all kinds of water sports and cruises, the hotels here recommend that, for safety reasons, guests use only the hotels' authorized watersports agents (at the marked kiosks along the beach).

Boating

See "Sailing" and "Sights and Attractions."

Fishing

Arrange fishing trips through your hotel or by contacting **Chubasco Charters** (☎ *322-8148)* or **Born Free Charter Service** (☎ *363-2003 or 393-4144)* for deep-sea adventures, or Island Drifter Ltd. (☎ *326-5441)* for bottom and drift fishing, all on Paradise Island; or **East Bay Yacht Basin** (☎ *326-3754)*, **Nassau Yacht Haven** (☎ *393-8173)*, **Bayshore Marina** (☎ *326-8232)*, or **Lyford Cay Marina** (☎ *326-4267)*, all on New Providence.

Diving

Whether you're a certified diver or want to learn scuba, you can arrange to go down under through your hotel or by contacting one of Nassau's dive operators directly. Among the best are **Bahama Divers** (☎ *393-5644 or 393-1466),* **Dive Dive Dive Ltd.** (☎ *362-1143 or 362-1401),* **Sun Divers Ltd.** (☎ *325-8927),* and **Diving Safaris Ltd.** (☎ *393-2522 or 393-1179).* Also excellent are **Nassau Scuba Centre** (☎ *362-1964, 362-4688, or (800)327-8150)* and **Stuart Cove's** (☎ *362-4171, 327-7862, or (800)468-9876),* both of which specialize in underwater photography (still and video). Stuart Cove's also snares the adventurous with its shark dives. (They're quite safe!)

Helmet diving

Somewhere between snorkeling and scuba, helmet diving allows you to go down about twelve feet while air is pumped into your helmet through a long tube. Try this sport with **Hartley's Undersea Walk** (☎ *325-3369)* at Nassau Yacht Haven, near the Paradise Island bridge.

Golf

Courses are at the **Crystal Palace PGA Course**, 18 holes, (☎ *27-8231);* the **Coral Harbour Golf Club,** 18 holes, (☎ *326-1144);* the **Ramada South Ocean Golf & Beach Resort**, 18 holes, (☎ *326-4391);* and the **Paradise Island Golf Club**, 18 holes (☎ *326-5925).*

Horseback Riding

Paradise Island (☎ *326-1433) •*
   Rates at the Paradise Island Riding Stables are about $22 an hour.

Sailing

On Nassau and Paradise Island, there are many ways to spend time afloat, for a half day or full day. You can make sailing arrangements through your hotel or by contacting charters at **Nassau Yacht Haven** (☎ *393-8173)* and **East Bay Yacht Basin** (☎ *326-3754)* in Nassau or **Hurricane Hole Marina** (☎ *326-5441)* on Paradise Island. Several companies host sightseeing sails, glass bottom boat trips and **snorkeling** cruises with live bands, lunch and visits to uninhabited cays such as Rose Island, Discovery Island and Blue Lagoon Island.

Also offering scuba diving, **Island Fantasy Ltd.** (☎ *393-3621 or 323-1988)* specializes in small groups for their snorkeling excursions on a fishing boat, which include cocktails, buffet lunch and stops at a deserted beach. Departing from downtown Nassau and Paradise Island, **Topsail Yacht Charters** (☎ *393-0820)* takes intimate groups snorkeling on sail boats, serving lunch and drinks and stopping at Rose Island. Ask about their champagne cocktail cruises and dinner cruises just for two. For real partying to the sounds of a live calypso band, try **Robinson Crusoe Shipwreck Cruises** (☎ *322-2606).* You'll sail to an uninhabited island aboard an 85-foot catamaran with three decks. Lunch, wine and use of snorkel gear are included. Twice a week, there are also dinner/dancing cruises. Another good company for snorkeling cruises to an uninhabited island, with lunch and drinks, is **Sea Island Adventure** (☎ *325-3910 or 328-2581).*

For a truly romantic day, charter a boat to Rose Island (at a time when other boats won't be around). The beach looks as if it were plucked from a postcard, and you'll have it all to yourselves. **Calypso cruises** (☎ *363-3577 or 363-3578)* runs moonlight dinner cruises, as well as daytime sails to Blue Lagoon Island (once a pirate's haven) for snorkeling, beachcombing and lunch. You'll eat in the elevated party pavilion, where there is usually a live band. The view from here of the Atlantic and of the long stretch of white sand is wonderful. Although the pavilion is often crowded with people from cruise ships and noisy with limbo contests, there are plenty of tranquil spots throughout the island. In the center, the land forms a C, cupping the calm Blue Lagoon, with windsurfers, big-wheeled aqua-cycles, and other water toys. Since the water here is so still, it's too murky for swimming, but there are excellent swimming beaches all around the island. Bordered by groves of palms, paths snake across the island, leading to snorkeling spots and quiet sandy coves. Hammocks hang between trees. A volleyball net is strung across the sand, and there is a play area for children.

Snorkeling See "Sailing."

Tennis

Most of the large hotels have tennis courts. The sports complex across from the Crystal Palace has **squash** and **racquetball courts** as well. You can also play these sports at the Nassau Squash and Racquet Club *(Independence Drive;* ☎ *322-3882)* and at the British Colonial Beach Resort.

Parasailing

Enjoy this sport on Cable Beach at the **Ambassador Beach Hotel**, the **Crystal Palace**, and the **Nassau Beach Hotel**, and on Paradise Island at the **Radisson Grand Hotel**.

Water-skiing

Most of the larger beach hotels offer water-skiing.

Windsurfing

The **Ambassador Beach Hotel**, the **Crystal Palace** and **Coral Harbour Beach Villas** all have windsurfing.

NIGHTLIFE

The Crystal Palace and Radisson resorts flank the high-tech **Fanta-Z** disco. Many other hotels have night clubs and discos. **The Paon**, for instance in the Radisson Grand, has a computerized sound system that will shame any New York disco.

In Nassau, **The Palace** on Elizabeth Avenue has a live band that plays a mix of calypso, reggae and disco. **The Ritz Waterside Nite Club**, on Bay and Deveaux streets, is an indoor/outdoor disco by **Captain Nemo's Restau-**

rant, which has live bands on weekends. DJs and live bands appear periodically at **Parliament Inn** downtown. **The Goombay Club** is another popular dance spot. At the **Rock 'n Roll Cafe** in Cable Beach, happy hour runs from 10 p.m. to 2 a.m. Another popular disco is **Club Waterloo**, on East Bay Street.

The casinos in Cable Beach and Paradise Island are two of the most popular places to be after dark—and for some, during the day as well. The Crystal Palace casino in Cable Beach gives visitors a bright, modern alternative to the more traditional-looking Paradise Island casino. Glittery Las Vegas-style performances are put on in the Paradise Island cabaret theatre and The Crystal Palace casino. When you're ready to laugh, make reservations for an evening at **The Joker's Wild Comedy Club** in Atlantis, Paradise Island. Shows are Tuesday through Saturday.

Avoid the nightclub tours offered by some companies—you'll have much more fun doing the clubs on your own.

DINING OUT

For some real home cooking, have lunch at one of the beach parties often hosted on Saturdays on Western Esplanade, across from Fort Charlotte, or on other shores. You won't spend much, and you'll have a chance to mingle with Bahamians over music, drinks, hearty food, and swimming. Check newspapers or ask at your hotel for details.

PERSONAL FAVORITES

Sun And..., where the French and Bahamian cuisine is fast rivaling that at Graycliff, the island's only "Relais et Chateau."

Traveller's Rest, near the airport, for its beachfront locale and delicious local food.

CABLE BEACH/NASSAU

EXPENSIVE

Sole Mare   ★★

Carnival's Crystal Palace Resort & Casino, Cable Beach; *327-6200* •
Although this gourmet restaurant is located in the casino building, you don't have to be a gambler to enjoy the delicious Northern Italian food. The Sunday buffet brunch is popular. Seafood and veal are served in addition to a variety of pasta dishes.

Open Tuesday–Sunday. Major credit cards.

Le Cafe de Paris   ★★

Le Meridien Royal Bahamian hotel, Cable Beach; *327-6400* • This elegant gourmet French restaurant is highlighted by French doors, fanlight windows and a pianist who plays during dinner. Among the well-prepared and presented selections, you might find onion soup, seafood bouillon, escargot, endive salad with roquefort dressing, veal sweetbreads, stuffed chicken, lamb chops with herbs and poached salmon. Breakfast is also served. *Major credit cards.*

Buena Vista ★★★

Delancy St., downtown Nassau; ☎ *322-2811* • A circular driveway leads to the gourmet restaurant in an 18th-century colonial mansion. The candlelit dining areas are decorated with paintings and hanging plants. The menu might include smoked dolphin fish, avocado stuffed with lobster, escargot, Cajun salmon, leg of lamb and charcoal broiled tenderloin. For dessert, try the baked Alaska and calypso coffee. A pianist entertains with soft music. *Major credit cards.*

Roselawn ★★

Bank Lane, downtown Nassau; ☎ *325-1018* • This restaurant is a stone's throw from Rawson Square. Pasta is made on the premises and Bahamian seafood as well as Continental cuisine are served. There is entertainment at dinner. *Roselawn is closed on Sunday, and reservations are a must.* *Major credit cards.*

Graycliff ★★★

West Hill and Blue Hill Rd., downtown Nassau; ☎ *322-2796* • This is considered one of the finest restaurants in the Bahamas. It is located opposite Government House in a beautiful old mansion, and meals are served in charming and tasteful settings that include antiques, Royal Copenhagen china and British silverware. Although the cuisine is elegantly Continental, the chef also knows his way around Bahamian cooking. Visiting celebrities as well as ordinary mortals beat a path to Graycliff's at least once before leaving the island. Reservations are required. *Major credit cards.*

Sun And . . . ★★★

Lakeview Dr., off East Shirley St., downtown Nassau; ☎ *393-1205 or 393-2644* • In an old mansion not far from Fort Montague, this restaurant serves French and Bahamian dishes including conch chowder, braised duckling and sweetbreads with asparagus tips. Guests, who are asked to dress up, may dine alfresco or on a palm-shaded patio or in the indoor-outdoor areas around the pool. Sun And . . . is closed on Mondays. Reservations are requested. *Major credit cards.*

MODERATE

Poop Deck ★★

Nassau Yacht Haven Marina, East Bay St., downtown Nassau; ☎ *393-8175* • Just east of the Paradise Island bridge, this restaurant overlooks the picturesque, busy marina. Planes swoop down toward the airport on Paradise Island, across the water. Antique nautical items, such as an old diving helmet and aged brass portholes, decorate the walls. Hanging plants flutter in the breeze. To sit at the best tables, at the marina edge of the balcony, arrive just before noon or early for dinner. (However, single diners are not seated at these front tables!) Specialties, which change daily, include boiled fish and johnny cake, chicken souse with grits, okra soup, charbroiled pork chops with mashed potatoes and spiced apple sauce and Cajun-fried grouper nuggets. Grouper fingers, cracked conch, chicken wings, burgers, salads and sandwiches are also on the menu. This is one of the few places that serves guava duff, a prized local dessert. Other sweet surrenders include rum cake, key lime pie and coconut pie. Open noon to midnight.   ***Major credit cards.***

The Rock 'n Roll Cafe

Cable Beach; ☎ *327-7639* • Steak and seafood are the stars of the show at this beachfront Hard Rock Cafe clone. Walls are decorated with posters and photos of musicians, gold records, album covers and electric guitars. Rock music plays in the background. So the old world elegance of the dining rooms provides an amusing contrast, especially when the place is packed with rowdy young folks during late night happy hours (10 p.m. 'til 2 a.m.). Highbacked wooden chairs and white tablecloths complement the French doors and fireplace, but they somehow seem incongruous with Bob Marley, the Beatles, and Fats Domino, whose faces gaze at diners from walls. For lunch, try the conch chowder, mozzarella sticks, nachos, grouper fingers, burgers or sandwiches. The limited dinner menu might include Cajun snapper and blackened New York steak. Stop by the rock 'n roll shop on the premises.

Captain Nemo's

Bay and Deveaux St. dock, Nassau; ☎ *323-8426 or 323-8394* • Overlooking the harbor and Paradise Island, this steak and seafood restaurant is found at the end of a dock. Plants and fans hang from the ceiling in the open-air dining room. Take your pick of an array of tropical drinks. Begin your meal with conch chowder or conch fritters, then try seafood kebob, crab and lobster pie or filet mignon. For dessert, guava duff is served with hot brandy sauce. There's a daily happy hour from 3 p.m. to 6 p.m., and people dance to a live band on Friday and Saturday nights. The Ritz disco is nearby.   ***Major credit cards.***

The Deep End Cafe & Bar

Bay Street, next to the Dolphin Hotel; ☎ *323-3849* • Look for the surfboard painted to resemble a shark that hangs above the doorway. Breakfast, lunch and dinner are served at this cozy cafe, where the specials change daily. You might find stir-fried beef, shrimp or chicken; grilled fish; pasta; and seafood or dessert crepes. The pizza made on French bread or pita moves quickly, and the steaks and kebabs are also popular. On weekends, people come for the raw bar, which features oysters, clams and, of course, conch. The outdoor dining can be a bit noisy with all the Bay Street traffic, but you can gaze at a slice of the Atlantic over the seagrapes and between the palms. Closed Sundays.
                                                          A, M, V.

MODERATE TO INEXPENSIVE

Green Shutters Inn

Parliament St., across from the Royal Victoria Gardens, downtown Nassau;
☎ *325-5702* • Green Shutters has all the flavor of an English pub.
From its decor to its fish and chips, steak and kidney pie and beer, it
is all British and good for a luncheon stop.   ***Major credit cards.***

Pick-A-Dilly

Parliament Inn, 18 Parliament Street, downtown Nassau; ☎ *322-2836* •
As you enter the flower-filled courtyard, check the climate on the
hanging "weather rock," a chunk of coral stone. Treat yourself to a
frozen daiquiri, made with soursop, mango, coconut, banana or some
other tropical fruit, or try a Bahamian specialty: gin and coconut
water. You'll choose among blackened salmon, chicken stir-fry, burgers, sandwiches, pasta and other dishes. Open 8 a.m. to 9:30 p.m.
except Sunday.

Coconuts and Le Shack

East Bay Street, Nassau; ☎ *325-2148* • Featuring steak and seafood,
Coconuts is an attractive restaurant at the edge of the harbor. You'll
enter through a plant-filled courtyard with a small trickling fountain.
Each of the three casual dining rooms has its own personality. Open
for cocktails and dinner 5 p.m. to 11 p.m. Next door, waterfront **Le
Shack** is a lively bar and cafe. Tables sit on the wooden deck edged by
tall palms, and in a covered gazebo. Patrons gaze out to the masted
sailboats studding the harbor and to Paradise Island across the water.
Open daily, 11 a.m. "until." Happy hour Monday through Friday, 5
p.m. to 7 p.m.

Tamarind Hill Restaurant & Music Bar

Village Rd., Nassau; ☎ *393-1306* • Dine alfresco or sit inside by one of
the tall windows at this hilltop restaurant that specializes in Bahamian
and West Indian cuisine. Good choices are the roti (East Indian bread
filled with curried meat or vegetables), barbecued ribs, cracked conch
and broiled grouper. Happy hour (Monday through Friday from 5 to
7 p.m.) is a popular time to make an appearance. The Tequila Sunrise
Party livens up Saturday afternoons and evenings (4 to 7 p.m.), and
the Reggae Sunsplash Party is the place to be on Sundays. Open noon
to midnight Monday through Friday and 4 p.m. to midnight on Saturdays and Sundays.

Prince George Roof Top Cafe Restaurant & Lounge

Prince George Plaza (upstairs), Bay St., downtown Nassau; ☎ *322-5854* •
There's no charge for the view of the harbor at this appealing restaurant in the heart of downtown Nassau. Diners are seated both downstairs in the cafe and outdoors on the rooftop overlooking busy Bay
Street. The menu is thoroughly international, featuring Greek, Continental and Bahamian dishes. Local boil fish and Johnny cake move
quickly at breakfast, while the lunch buffet offers everything from

soups and salads to pizza. Dinner selections include stuffed broiled lobster, shrimp kebab, skewered scallops with bacon, steak, barbecued ribs and blackened snapper. Open from 11 a.m. to 11 p.m. Closed Sundays.

Grand Central ★

Charlotte St., off Bay St., downtown Nassau; ☎ *322-8356* • This attractive restaurant and bar in a small, Greek-owned hotel near the straw market makes a convenient lunch stop during a day of shopping. The cheerful decor is highlighted by blond wood, floral wallpaper with matching curtains and a Day-glo blackboard scrawled with the daily specials. Bahamians highly recommend the cracked conch, steamed grouper, pork chops, turtle steak and minced lobster, all served with peas and rice or yellow rice. The restaurant usually closes early (8 p.m.), but may stay open later during the busiest seasons, so check before going.

The Palm ★

Bay St., opposite John Bull, downtown Nassau; ☎ *323-7444* • This cheerful restaurant in the heart of Nassau's shopping district draws just as many locals as tourists. Perhaps this is because of the homestyle cooking. Visitors breakfasting alone might be given a local newspaper for company. The very spicy conch salad is excellent here, and the grouper fingers, peas and rice, cracked conch, pasta, soups and sandwiches are also delicious. Wash it all down with an ice cream soda.

Major credit cards.

INEXPENSIVE

Three Queens ★★

East Wulff Road; Nassau; ☎ *393-3512* • For some local color and delicious food, this is a good choice. Stop by for the buffet lunch, when you might sample curried chicken or steamed snapper. For dinner, try the minced lobster, cracked conch, steamed grouper, fried chicken or turtle steak (when in season). Johnny cake is served on the side. If you'd like to sample a Bahamian breakfast, order the "boil fish." Open until midnight. *Major credit cards.*

Basil's ★

Blue Hill Rd., Nassau • Slightly off the beaten track, Basil's caters very much to a local clientele. Visitors would do well to sample its conch fritters.

The Shoal & Lounge ★

Nassau St., Nassau; ☎ *323-4400* • Few Bahamians talk about the Shoal without mentioning the delicious boil fish served here. Attracting quite a few families, this casual local restaurant is also celebrated for its crawfish salad, grouper fingers, steamed or cracked conch, steak, and mutton. Fried plantain and mountains of peas and rice come on the side. The lounge adjoining the dining room is a good place to mingle with Bahamians. A 20-minute stroll will get you here from Bay Street.

Coco's Cafe ★

Marlborough St., across from the British Colonial Hotel, downtown Nassau; ☎ *323-8778 or 323-8801* • Three meals a day are served here amid bright art deco decor. The Bahamian and American fare includes broiled fish, steaks, veal, hamburgers, pasta and large salads. Open 8 a.m. to 9:30 p.m. except Sunday. ***Major credit cards.***

Johnson's Take-Away ★

Shirley St. and Ball's Alley; ☎ *393-0071* • You might be mistaken for a resident at this unassuming "pick-up-and-run" spot known for its generous portions of tender cracked conch, chicken, potato salad, cole slaw and peas and rice. Open Monday through Saturday from 9:30 a.m. to 12:30 a.m.

Mandi's Conch ★

Arundel and Mount Royal Ave., Palmdale, Nassau; ☎ *322-7620* • Bahamians prepare mild-flavored conch in countless ways, and you can sample a variety of incarnations here. Try the conch fritters, conch chowder, stewed conch, conch salad and of course good old cracked conch, all accompanied by cole slaw and french fries. Open daily (except Sunday) from 11:30 a.m. to 11 p.m.

Choosy Foods ★

Market St., off Bay St.; ☎ *326-5232* • Near the Straw Market, this local natural foods dining spot serves good seafood lasagne, conch salad, conch burgers and fruit-stuffed grouper.

Traveller's Rest ★ ★

West Bay St., near airport; ☎ *327-7633* • As you approach this popular restaurant across the road from a narrow beach, you might find children selling cantaloupes or other fruit out front. Many people enjoy dining on the patio, near the tall palm trees on the front lawn. Inside, wicker lamp shades hang from the ceiling and paintings of colorful aquatic scenes decorate the walls. Your gracious hostess is likely to be owner Joan Hanna, a former schoolteacher from Canada, whose Bahamian husband is a local politician and head of the musician's union. Scribbled on the chalkboard menu, you'll see "smudder" (smothered) grouper, steamed conch, turtle steak, grouper fingers, minced lobster and the like. If you happen by on a weekend, you might be treated to conch salad. Open daily, 11 a.m. to 11 p.m. ***Major credit cards.***

The adjacent **Sea Grape Boutique** sells bright Androsia resortwear, fashioned into skirts, shirts, shorts, dresses and bathing suits. Straw hats are also on sale, along with belts, shoes, jewelry, stuffed animals and other toys.

This tiny boutique even accepts American Express, MasterCard, and Visa.

SNACKS

Roscoe's   ★
East Bay Street, just west of Paradise Island bridge, Nassau; ☎ *322-2810*
• How about a special lunch to take to the beach? Stop by this gourmet deli in a beautiful former home that dates back to the 1880s.
You'll enter through wrought-iron gates. On sale is everything from
smoked salmon and mussels to fancy meats, all kinds of cheeses, pasta,
caviar and baked goods. If you prefer to eat here, choose a table out
back in the lovely garden, where flowers are surrounded by tall bushy
trees. Those staying in places with kitchens may want to stock up on
international coffees and other goodies.

The Swiss Pastry Shop   ★
Near Le Meridien Royal Bahamian hotel, western Cable Beach; ☎ *327-
7601* • The spicy conch patties are excellent here, and the meat patties
get raves as well. Delicious guava duff is also sold, along with all kinds
of breads and European chocolates. Closed Tuesday and Sunday.

PARADISE ISLAND

EXPENSIVE

Cafe Martinique   ★ ★ ★
Opposite Atlantis, Paradise Island; ☎ *363-2222* • As its name implies,
the cuisine is gourmet French. This popular (and very expensive) restaurant is situated in a palm-shaded spot across from Atlantis, Paradise
Island. With tall windows facing a lagoon, the setting invites dining at
what some consider one of the best Continental restaurants in the
Bahamas. The candlelight, the linens and the romantic music add to
the elegant atmosphere. The menu runs the gamut from escargot and
goose liver pâté to filet mignon and roast duckling in Grand Marnier.
Since the elaborate dessert souffles are so tempting and time-consum-
ing to prepare, the dessert menu precedes the dinner menu, and your
waiter will ask you to order your last course when you place your dinner order. *Men are required to wear jackets.* Dinner only.

Major credit cards.

The Courtyard Terrace   ★ ★ ★
The Ocean Club Golf & Tennis Resort; ☎ *363-2222* • At this elegant
alfresco restaurant, diners sit at the edge of a pool with a fountain,
surrounded by palms. The gourmet meals are served on Wedgwood
china, with crisp Irish linen. Candles flicker in the breeze. Live music

floats down from the balcony above the central staircase that leads to
this outdoor restaurant.   *Major credit cards.*

The Rotisserie   ★ ★
The Radisson Grand; ☎ *362-2011* • This is the hotel's upscale dining
room overlooking the ocean. Only dinner is served. Specialties are
meat, fish and poultry grilled or broiled over open flames.

Major credit cards.

Villa d'Este ★★

Atlantis, Paradise Island; ☎ *363-2222* • This restaurant, serving delicate Italian specialties, is situated in the casino area. It is open for dinner nightly and features entertainment. It attracts much of the casino crowd. Jackets required for men. Reservations required.

Major credit cards.

Le Cabaret Theatre ★

Atlantis, Paradise Island; ☎ *363-2222* • The nightly revue, much like the Folies-Bergère, presents women dancers, often innocently barebreasted, in spectacles with performers ranging from comedians and acrobats to animals. Jackets required for men. Reservations required.

Major credit cards.

The Boat House Grill ★★★

Across from Atlantis, Paradise Island; ☎ *363-2222* • The atmosphere is convivial at this nautical restaurant where diners sit family-style. Steak and seafood are cooked on grills in the center of the large tables, some of which have partial views of the lagoon. Note that having the kitchen at your table can make for a warm evening, so dress lightly. Dinner only. Reservations recommended.   *Major credit cards.*

MODERATE

Blue Lagoon ★★

Club Land'Or; ☎ *363-2400* • Overlooking the Paradise Island lagoon, which sparkles with lights in the evening, this restaurant specializes in seafood. Dinner only is served Monday through Saturday, 5–10 p.m.

Major credit cards.

INEXPENSIVE

The Blue Marlin ★★

Hurricane Hole Plaza; ☎ *363-2660* • Overlooking the harbor near the Paradise Island bridge, this restaurant serves lunch and dinner and hosts a happy hour from 4 p.m. to 6 p.m. During the day, sunlight from the large picture windows bathes the terra cotta tiles and potted plants. Try a daiquiri made with tropical fruit. Bahamian favorites are on the menu, including conch fritters, conch salad, cracked conch, grouper fingers and snapper creole, served with peas and rice. After dinner most nights, the chefs and waiters join other performers in a musical production that features Junkanoo music and costumes. Glass-eating and steel drum music might be part of the entertainment.

V, M, A.

Island Restaurant ★

West of Paradise Island bridge, by the former airport; ☎ *363-3153* • While waiting for lunch, watch the educational programs or soap operas on the television or eavesdrop on the animated philosophical and political discussions at the bar. The friendly staff serves three meals a day, featuring Bahamian dishes such as stewed fish and grits for breakfast, steamed conch for lunch and turtle steak for dinner. Open 7:30 a.m. to 11 p.m.

WHERE TO STAY

Nassau's variety of accommodations gives visitors a wide choice. There are hotels, housekeeping apartments and guesthouses to suit almost any need and pocketbook. Places to stay are located along Cable Beach, in downtown Nassau, out on Paradise Island and at a sprawling, self-contained resort at the island's southwestern end. Carnival's Crystal Palace, the Radisson, Nassau Beach, and Ambassador Beach hotels are all within easy walking distance of each other. The British Colonial Beach Resort is the only downtown hotel on a beach. If you want to be near a casino, stay in Cable Beach or on Paradise Island. Staff at all hotels are happy to help you arrange scuba diving, snorkeling cruises, golf, tennis, horseback riding and any other activities whether or not they are available at the accommodation itself. During spring break, the more modest hotels in Cable Beach, downtown Nassau and Paradise Island often cater to the American high school and college student crowd. Unless you plan to join the (often noisy) fun, this may not be the best time to book a room at these hotels.

PERSONAL FAVORITES

The Ocean Club Golf & Tennis Resort, on Paradise Island, for its beach-front elegance.

Graycliff, in Nassau, for its historic mansion and plant-filled patios.

CABLE BEACH

Most Cable Beach hotels that aren't close to the casino (which is between Carnival's Crystal Palace and the Radisson) provide complimentary shuttle service there.

EXPENSIVE

Wyndham Ambassador Beach

Across from the Crystal Palace golf course, this modern 385-room hotel welcomes guests with inviting public rooms done in subdued colors. The pleasant guest rooms have ample tiled baths and dressing areas. Guests have a choice of restaurants and bars, including a dining room with Italian cuisine. Sun worshipers gravitate either to the pool or step out to the hotel's beach. Watersports facilities are available and guests can perfect their tennis, raquetball or squash skills at the nearby Sports Centre.

Carnival's Crystal Palace & Casino

This lavish, multicolored extravaganza shares the casino with the neighboring Radisson, formerly part of this hotel. The hotel's towers, striped with pinks, purples, mauve, magenta and turquoise, really bloom when lit at night. While somewhat startling for the outside, the colors are used attractively in room decoration for walls, carpeting, sconces and other furniture. However, as chic as the art deco decor of rooms is, the workmanship leaves something to be desired. Also, the neon bedside lights are too dim for reading. Rooms have floor-to-ceiling windows with balconies overlooking the ocean.

Carnival's section of the beach is more crowded and not as broad as that of the Radisson next door. The slide that spirals into the duplex waterfront swimming pool is irresistible, though, for adults as well as kids. A profusion of restaurants caters to all tastes. There are in-hotel boutiques as well as a straw market. The Palace Theater puts on the expected colorful Las Vegas-like revue with feathers, sequins and bare breasts. Off the sprawling casino, the laser-lighted Fanta-Z disco sweeps on until the small hours. High rollers can book a computerized suite, for a mere $25,000 (yes, three zeros) a night. They'll be greeted by a robot that resembles Grace Jones and performs all kinds of electronic miracles. Actually, they get the room "free." The cost is covered by the amount that they've lost in the casino. One man recently gambled away $70,000!

Forte Nassau Beach Hotel

Balconies of the pleasant guest rooms overlook the large pool and the beach, where all kinds of watersports are available. Landlubbers can play tennis or make arrangements to golf at the nearby course. Lined by palms and manicured bushes, stone walkways meander through the tranquil grounds. Wrought-iron garden furniture sits on lawns. At Club Premiere, the hotel's 180 upscale rooms all have balconies and ocean views, dressing alcoves, secretarial service and a separate concierge. Those who find this hotel too peaceful at times can pop right next door to Carnival's Crystal Palace & Casino, with its crowds and glitter.

Le Meridien Royal Bahamian

For a pampered stay in a serene setting without the hordes and noise of a large hotel, this is the place. The columned six-story pink manor house with its marble-floored, Georgian-furnished entrance lobby opens onto a courtyard with a fountain. One end of the paved courtyard leads to an area of pink villas, some with their own pools, set among attractive landscaping. The pampering continues with plush rooms, some with balconies overlooking the sea and the hotel's secluded beach. (However, be sure to request a renovated room.) There are dressing areas, and an array of toiletries. Beds are turned down at night, and a helpful concierge is at hand to take care of any special needs. Guests can have drinks in the Balmoral Bar or on its terrace. Breakfast and dinner are served either indoors or outside on the patio of the gourmet Cafe de Paris, which is adjacent to the pool. For lunch, the Hamak bar and restaurant sits on the beach. Tennis courts are on the grounds, and the hotel's spa has universal gym equipment and exercise rooms, which are free to guests. Massages and mud baths, arranged by appointment, are the only spa services for which there is an extra charge. For gamblers, there is complimentary transport to the Crystal Palace Casino.

MODERATE

Radisson Cable Beach Casino & Golf Resort

Formerly part of Carnival's Crystal Palace next door, this high-rise hotel has undergone a major facelift. The beach here is wider and longer than that of its neighbor. On your way to the swimming pool and shore, you can walk over a bridge through a cave and under a cascading waterfall without getting wet. The Radisson shares the casino, as well as the 18-hole golf course, fitness center and tennis, squash, and racquetball courts, with the Crystal Palace. Guest rooms are comfortably decorated, but note that hallways are long so you may have a bit of a hike from the elevator to your room. Views take in the ocean, the garden and the lagoons. In and around the casino, you'll have a slew of restaurants to choose among, along with a disco and a theater.

Days Inn Casuarinas of Cable Beach

Located on two sides of the road, Casuarinas welcomes guests with a flower-filled courtyard, two swimming pools, a tennis court and a narrow beach. Rooms on the ocean side are a bit more expensive than those across the street. All come with refrigerators, wet bars and balconies. The one- and two-bedroom apartments make this modest property attractive to families. The Round House is in a circular building on the beach side. Albrion's is the second restaurant. Casuarinas is located at the quiet end of Cable Beach, about a mile from the casino.

CORAL ISLAND/SILVER CAY

EXPENSIVE

Villas on Coral Island

Between downtown Nassau and Cable Beach • Somewhat out of the way, this unusual hotel is adjacent to the Coral World Undersea Observatory and Marine Park. Each of its 22 rooms is really a suite with living, dining and kitchen areas. Best of all, each has its own enclosed swimming pool. All rooms are oceanview, with VCRs (the video library is complimentary), minibars, ice makers and microwaves. Gleaming with Italian marble, the gorgeous baths feature oval tubs with windows that overlook the ocean crashing against the jagged rocks. The small sandy beach, which you'll see as you come over the bridge to the island, gazes out to the observatory at Coral Island (formerly Coral World). A restaurant is on premises, but room service is also available for breakfast and dinner. (Continental breakfast is included in the rates.) After guests have toured the marine park, they can take the free bus and ferry to Cable Beach, Paradise Island and downtown Nassau for shopping, dining and gambling. However, this complimentary transportation is available only during the day. If you go out at night, you'll need a taxi.

DOWNTOWN NASSAU

EXPENSIVE

Graycliff Hotel ★★★

This historic mansion, set behind a wall opposite Government House, has become a sought-after accommodation. The columns at the entrance, the wide porch and the latticework set it apart from the run-of-the-mill hotel. It houses a five-star restaurant that boasts a world-wide reputation. A plaque celebrating its five stars and its *Relais et Chateau* designation is affixed to its outside wall. Staying as a guest in one of the 14 rooms is like accepting an invitation to the home of a wealthy friend. Each large room is different and each bears a name, such as Pool Cottage, Yellowbird or Hibiscus. Some have walk-in closets and dressing rooms, and many have beautiful tile floors. All are furnished with a melange of comfortable, eyepleasing pieces, including well-polished antiques. The varied bathrooms are commodious and invite lingering showers or bubble baths. A stone walkway and lush greenery surround the pool. The hotel seems to have endless dining areas, including porches, patios, and poolside. One dining room off the main sitting room has bamboo growing outside the window. Hotel additions include a jacuzzi, sauna, gym and solarium.

MODERATE

British Colonial Beach Resort—Best Western ☆☆

The only downtown hotel that is directly on a beach (albeit an artificial one), this hulking building is an architectural landmark. It stands at the end of Bay Street and sprawls over eight garden-sprinkled acres. However, as handsome as it is from the outside, readers have complained that the dining and front desk service can be much too slow, even by relaxed Bahamian standards. The spacious guest rooms face the ocean, the harbor and the city. Fringed with palms, a large free-form pool overlooks the beach, which provides a good vantage point for watching the nearby cruise ships. Guests may play shuffleboard and tennis, or make arrangements for an endless array of other sports. The hotel's steak and seafood restaurant is called Blackbeard's Forge. It is named in honor of the pirate who lived on the site when it was Fort Nassau and hid from the Royal Navy in a well that is still on the grounds.

Buena Vista ☆☆

Delancy St. • A nineteenth-century mansion near Government House, Buena Vista sits on a hill in a residential neighborhood. Downtown Nassau and the beach are within walking distance. A grassy area with bushes and shady trees borders the circular driveway. After crossing the veranda and entering the reception area, it seems as if you have stepped into a comfortable, lived-in, private home and well-used living room. A central staircase leads up to the second floor and five, spacious, eclectically furnished rooms. All have refrigerators. The Buena Vista restaurant rivals the best and most elegant of eating places, with candlelight, fine china and crystal in the several dining areas hung with paintings and plants. Only dinner is served here, but other restaurants are not far.

INEXPENSIVE

The Parliament Inn

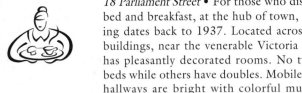

18 Parliament Street • For those who dislike large, bustling hotels, this bed and breakfast, at the hub of town, may be the answer. The building dates back to 1937. Located across the street from Government buildings, near the venerable Victoria Gardens and the Cenotaph, it has pleasantly decorated rooms. No two are alike. Some have twin beds while others have doubles. Mobiles dangle in the cozy rooms and hallways are bright with colorful murals and wallpaper. Doorway moldings are painted in bold hues. Some of the inn's eye-catching artwork was done by Tony McKay, the Bahamian musician also known as the Obeah Man. Pick-A-Dilly, the indoor-outdoor bar and restaurant, is especially lively on afternoons and evenings when a band performs or a deejay entertains. Bay Street is nearby and a beach is several blocks away.

Dillet's Guest House

Hardly 10 minutes away from downtown Nassau, in the area called Chippingham, Dillet's Guest House was once a family home. It is now run by a Dillet descendant as a charming bed and breakfast. There are seven rooms available, some with private sitting areas and kitchenettes. Ceiling fans as well as air conditioning keep vacationers comfortable, and the common living room has a fireplace for cool nights. Tea is served in the afternoon, and continental breakfast each morning. Other meals can be arranged at additional cost. Discounts are available for senior citizens.

PARADISE ISLAND

EXPENSIVE

Pirate's Cove Holiday Inn

This high rise looks down on a calm, quiet sandy cove cupped by pines and palms. Paddle boats, rafts and other aquatic toys lure guests to the beach. A waterfall pours into the swimming pool, by the open-air bar in a replica of a wrecked ship. Nearby, two rock-enclosed, flower-draped whirlpools, shaded by palms, are prime romantic spots. There's a sandy volleyball court, and scuba instruction is available. An exercise room is off the snazzy lobby, which gleams with granite tiles and brass rails. The comfortable guest rooms, most with two double beds, some with kings, differ in price according to floor and view. Ask about non-smoking rooms.

Ocean Club Golf & Tennis Resort

This posh resort was once the home of A&P heir Huntington Hartford. At press time it is undergoing a major restoration and renovation. Guests checking in are escorted to their rooms by the concierge. Rooms are furnished with double beds, television, dining areas and ceiling fans for those who eschew air conditioning. Some have patios or balconies, and views take in the gardens or the ocean. Villas are also available, some of which have marble whirlpool baths. The Courtyard Terrace can be a romantic dining spot at night. The lavishly landscaped grounds bring vistas that include the terraced Versailles Gardens and a filagree gazebo overlooking the harbor. Seen from the spacious pool patio, a medieval French cloister makes a dramatic sight when illuminated at night. The long, broad white sand beach is wonderful for swimming and sunbathing. Perched on a bluff, the beach bar and lunch-time restaurant overlooks the sand. Watersports, golf and tennis are always on tap for the energetic.

Atlantis, Paradise Island

Formerly the Paradise Island Resort & Casino, this beachfront complex is undergoing major changes. By the time you arrive, you may find that the huge outdoor aquarium, part of a 14-acre waterscape, has been completed. One of the highlights will be a see-through pedestrian tunnel running beneath a lagoon filled with sharks and stingrays. A 100-foot suspension bridge will swing above this Predator Lagoon. Other exhibits will feature colorful tropical fish and coral. There will even be a natural turtle sanctuary. Three underground caves, more than three dozen waterfalls, cascading water slides and five swimming pools will also be on the grounds. You'll be able to take in the lush vegetation while floating on the resort's quarter-mile river. Guests, who are accommodated in the Beach Tower, Coral Towers or villas, may choose among the resort's dozen restaurants. With all this, the flashy casino and its Las Vegas-style productions at Le Cabaret Theatre almost pale by comparison. Camp Atlantis offers supervised activities for the younger editions.

Harbour Cove/Paradise Island Fun Club ☆☆

This harborside resort is now all-inclusive. An L-shaped swimming pool with a "sip & dip" bar sits at the edge of the water, next to a small artificial beach. The view of the Paradise Island bridge, the boat-filled harbor and Nassau's marinas is stunning. You can also take in these sights while working out in the spacious exercise room with floor to ceiling windows, or while dining at the open-air restaurant. Done in blond wood and wrought iron, with mirrored sliding closet doors, guest rooms are quite attractive. They vary in size and view. Tennis clinics, use of snorkel gear, cocktail parties, bicycle tours, nightly live entertainment and three meals a day are all part of the package.

Radisson Grand Resort Paradise Island

All rooms in this high-rise have balconies that look out to the ocean. The lobby's focal point is a fountain and waterfall that empty into a pool surrounded by lush foliage. Chairs are arranged before the floor-to-ceiling windows and there are hanging baskets and lazily revolving ceiling fans. The rooms are tastefully decorated and the latest disco innovations lure stay-up-late guests from other Paradise Island evening attractions, most of which are within walking distance. An excellent beach stretches in front of the hotel and all water- and other sports are on tap, including tennis.

Club Land'or

The main focus of this resort is time sharing, but some hotel rooms are available. It is a part of Resorts Condominiums International. All units have living-dining areas and kitchenettes. Some of the rooms have balconies. The beach is about a 10-minute walk away and the attractive pool patio overlooks the lagoon. Each day except Sunday there is a happy hour in the Oasis Lounge, and the Blue Lagoon restaurant serves breakfast and dinner on the third floor. There is a once-a-week trip to Rose Island. The ferry to Nassau is across the road.

MODERATE

Club Med Paradise Island

This popular 21-acre beachfront Club Med village appeals to couples and singles who like lots of activites and the one-price-fits-all rates. It consists of various buildings with air-conditioned double rooms, each with a private bath. Single rooms can be had depending upon availability, but with a surcharge. Flights directly to the island can be arranged from many U.S. cities, including airport transfers. Recreational facilities are included in the cost except for golf, excursions and craft supplies.

Bay View Village

Paths wind through nearly four acres of lush, tropical gardens at this condominium run like a hotel. The one-, two-, and three-bedroom units and town houses are individually decorated by their owners. But they all come with patios or balconies, built-in safes, ironing boards, irons, microwave ovens, TVs and hair dryers. Some have audio cassettes as well. Dishwashers are in larger units and villas have skylights in the master bedroom baths. After playing tennis (the court is lit for night games), guests may cool off in one of the three swimming pools.

Comfort Suites   ★★★

A two- and three-story multiwing building, this quiet hotel sits just across the street from busy beachfront Atlantis, Paradise Island resort and casino. (In fact, Comfort Suites guests can sign meals to their rooms when dining at the neighboring casino resort.) Glass-paned

French doors lead to the lobby, tiled in gleaming marble and decorated with leafy plants. Fans hang from the open beams of the high-pitched ceiling. Each "suite" is actually one room with a king-sized bed or two doubles plus a sofabed in a sitting area. Amenities include minibars, in-room safes (for which there is a daily charge) and sinks outside the rest of the bath. For the most privacy, ask for a room that's not along a walkway. The open-air restaurant (serving breakfast and lunch) overlooks the patio surrounding the pool, with its swim-up bar. Continental breakfast is included in the rates. Non-smoking rooms are available.

Paradise Paradise

The atmosphere of this modest beach hotel is relaxed. Rooms have minibars, dressing areas and double or king-sized beds. Some have balconies. Young staff members are ever-present to see to your needs. Because the emphasis is on sports here, the ratio of activity directors to guests is higher than at the larger hotels. Guests work out at the basketball hoop, the volleyball court and the small kidney-shaped pool. There is a bicycle tour every morning, and all activities are included in the room rate. The long inviting beach is seldom crowded and changing rooms are at the disposal of guests who arrive early or stay around after check-out. The restaurant patio overlooks the ocean.

Sunrise Beach Club & Villas Hotel

Offering time-shares, condos and hotel rentals, this jungled resort draws many Europeans. From the entrance, a stone path curves past tall tropical trees, colorful flowers and thick bushes. A waterfall flows into one of the swimming pools, which is shaded by palm fronds. Picket fences enclose the downstairs patios of nearby units. Apartments come with kitchenettes and one, two, or three bedrooms, so this resort is popular among families and groups of friends. There's no restaurant, but several Paradise island dining rooms are not far. Since people who stay here are looking for real escape, there are no telephones in rooms. The second swimming pool overlooks the ocean. Although this resort borders the beach, most units are not on the shore. Instead, most face gardens, courtyards and waterfalls.

Villas in Paradise

These villas are designed for those who treasure privacy and want to feel at home. The one-, two-, three-, and four-bedroom villas, only about a five-minute walk from the beach and casino, also have their own pools. Some are huge, with nice touches such as Oriental rugs. A car or jeep is included in villa rates for a day or two if you stay a minimum number of nights. For both suites and villas, washer/dryers are on the premises and there's a small surcharge for daily maid and pool service.

Golden Palm Resort

East of the Paradise Island bridge, this attractive Bahamian-owned hotel offers modern one- and two-bedroom apartments. The larger units are duplexes. All have balconies and the decor includes tiled and carpeted floors, louvered wooden doors and fanlights. Waterfalls splash into a brook and the free-form swimming pool, nestled in a courtyard lush with palms, banana trees and other greenery. Wooden bridges crisscross the pool. Golden Palm Resort attracts many Germans and other Europeans.

SOUTHWESTERN NEW PROVIDENCE

MODERATE TO EXPENSIVE

Ramada South Ocean Golf & Beach Resort ☆☆☆

About 15 minutes from the airport but a half-hour drive from downtown Nassau, this sprawling resort is in a quiet corner of the island. Guests keep themselves busy with a nice stretch of beach, two pools, four tennis courts and an 18-hole golf course. Scuba diving and windsurfing are available along with parasailing and other aquatic diversions. Rooms are smartly decorated and most have louvered doors leading to balconies or patios. However, those on the ground floor, whether facing the pool area cafe or the gardens, have little privacy and can be noisy for guests wanting afternoon naps. Second-story rooms are quieter. Tapes from the hotel's extensive video library can be rented to play in your room. The in-room safety deposit boxes are good for passports, tickets, jewelry and cash, but too small for 35mm cameras and the like. Front-desk safes are available for a small fee. Papagayo is the Italian restaurant, while Casuarina serves Bahamian food. There is also a beach pavillion for light fare, as well as a beach bar and golf lounge. Transportation to town costs between $4 and $6 each way.

Freeport

FREEPORT

Visitors wander through Garden of the Groves in Freeport, Grand Bahama.

THE SECOND CITY

Freeport, with an array of restaurants, clubs, sports and two vast casinos, is located inland on Grand Bahama. This island of about 41,000 people has taken its place after New Providence as the second most important in the Bahamas chain. An orderly city with excellent roads and broad, landscaped highways bordered by stately palms and pines, Freeport is quite young as cities go. Since it is shy on historical attractions and sightseeing shrines, those who thrive on sunbathing, watersports, fishing, golf, gambling, dining and nightlife will find it made to order. For theatergoers, the Regency Theatre on East Mall often presents local and imported plays.

High-rise hotels, apartment buildings, condominiums and time-sharing complexes stand against the cerulean sky and sparkling waters. Residents of Freeport and adjoining Lucaya (the islands' beach resort), have attractive homes surrounded by well-kept lawns and flowering shrubs. Some of the nicest are along Midshipman Road and in the Fortune Beach area cul de sac. The many Europeans, Canadians and Americans now living in Freeport/Lucaya make it a truly international city. Many Americans have spilled over from Florida and other states for retirement and vacation homes. The late American band leader Count Basie lived in Bahamia, an exclusive neighborhood popular with sightseers.

As you enter Freeport along West Sunrise Highway, the lofty Princess Tower and the casino next door become unmistakable landmarks. Through Moorish domes, minarets and intricate tilework, they strive for the exotic. Along with the low-rise Princess Country Club across the road, they form the Bahamas Princess Resort & Casino.

Alongside the Princess Resort's tower, a Japanese torii gate welcomes you to the sprawling International Bazaar with its shops and decor representing countries around the world. Visitors may purchase international wares and dine on a wide selection of international cuisines. The Bahamas Tourist Office is also in the busy bazaar. Here, through the government's free **People-to-People Program,** you can arrange to do things with individual Bahamians or families who volunteer their time to make your stay more enjoyable. Whether or not you participate in the People-to-People Program, you may want to check the local newspaper for the weekend barbecues or beach parties sponsored by churches, lodges or schools to raise money. There is always music as well as spirited domino games, and you'll have an inexpensive home-cooked meal of treats such as conch fritters, curried chicken and ribs.

If you're staying at a hotel or guest house with cooking facilities, you can buy fresh seafood at the Harbour Fish and Lobster House in Freeport's downtown industrial area. Fresh fruits and vegetables are sold in the market outside the grocery store in the downtown shopping area and fresh-baked goods can be found at Mum's and Western bakeries.

In the Lucaya area, across from the Lucayan Beach Resort & Casino, the Atlantik Beach Hotel, and the Radisson Resort on Lucaya

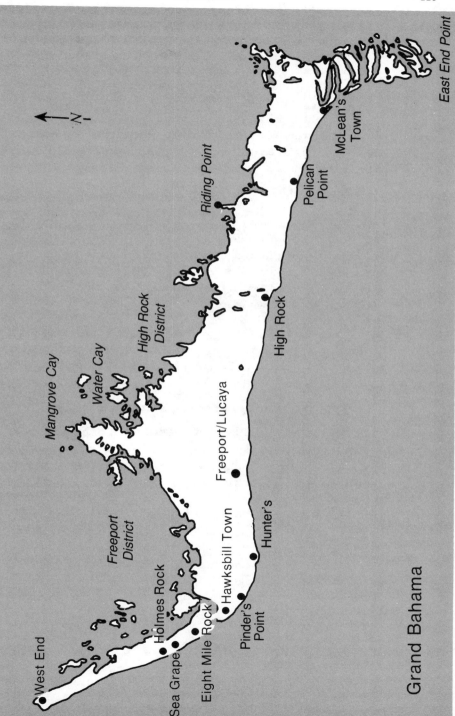

West End

Sea Grape

Holmes Rock

Eight Mile Rock

Pinder's
Point

Hawksbill Town

Hunter's

Freeport/Lucaya

*Freeport
District*

Mangrove Cay

Water Cay

*High Rock
District*

High Rock

Riding Point

Pelican
Point

McLean's
Town

East End Point

Grand Bahama

-N-

Beach is the Port Lucaya shopping complex. Spread along the marina, the various buildings and plazas house shops, a marina, restaurants, a bandstand and other attractions. At UNEXSO, near Port Lucaya Marketplace and the Lucayan Beach Resort & Casino, a not-to-be-missed experience for visitors is swimming with playful dolphins. A ferry connects the hotels and condos along the channel to those along the beach. A peaceful, pleasant stroll along Royal Palm Way will take you past some attractive private homes bordered by Cook Island pines, casuarinas and colorful flowers—but no royal palms.

Local buses running among Lucaya, Freeport's International Bazaar area, and downtown Freeport cost about $1. Near Pub on the Mall restaurant you can get a bus to Lucaya Beach for windsurfing, water-skiing, and other watersports. Rent a car or a moped through a hotel for a short trip to one of the more remote, uncrowded Lucaya area beaches, such as beautiful Taino and others off Midshipman Road. The 40-acre Lucayan National Park, about 25 minutes by car east of downtown Freeport, has a wide, secluded beach with high dunes. The lush Garden of the Groves is also worth a visit. Another pleasant nature reserve is the Rand Memorial Nature Centre, not far from the International Bazaar area. A drive along the western coast will take you through tiny old settlements and to restaurants overlooking the ocean.

THE GROWTH OF GRAND BAHAMA

Until the sixties, Grand Bahama had developed in fits and starts, beginning at its west end. Then Wallace Groves, an American from Virginia, saw trade and other growth possibilities. With loans and the enthusiastic encouragement of the colonial government, he began building the city of Freeport and developing its deepwater harbor for the expected boom in trade and commerce. Since the 1964 opening of its first tourist hotel, the Lucayan Bay, Freeport/Lucaya has blossomed with hotels and resorts. Sensing that his new city could not thrive on tourism alone, Groves set out to attract industry as well. His foresight has resulted in an industrial area that now supports oil refineries, cement production, pharmaceuticals and other types of manufacturing.

Most of what little history there is can be found in the small settlements such as Pinders's Point, Eight Mile Rock and Seagrape, along the western coast. Before the advent of tourists, and when there was Prohibition in the United States, this section of Grand Bahama was notorious. It was an important operating point for smugglers and

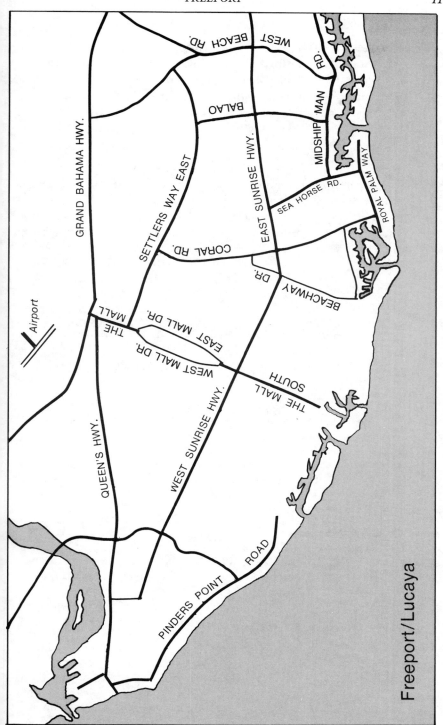

Freeport/Lucaya

rumrunners who used the area much as their predecessors, the pirates, had.

When it appeared that tourism would develop at the western end of the island, the Grand Bahama Hotel and Country Club was erected. This expansive resort with lush plantings, a golf course, tennis courts, a giant pool, a marina and countless other amenities, fell upon hard times when growth took place at Freeport, some 25 miles to the east. It was resurrected as the now closed Jack Tar Village.

Today tourism on Grand Bahama continues to grow. Perhaps taking its cue from Christopher Columbus, the first Italian and Westerner known to arrive here in the "New" world, a new resort has cropped up with an Italian accent. Attracting mainly visitors from Italy, the all-inclusive Club Fortuna Beach Resort, which opened in late 1992, features Italian cuisine and even bocce ball on the beach.

WHAT TO SEE AND DO

PERSONAL FAVORITES

The Dolphin Experience, for the chance to play with Flipper's cousins.

Port Lucaya, for its colorful restaurants and shops in a waterfront setting.

SIGHTS AND ATTRACTIONS

A number of buses take visitors on tours of Freeport/Lucaya and the vicinity. Tour attractions are celebrity homes, the historical West End, several beaches, nature reserves and the industrial area. Some tours stop for shopping and lunch or a snack. One of the tours is aboard a red, double-decker bus from London. Prices range from about $10 to $15. Check hotel tour desks for details.

The Dolphin Experience

At the UNEXSO dock across from the Lucayan Beach Resort & Casino;
☎ *373-1250 or 800/992-DIVE* • Dolphins in this program are free to leave, but they always return to home base. Don't pass up the chance to caress their smooth skin or to swim or scuba dive with them. Even if you only participate in the "Close Encounter," you can get right into the water with these playful aquatic mammals, who allow you to stroke and hug their powerful six- or seven-foot bodies. Afterward you can view your performance on video and purchase a copy for about $30. Originally from Mexico, the dolphins are part of an experiment in human/dolphin interaction. After being taught to follow a boat back and forth between an enclosure and a reef a mile away, they are now released into the open sea regularly to swim with scuba divers.

The trainers periodically test the dolphins' ability to use sonar and to retrieve objects from the divers. Call for reservations.

Close encounter: $22 (including a chance to dangle your feet in the water and allow the dolphins to rub their smooth bodies against you). Dolphin Dive: $100 (certified divers only). Make reservations several weeks ahead.

A vacationer strokes Flipper's cousin in Lucaya, Grand Bahama.

Garden of the Groves

Off Midshipman Road, about eight miles east of downtown • This 12-acre garden is named for Freeport's founder, Wallace Groves, and his wife. The entryway is lined with greenery and stalls selling t-shirts and straw goods. The garden has a thousand species of flowers, ferns, shrubs and trees. Among its attractions are waterfalls and hanging gardens. You can walk under one of the waterfalls and stay dry. Many Bahamians get married in the chapel here or have their wedding pictures taken with the garden as a backdrop. On Midshipman Road along the way, you'll pass some handsome one-family homes.

Open daily (except Wednesday) 9:30 a.m. to 5 p.m. Free admission.

Grand Bahama Museum
Garden of the Groves • This tiny museum is just inside the entrance to the Garden of the Groves. Here you'll find artifacts of the Lucayan Indians, who came by canoe from South America and inhabited the island when Columbus arrived. You'll learn that English words such as canoe, hurricane, potato and barbecue were taken from the Lucayan language. Displays might also include colorful costumes worn for the Bahamian traditional Junkanoo parades on New Year's Day, Boxing Day and Independence Day.   ***Admission: $2.00.***

Hydroflora Gardens ★★
East Beach Drive; ☎ *352-6052* • This garden demonstrates hydroponics, the growing of plants in water. Visitors are given complimentary Bahamian flowers, and they learn the history of the conch shell, which has its own museum here. These gardens are about a 20-minute stroll from the International Bazaar area or a 10-minute bus ride from Port Lucaya Marketplace.
Open Monday to Sat. 9:30 a.m. to 5:30 p.m. Admission: $2.

Lucayan National Park ★★
Eastern End • This 40-acre park made up of four different ecological zones has coca plums, seagrape, ming trees, wild tamarind, mahogany and cedar, among many other types of vegetation. Gold Rock Creek flows through the park to the ocean and there is a beautiful, wide, secluded beach. Two cave openings are accessible by stairways and ramps, and there is over a mile of footpaths and elevated walkways.
Free admission.

International Bazaar ★★
Entrance through Torii gate on West Sunrise Highway, next to Princess Tower Hotel and casino • This is a complex of international shops, boutiques and restaurants with architecture, goods, food and souvenirs reminiscent of a variety of countries. Most Freeport/Lucaya visitors eventually find their way here. At the **Bahamas Arts & Crafts Market**, various booths sell locally made jewelry, paintings and other crafts.
Open daily (except Sundays) until midnight. No admission charge.

Perfume Factory
Near International Bazaar • Perfumes, made from local flowers, are manufactured here, and the entire process may be seen in operation. Visitors may make purchases, selecting from among several fragrances.

Port Lucaya Marketplace and Marina ★★
Near the UNEXSO dock, across from the Atlantik Beach Hotel • The pastel shingle-roofed buildings of this youthful shopping, dining and amusement center are very pleasing to the eye. Clusters of bougainvillea festoon buildings, fireman's red British telephone booths actually work, and a bandstand sits close to the channel, where gleaming white yachts and other boats wait to take visitors on an array of trips. Many

restaurants are on second stories, giving views of the marina. Food ranges from hamburgers and ice cream to English pub fare and Bahamian. You can buy such things as perfume, leather goods, old coins, crafts and resortwear. Pussers, for example, a very British combination restaurant, pub and boutique, sells upscale slacks, shirts and other accessories for men and women. When we recently looked in, men's cotton suits were on sale for $150.

Other upscale shops in the Marketplace are Just for Kids, which sells children's clothing; Marroquinera of Colombia, which carries leather goods; Androsia, with colorful women's wear; and the Island Galleria, which offers china and crystal. A straw market sells traditional Bahamian straw products, and women (or men!) can have their hair cornrowed nearby.

Count Basie, the legendary jazz pianist and band leader who lived on Grand Bahama until his death, first had the idea for this attractive plaza and promenade. Live music spills out from the lacy gazebo bandstand and a steel band plays every day except Sunday. Many of the shops and restaurants are open late and can be pleasant spots for sunset watching.

Rand Memorial Nature Centre

Settlers Way East • Named for and financed by James H. Rand, a former president of Remington-Rand, this 100-acre park has 200 species of birds, and more than 400 varieties of plants. On the guided tour, you are followed by friendly birds. You can photograph the national bird, the pink flamingo, in all its glory at a tropical pool. You will also learn where the "straw" at the straw markets really comes from, and you'll see how bubble gum grows.
Open Monday through Friday and Sunday. Guided tours at 10:30 a.m., 2 p.m., and 3 p.m. and on Sunday, 2 p.m. and 3 p.m. $2.00.

Straw Market

Next to the International Bazaar • Freeport/Lucaya's Straw Market carries the same kinds of handcrafted items found in straw markets throughout The Bahamas. Items include hats for both sexes, baskets, and place mats, as well as wood carvings, necklaces and a variety of objects fashioned from the ubiquitous conch shell.   ***Open daily.***

SPORTS

Diving

Novice and experienced scuba divers gravitate to Freeport/Lucaya to take advantage of the extensive services and facilities of the **Underwater Explorer's Society (UNEXSO)**, across from the Lucayan Beach Resort & Casino. Along with a pool designed for introductory scuba lessons, there's a decompression chamber on the premises (but don't worry—it's hardly ever used). In addition to giving scuba lessons (both the resort course and certification), leading expeditions to exciting dive sites and teaching photography courses (both still and video), UNEXSO also runs the Dolphin Experience. Through this program, you can learn all about these friendly mammals and dive with them. (see "Sights and Attractions.") If this sounds too tame, ask about the shark feed dives. Just in case your friends back home won't believe the stories of your adventures, you can buy videos taken of you diving with sharks or dolphins. The UNEXSO store sells the latest in wet suits, snorkels, masks, fins and other underwater gear as well as shorts, bathing suits, t-shirts, dive books and underwater videos.

The introductory scuba resort course is about $90 and the five-day certification course runs about $300. A single tank dive will cost about $35. Dive packages range from about $85 for three dives to about $250 for 10. ☎ UNEXSO at *809/373-1250* in the Bahamas, *305/359-2730* in Florida, and *800/992-DIVE* from the rest of the U.S.

Fishing and Boating

For deep-sea fishing, boats leave daily from the marina adjacent to the Lucayan Bay Hotel at 9 a.m. and 1 p.m. Bait and tackle as well as soft drinks and ice are included in the price. Make reservations through your hotel tour desk or bell captain. The cost is about $50 (or $20 for spectators).

Cruises include sightseeing trips as well as **snorkeling** excursions. The *Mermaid Kitty,* said to be the world's largest glass-bottom boat, leaves from the Lucayan Bay Hotel dock at 10 a.m., noon, and 2:30 p.m. and visits tropical fish-filled coral reefs and a shipwreck. You can also see a diving show. The cost is about $12 for adults and about $8 for children. Other cruises allow time for swimming and lunch on a deserted beach. Sailing trips can be arranged through hotels. Check hotel tour desks for further details.

Golf

There are several good golf courses in Freeport/Lucaya: Bahama Reef, nine holes, is not far from the Radisson Resort on Lucaya Beach; Lucayan Park Golf & Country Club, 18 holes, caters to guests of the Atlantik Beach Hotel; Fortune Hills Golf & Country Club, a nine-hole course; 18-hole Princess Ruby, one of two courses operated by the Princess hotels; and 18-hole Princess Emerald, the other one, designed by Dick Wilson.

Horseback Riding

Pinetree Stables takes groups out at 9 a.m., 11 a.m., and 2 p.m. every day except Monday. Riders have a choice of English or Western saddles. Adults $22 per hour.

Tennis

Courts are at accommodations including the Princess, the Radisson Resort on Lucaya Beach, the Shalimar Hotel and Silver Sands Sea Lodge.

Parasailing and Windsurfing

These sports are available at the Atlantik Beach Hotel and the Radisson Resort on Lucaya Beach.

Water-skiing

The Princess and Radisson Resort on Lucaya Beach offer waterskiing.

NIGHTLIFE

Freeport Inn is the nightspot to go to if you want to party with an almost completely Bahamian crowd. The live band plays Bahamian music as well as disco, and the club attracts mainly young people. While people tend to dress up to go dancing at **Studio 69** on Midshipman Road, jeans and sneakers are the attire for many at **Sultan's Tent** in the Princess Tower, which plays more calypso than most other clubs. **Yellow Bird**, at Castaways Resort, features Bahamian music. You can listen to live jazz at **Skipper's Lounge** in the Bahamas Princess Country Club. With potted plants and a gleaming black bar, snazzy **Club Estee,** in Port Lucaya, adds to Freeport's after dark scene. Happy hour here is a good time to mingle with other vacationers.

The Princess Casino adjoins the tower of the Bahamas Princess Resort. There is always a flurry of activity. Visitors to the casino's nightclub are treated to a Las Vegas-style act complete with magicians, comedians and glittering, scantily dressed male and female dancers. The **Lucayan Beach Hotel Casino**, although not as busy, attracts many guests from the beach area and also hosts a spirited casino show. If you like to laugh, check out the **New Jokers Wild**, a comedy club on Midshipman Road.

DINING OUT

NOTE: Some restaurants will add a service charge to your bill if you pay with "Traveler's cheques."

PERSONAL FAVORITE

The Pusser's Company Store & Pub, in Port Lucaya, for its British atmosphere and food.

EXPENSIVE

Luciano's

Port Lucaya; ☎ *73-9100* • Residents rave about the Bahamian and Continental steak and seafood served here amid sophisticated surroundings. Save this one for a special night out. Jackets required. Closed Sundays.

The Rib Room

Bahamas Princess Resort & Casino; ☎ *352-6721* • The atmosphere of this restaurant is warm in the evening, with candlelight against dark beams, and there is a variety of gourmet dishes on the menu. Steak, of course, is the star of the show. Dinner only. *Major credit cards.*

EXPENSIVE TO MODERATE

Fatman's Nephew ★
Port Lucaya; ☎ *373-8520* • Upstairs from the Pusser's Pub, this restaurant and lounge continues the legacy of the late Fatman, who ran a popular local eatery for years. Bahamian favorites served here include conch fritters, turtle steak, grouper fingers and peas and rice. From the balcony, you'll have a wonderful view of the Bell Channel Waterway.

Guanahani ★
Bahamas Princess Resort & Casino; ☎ *352-6721* • Guanahani was the Indian name for San Salvador when Columbus "discovered" this Bahamian island. Near the pool, this glass-enclosed restaurant featuring barbecued ribs and chicken is surrounded by lush plants and is attractively lit at night. *Major credit cards.*

Ruby Swiss ★
West Mall and West Sunrise Highway; ☎ *352-8507* • Across from the International Bazaar and Casino, this restaurant specializes in gourmet Bahamian and European cuisine. Live calypso music accompanies dinner. Reservations are necessary.

Pub on the Mall ★
Mall & Sunrise Hwy.; ☎ *352-5110* • Right across from the International Bazaar, this lively pub serves English, Bahamian, and American food as well as a variety of imported beers. Closed Sundays.
Major credit cards.

MODERATE TO INEXPENSIVE

The Brass Helmet Restaurant and Bar ★
Upstairs from UNEXSO, Lucaya; ☎ *373-2032* • Among the most popular menu items are cracked conch, steak and Jamaican beef or chicken patties. An unusual piece of decor, the head of a huge, fierce looking shark has "burst" through one of the walls of the restaurant. An old copper diving helmet sits atop an aged wooden crate. Other antique diving gear is hung on walls. A large-screen TV plays underwater videos.

The Pusser's Co. Store & Pub ★★
Port Lucaya; ☎ *373-8450* • Dine inside or alfresco on the patio at this upscale pub. Outside, sit at marble-topped, cafe-style tables. Inside, the dark wood tables and paneling create a warm atmosphere. Shepherd's pie, steak and ale, fisherman's pie and other pub fare are on the menu along with sandwiches, grilled fish and burgers. The adjoining store sells sportswear (for men, women, and children), model ships, scrimshaw chess pieces, oversized mugs and other items.

Japanese Steak House

International Bazaar; ☎ *352-9521* • The Japanese Steak House is a welcome find in the labyrinth of the International Bazaar. It has a pleasant atmosphere, and food is dramatically prepared at hibachi tables. Closed Sundays.

The Buccaneer Club

Queen's Highway, Deadman's Reef; ☎ *349-3794* • This restaurant is a good reason for getting out of town. It is on the beach and its grounds have lush palms and other foliage. The menu consists of European and Bahamian selections. From November through April, when the restaurant is open, it sponsors beach parties with food, volleyball and other activities for an all-inclusive price. Call for free transportation from your hotel. Open only for dinner, the Buccaneer is closed on Mondays.

Churchill Pub

Near International Bazaar; ☎ *352-8866* • This English-style pub, named for Sir Winston Churchill and next to the straw market, serves dishes such as roast beef with Yorkshire pudding, but it is also known for its cracked conch. In addition to a happy hour Monday through Friday, there is entertainment several nights a week. The pub is open until 4 a.m.

Marcella's

East Mall at Kipling Lane; ☎ *352-5085* • Before digging into an Italian meal here, try a frozen daiquiri. Many people consider Marcella's the best place to find authentic Italian food in Freeport. It has also become a popular evening hangout.

The Captain's Charthouse

East Sunrise and Beachway Dr.; ☎ *373-3900* • In this restaurant the hearty fare runs to steaks, chops, shrimp, lobster and the like. The decor is tropical, and island music adds to the lively atmosphere. Call for complimentary transportation.   ***Major credit cards.***

INEXPENSIVE

Papa Charlie's Lounge

Port Lucaya; ☎ *343-1451* • This is a good choice for Bahamian conch salad, conch fritters, hot dogs, sandwiches, and other light fare.

George's Restaurant and Disco

Port Lucaya; ☎ *373-8513* • Try George's for an authentic Bahamian breakfast of boiled or stewed fish, chicken souse or corned beef and grits.

The Curry Pot Restaurant and Bar

Port Lucaya; ☎ *373-9121* • Try the curried chicken, mutton, lobster, conch or fish at this local eatery that specializes in homestyle cuisine. There's a daily happy hour from 6 p.m. to 8 p.m.

The Outriggers ★

Smith's Point, past Taino Beach; ☎ *373-4811* • A very small, very local restaurant, the Outriggers serves minced lobster, cracked conch, grouper, conch salad and other Bahamian specialties.

The New Office ★

Logwood Rd.; ☎ *352-8997* • The Bahamian specials at this casual dining spot that serves three meals a day include okra soup, curried chicken, steamed mutton, chicken souse and barbecued ribs. The Office, open daily from 8 a.m. to 5 a.m., has a live band and a disco.

The Pancake House ★

East Sunrise Highway; ☎ *373-3200* • This popular restaurant specializing in Bahamian home-style cooking has nothing to do with the American chain with a similar name. In addition to 12 different kinds of pancakes, the menu includes stewed fish and grits, shrimp, steak and sandwiches. Breakfast is served all day.

Kristi's ★

West Atlantic Drive; ☎ *352-3149* • Open for breakfast and lunch, this eatery whips up great homestyle soups and quiches. A variety of sandwiches and salads is also served, along with hot daily specials.

Scorpio's ★

Explorer's Way and West Atlantic, ☎ *352-6969; and Port Lucaya,* ☎ *373-8503* • Cracked conch, steamed grouper and minced lobster are just a few of the dishes served at this restaurant recommended highly by Bahamians. But locals say the original in-town restaurant is better than the newer one at Port Lucaya. Take-out service is available from 7 a.m. to 3 a.m. every day.   ***Major credit cards.***

Freddie's ★

Pinder's Point; ☎ *352-3250* • Open from 11 a.m. until 11 p.m., Freddie's serves grouper, steak, minced lobster, pork chops, cracked conch and other local dishes. Early-bird specials are on the menu from 5 p.m. to 6:30 p.m. Freddie's is closed on Sundays.

Blackbeard's ★

Fortune Beach; ☎ *373-2960* • The location, right on the beach, makes this an especially pleasant place to have a drink, mingle with locals and sample Bahamian specialties like peas and rice and cracked conch.

Traveller's Rest ★

William's Town, off Beachway Dr.; ☎ *373-4884* • This informal restaurant, overlooking a narrow beach, is off the beaten track. Conch is served in burgers, fritters and salads. Hearty chowders, rice and peas, and fish are also on the menu.

PERSONAL FAVORITE

Deep Water Cay Club, off the East End of Grand Bahama, for its fishing and friendly atmosphere.

WHERE TO STAY

FREEPORT

EXPENSIVE

Xanadu Beach & Marina Resort

Readily recognizable as the pyramid-topped high-rise with a cluster of villas at its base, Xanadu was once the hideaway of multi-millionaire recluse Howard Hughes. Today's hotel is a modern, refurbished accommodation with comfortable, well-furnished, balconied rooms set on a peninsula formed by its own beach and its 72-slip marina on the canal waterway. When not basking on the beach, guests may use the pool where there is a bar and drink service. All watersports are offered, with golf at the Ruby or Emerald courses short trips away. Tennis is on premises. Dining is offered at several locations. Pre-dinner cocktails can be had at one of the bars in either the tower building or the pool wing.

MODERATE

Bahamas Princess Resort & Casino

This large resort, on both sides of West Sunrise Highway, results from the combining of Freeport's two Princess hotels. Guests enjoy the ample facilities of both establishments, which include dining at nine restaurants, a range of sports, other recreation and, of course, the casino. Two golf courses are on tap and guests not using either of the two pools have free transportation to Xanadu beach. The winding, shop-filled streets of the busy International Bazaar are a step away and the new Port Lucaya shopping center is a short bus ride away. The two hotels, the Princess Tower (adjacent to the casino), and the Princess Country Club, are pleasantly landscaped and are an imposing sight seen together. The domed tower building has a Middle Eastern theme brought together in a lavish, blue tiled Moorish lobby with a grand piano in the center. The Country Club buildings (where the less expensive guest rooms are located) are spread out, with much activity centered around the pool with its waterfall and swim-under bridge. All rooms are cheerfully furnished and those in the tower have panoramic views of the city. However, some Country Club rooms are a long walk from the lobby and a few of the others get little sunlight and have uninspiring views.

Running Mon Marina & Resort

Born in July 1991, this small, crisp-looking hotel in Bahama Terrace offers facilities for sailers as well as other sun worshippers. It is particularly appealing to families. All the pleasantly furnished rooms in the two-story U-shaped building have kitchens and look out at the sparkling boats moored in the marina. A suite sporting two baths (one with a Jacuzzi) is available. Drinks are served at the Compass Bar on the second level, and the Mainsail Restaurant is just below. In addition to American food, traditional Bahamian fare is also served. Dinner specialties include lobster tail, grouper and, of course, conch, done in a variety of ways. A swimming pool is on premises, and the hotel provides complimentary transportation to the nearby beach, the International Bazaar, and the casino. The staff will be happy to make arrangements for fishing, watersports, sightseeing and other activities.

LUCAYA

EXPENSIVE

Club Fortuna Beach

Here at Italy's answer to Club Med, it's easy to forget you're in the Bahamas. You'll be surrounded by guests and staff speaking Italian (though English is also heard). The food, served at sumptuous buffets in a huge open-air dining hall, is Italian as well (except during the weekly Bahamian night). And you can learn to play bocce ball on the beautiful broad beach (that at low tide is also long). Club Fortuna attracts a young crowd, and since most guests are European, topless bathing is commonplace. Daily sports tournaments and musical games keep the pool and shore filled with laughter and excited voices.

Each night, the energetic staff puts on a spirited bi-lingual show (but if you like to turn in early, ask for a room away from the theater). The attractive guest rooms don't have TVs or telephones at press time, but plans are in the works to install them. Rates include three meals a day, soft drinks during meals, windsurfing, kayaking, use of snorkel gear, archery, volleyball, tennis (on courts lit for night play) and bocce ball. There's an additional charge for alcohol, scuba diving (you can arrange to be certified here), banana boat rides and moped rental.

MODERATE

Atlantik Beach Hotel

This sixteen-story hotel sits on Lucaya Beach. The lobby has been redone in beige and sea green, with pale travertine marble setting the overall tone. Guest rooms reflect the same color scheme, where sparkling mirrors abound and television sets are hidden in blonde wood armoires.

The hotel's beach, always one of its prime assets, has many amenities for enjoying the sand, the surf and the sun. The usual array of resort activities are available, including parasailing with colorful chutes billowing against the blue sky. Snacks are obtainable at the beach, and more substantial fare can be had indoors or out at the Butterfly Brasserie which looks out on the swimming pool. Dinner, with an emphasis on Italian cuisine, is served at Alfredo's, where quarry tile floors and Roman columns create the rosy, sun-baked look of old Italy.

For golfers, there is complimentary transportation to the hotel's Lucaya Golf and Country Club, and the Port Lucaya Marketplace is just across the road. Cars for island exploration are also rented at Hertz or Sears in the hotel or across the road at Avis and National.

Lucayan Beach Resort & Casino ☆☆☆

This upscale hotel is set along a beautiful section of Lucaya's long beach. It sprawls low and is noted for its lighthouse tower, which soars above the two- and three-story wings. Rooms are spacious, with generous walk-in closets. The large baths are marble, but the over-the-counter lighting could be brighter for makeup and shaving. All rooms have TV and king-size or oversize twin beds, with terraces or balconies, depending upon location. The casino is large and bright with all the traditional games of chance, along with a bar and cocktail area. It is never as noisy or crowded as the one at the Bahamas Princess. A Las Vegas-style casino show entertains at night. Tennis courts are across the road as is the complimentary ferry to Reef Tours, which offers boating, sailing and fishing trips on a glass-bottom boat. Right across the road is the Port Lucaya Marketplace, the waterfront array of restaurants and shops.

Radisson Resort on Lucaya Beach ☆☆

Although this hotel (formerly the Holiday Inn) has been updated, with renovations indoors and out, guests still have to pick their way through an obstacle course of luggage in the lobby. This perked-up room is brighter and mirrors have been added, but a furniture rearrangement would make it much less crowded when guests are arriving and departing. The beach remains among the strip's best. Live music and festive crowds are almost constant. Be sure to request a room well away from the laundry and exhaust system. The persistent hum can be heard even with the balcony door shut and the TV and air-conditioner going. The disco is open until all hours and young folks seem to love it. Port Lucaya Marketplace is across the road as are UNEXSO, the dive center and car rental offices.

Port Lucaya Resort and Yacht Club ★★

Adjoining Port Lucaya Marketplace and a brief stroll from a gorgeous beach, this hotel opened in September, 1993. Ten 2-story buildings encircle the spacious pool and Jacuzzi area, which is overlooked by first-floor guest rooms and the restaurant. Second-story rooms have views of the 50-slip marina (accommodating boats ranging from 40 to 125 feet). A live band entertains in the afternoons. Many guests are cruise ship passengers who spend a night or two.

Silver Sands Sea Lodge ☆☆

Modest studio and one-bedroom apartments are available here; all have balconies overlooking the pool, the ocean or the marina. The beach is within easy walking distance and the lodge has two tennis courts as well as paddleball and shuffleboard courts. The hotel's restaurant, La Phoenix, is popular among both locals and visitors. This hotel is isolated from the group of Lucaya hotels near the casino, but a few condos are nearby.

INEXPENSIVE

Coral Beach Hotel

Only a few of the studios and one-bedroom apartments in this condominium complex are rented to guests. Facilities include a pool and a stunning beach, where guests can sail and snorkel. Fishing is also available, and golf can be arranged. The Sandpiper, a popular nightspot, is in this hotel.

OFF EAST END

VERY EXPENSIVE

Deep Water Cay Club

Guests, mostly male, arrive looking forward to several days of bonefishing—or perhaps catching barracudas or permits—at this all-inclusive resort. Each morning they are sent out with a boat, a personal guide and a delicious box lunch. The guides know the waters intimately and never intrude upon other anglers, who are seldom seen in the shallows of the limitless jade and turquoise waters. In the evenings, vacationers gather at the bar lounge where they swap stories of fish and flies over drinks and hot hors d'oeuvres. The extensive fishing library comes in handy when settling disputes.

Guests dine *en famille* on imaginative meals served with wine, and they tend to retire early. When they return to their rooms, they find that the beds have been turned down, ice buckets are filled and hard candies have been placed on night stands. The rustic rooms have both ceiling fans and air conditioning, fluffy comforters and thick monogrammed towels. Embroidered pillows and shower curtains give away the hostess' touch. All cottages face the sea, and their porches sport umbrellas, fishing pole racks, easy chairs and, on some, hammocks. Don't look for newspapers or television. A two-bedroom villa is available for large parties and a saltwater swimming pool faces the main house.

Many guests fly in from Palm Beach and Miami onto the hotel's 2500 foot airstrip. Others take the small boat from McLean's Town, at the remote east end of Grand Bahama; make arrangements through the hotel to be picked up in Freeport for the approximately 45-minute drive to the dock.

THE OUT ISLANDS

Many visitors as well as Bahamians consider the Out Islands the most beautiful part of the Bahamas. These islands include all those other than New Providence and Grand Bahama, where Nassau and Freeport are located, and Paradise Island, which is connected to New Providence by a bridge. The government has changed the name from the Family Islands back to their old, more familiar appellation, the Out Islands.

Except for small towns here and there and a few large-scale resorts, nature in these islands has been left almost intact. Countless palm-shaded beaches lapped by clear turquoise waters lie undisturbed. Where there are roads, they are often bordered by nothing but wind-blown pines and bushes for miles. Bahamian waters maintain their crystal clarity because they are virtually unpolluted, especially in the Out Islands. Also, the islands are without streams and rivers and no silt or sediment collects to cloud them. Although the myriad creeks that interlace Andros, the largest of the Out Islands, appear to be rivers, or at least streams, they are waterways, fingers of the surrounding ocean.

While most fun for visitors revolves around watersports, there are also some natural and historical attractions. For seeing the sights, you can rent bicycles or cars or take taxi tours, but be prepared for bumpy roads and large old rattling cars in some areas.

Visitors to the Out Islands have more of a chance to meet and socialize with islanders than those who travel only to Nassau or Freeport. Some experiences have reinforced a belief among visitors that Out Island Bahamians are some of the most pleasant and hospitable people ever encountered during their travels. Many hotels are the centers of activity for their areas and locals are invited to hotel parties and other events. By the same token, residents often invite visitors to town happenings, such as beach parties, parades, dances and other celebrations. There is not much nightlife during the week, but on weekends something is always going on somewhere nearby. Entertainment is often low-key to say the least. Stop in a hotel or local bar, for example, and you might get to know some Bahamians over The Ring Game. The object of this popular pastime is to throw a ring attached to a long string so that it catches on a hook on the wall across the room. Experts practice throwing the ring over their shoulders or making it loop before catching. The Out Islands are not for those who are looking for casinos or hotel boutiques and beauty parlors. Don't expect phones, radios or televisions in most guest rooms or newspapers at hotels. Many accommodations and restaurants communicate by VHF or CB radio instead of phones.

Boats, bikes, mopeds and even golf carts are far more popular than cars on some islands. Many hotels do not use keys for rooms, but safety deposit boxes are available. Some accommodations have an honor bar system during the day—leaving it up to guests to write down the drinks they fix for themselves. Visitors may find that, even in the larger resorts, tap water may taste a bit salty, but most hotels supply filtered or bottled water for drinking. Although brief power "outages" are not uncommon, guest rooms usually have candles. Some Out Island accommodations close for several weeks during September and October. Although many of the hotels and guest houses have little or no air conditioning, most visitors are perfectly comfortable with ceiling fans and sea breezes. Most Out Island restaurants are in hotels and guest houses, although there are some good, locally operated eating spots.

On smaller islands, people usually wear several hats, appearing as taxi drivers, waiters, fishermen, carpenters, guides or hotel workers. One of the popular social events is helping unload mailboats, which arrive every week or ten days. At airports, where planes sometimes fly in only once or twice a week, there is also a gathering of onlookers watching their baggage-laden friends and family arriving and departing. After flights from the Out Islands, a tricycle or a carton of green bananas might come down Nassau or Freeport's baggage conveyor belt in between overstuffed cardboard boxes and suitcases tied with rope. Religion and superstition go hand-in-hand in the Out Islands. For instance, when local people kill a snake, they put it in the middle of the road, even if they end its life in the bush. This way everyone can see that Adam's enemy has been done in.

A seaside lounge looks inviting in South Andros.

The most developed islands are Abaco, Eleuthera and Exuma. Off the coast of Eleuthera, Harbour Island is known for its pink sand beaches, picturesque Dunmore Town, reminiscent of New England and its exceptional small hotels. Green Turtle Cay, in the Abacos, is another pretty island. Some island clusters, such as the Abacos, the Biminis and the Exumas, lend themselves to renting a boat and exploring on your own. During the winter, when the water is roughest and the temperature is coolest, boaters should be sure to rent at least a 21-foot powerboat.

Many travelers are surprised to find that the populations of some islands (such as Spanish Wells, off Eleuthera, and Man-O-War, Great Guana, and Elbow Cay, in the Abacos) are predominantly or almost exclusively Caucasian. Along with other areas, these islets were settled around 1648 by white Bermudians seeking religious and political freedom. They were later joined by British Loyalists fleeing America after the Revolutionary War. In the beginning, some of these Loyalists were against slavery and therefore did not keep enslaved Africans. However, as new arrivals cropped up, these sentiments were transformed into a desire to maintain the all-white status quo. Today, for the most part, these residents are friendly to visitors, no matter what color.

In April, George Town, in Exuma, is alive with the colorful Out Island Regatta. Many divers make their way to Andros, where the world's third largest barrier reef is just offshore, and Long Island, where they can learn to scuba dive among sharks. With its huge colony of pink flamingos, Inagua produces salt and is great for bird-watching. Bimini attracts dedicated fishermen. The other Out Islands with tourist accommodations offer visitors even more opportunities for rest and relaxation. Note that credit cards are not accepted everywhere, so be sure to carry "Traveler's cheques."

Until Andrew hit the Bahamas on its way to Florida and Louisiana in August, 1992, the Bahamas hadn't seen a real hurricane in nearly thirty years. Luckily, some islands were spared. Eleuthera suffered the most damage, in Governor's Harbour, Harbour Island, Current and Spanish Wells. Chub Cay in the Berry Islands and Bimini were also hurt.

GETTING THERE

The Abacos, Bimini and the Exumas are excellent sailing destinations, and more than a few boaters come from Florida. Others rent boats once they arrive in the Bahamas.

Resorts on some islands have their own or nearby airstrips and several work with charter pilots who fly guests in from Florida or Nassau. Resorts can also give vacationers tips on booking charter or commuter flights themselves. Paradise Island Airlines flies from Florida to Paradise Island (adjoining Nassau) and the Abacos. **Bahamas-**

air, the country's mass transit system, flies daily or weekly from Nassau to all the Out Islands. You may end up spending more time than planned between connecting flights, though, because Bahamasair flights are often delayed. Bahamians say, "If you have some time to spare, be sure to fly Bahamasair." As if this weren't bad enough, flights on this airline have also been known to leave *early.* Planes often make several stops, and they sometimes take off as soon as they're full, even if it's ahead of schedule. So be sure to reconfirm your seat a day or so before and to arrive at the airport in plenty of time. Despite all this, the Out Islands are well worth the hassles of getting to them.

USING TIME BETWEEN FLIGHTS

Even if your flights are on schedule, you could end up with long layovers at Nassau's airport, the hub of the Bahamas. Whether you plan to visit only one Out Island or to island hop, you may have to change planes in Nassau. Your flight from the U.S. may arrive in Nassau in the morning while your connecting flight to an Out Island departs in the late afternoon. Of course, there are other ways of getting to and around the Bahamas: you could take a long rough-around-the-edges **mail boat ride** between islands, sail yourself, fly a small airline from Florida or charter a plane from Florida or within the islands. But many people use Bahamasair, based in Nassau.

If you have most of the day in Nassau, by all means take a taxi into town (about twenty minutes away) or to Cable Beach (about ten minutes) to relax on the shore or get lucky at the casino. You can leave your luggage in airport lockers.

You might want to shop for that forgotten last minute gift. If so, check the variety of shops along Nassau's Bay Street or some of the more elegant boutiques along Bank Lane. Rawson Square, with its shaded benches and lively street activity can provide a pleasant resting place. Under the ficus and palms, and surrounded by oleander, you can watch cruise passengers venturing into town, taxi and carriage drivers soliciting fares, and Bahamians going about their daily chores.

Another shaded and quiet place for sitting is the park behind the Parliament buildings. There, local politicians and bureaucrats bustle about while citizens with court cases await their turn to enter one of the judicial buildings. Across the park, scholars and other readers enter the octagonal public library building. Up toward Shirley Street, in a wild and overgrown garden, stand the charred ruins of the once stately Royal Victoria Hotel.

Toward the water, on Prince George Dock, a stone's throw from the cruise ships, is the Junkanoo Expo building and the open-air pavilion where you can watch women fashioning intricate and astonishing hairdos for both locals and tourists.

West, on Bay Street, is the busy Straw Market, useful for finding souvenirs and gifts. A little farther on is the Pompey Museum, which was once a slave market. If you have time, you might check out the art gallery on the second floor.

If your feet are still in good shape, stop in at the Tourist Office on Prince George Dock just off the square. There, for two dollars, you can sign up for the walking tour. If you have a youngster in tow, the price is 50 cents for the child.

Depending on how much time you have between flights, the steep roundtrip taxi fare from the airport to town may not be worth it. Fortunately, you don't have to sit around watching planes taking off and landing. There are several pleasant places you can go that are not-too-expensive cab rides away: the Orange Hill Hotel, Traveller's Rest and the adjoining Sea Grape boutique, and the Airport Inn. Each of these establishments serves meals, snacks, and drinks. Traveller's Rest is especially appealing since patrons can dine on the veranda while counting the gorgeous shades of electric blue in the Atlantic across the road. If you bring your bathing suit, you can take a dip and change before you go. When it's time to return for your flight, the managements will graciously call you a taxi.

THE ABACOS

Often referred to as Abaco, this is actually a cluster of islands and islets, forming the second-largest grouping in the country. With some 650 square miles of land and many scenic coves, these islands are extremely popular among boaters. Each year in late June and early July, everyone is caught up in Abaco Regatta fever, which envelops Marsh Harbour, Elbow Cay, Green Turtle Cay and Treasure Cay. While the April Out Island Regatta in Exuma draws mainly locals, this event has traditionally attracted more tourists.

Despite growing development to lure vacationers, much of the untouched beauty of Abaco remains. The islands are thick with tropical pines, especially the feathery-needled casuarinas. Wild boar still roam some of the forests, providing meat for local tables and often for festive barbecues at local gatherings and at resorts. Islands including Elbow Cay, Great Guana and Manjack Cay are graced with some of The Bahamas' most scenic beaches. There are long stretches of tropical trees and flowering shrubs. Bearing trays of fruits and vegetables on their heads, local women still stroll majestically along quiet lanes. Most settlements have sprouted on the east side of the main island, which faces the Atlantic but is protected by offshore cays and reefs. Many visiting families enjoy renting private homes or staying in accommodations with housekeeping facilities.

DAYS GONE BY

The early Spanish explorers called these islands Habacoa, probably a corruption of *haba de cacao*, which describes the Abacos' rugged, bumpy limestone base. They found these islands of little value, except for capturing and enslaving Indians to replace those who had been killed off by excessive work and smallpox in Cuba and Hispaniola. By 1550, The Bahamas' Lucayans were completely wiped out. For years, piracy flourished amid the Abacos' many tiny cays.

Cape Cod seems transported to the Abacos.

As in nearby Eleuthera, 18th-century colonial Loyalists from New England, New York, the Carolinas and other parts of the Colonies settled here after the American Revolution. Believing that democracy and republicanism would be detrimental to their property and pocketbooks, they decided to move a piece of the British Empire to the Abacos. They chose these islands because of their proximity to the Colonies and promotional literature of the day that claimed that endless agricultural and commercial opportunities awaited them. However, they discovered that there was little fertile soil, and long droughts further thwarted their farming efforts. Many turned to fishing, developing communities on the smaller cays closer to reefs,

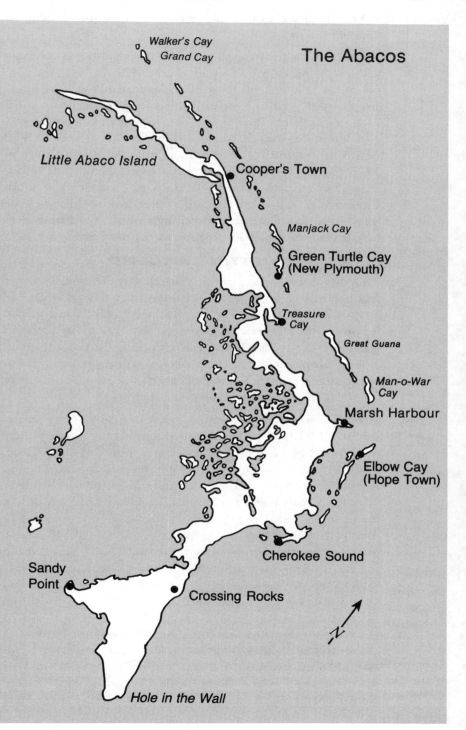

and to salvaging the cargo and wreckage of ships that fell victim to reefs and shallows.

In a country where some 85 percent of the population is of African descent, the Abacos are about 50 percent white. In 1967, the Abacos opposed the attempts of the black-dominated Progressive Liberal Party (PLP), led by Lynden Pindling, to gain a majority in the House of Assembly. But the PLP was victorious and formed a new government. Residents of Abaco were further put out when the PLP carried the Bahamas to independence from the British Crown in 1972. They tried to enlist the support of Queen Elizabeth II in their attempt to separate from the Bahamas to continue as a British Crown Colony. However, their request was denied. Although some areas in the Abacos remain predominantly white, these islands seem to have come to terms with progress, for the most part.

GETTING AROUND

Airports in the Abacos are at Walker's Cay, Treasure Cay, and Marsh Harbour. Ferries from Marsh Harbour take passengers to Elbow Cay, Man-O-War Cay and Great Guana Cay. Those headed for Green Turtle Cay catch the ferry near the Treasure Cay airport. If you plan to explore the Abacos, note that Green Turtle Cay is about a 45-minute powerboat ride from Elbow Cay or an hour from Marsh Harbour, and Treasure Cay is about a 45-minute bumpy drive from Marsh Harbour or a pleasant 60-minute sail away.

To get from the Marsh Harbour airport to Albury's Ferry Station (☎ *367-3147 or 365-6010*) you'll need to take a taxi (about $12 for two people). Ferries sometimes also depart from Union Jack Dock, which is closer to the airport, so be sure you're clear on which dock to go to. Boats depart two or three times a day for Elbow Cay, about 15 minutes away. Passengers are charged about $9 one way or $13 for same day round trip. For about the same price, ferries leave Marsh Harbour for Man-O-War Cay twice a day (about a 15-minute ride). If you arrive after the last ferry (around 4 p.m.), pray that you run into others going your way because you'll have to charter a ferry ($40 and up, per boat). A one-way ride between Marsh Harbour and Great Guana Cay (25 minutes) will cost about $10 per person ($12 for same day round trip). Guana Beach Resort & Marina picks up guests twice a day from Mangoes Restaurant in Marsh Harbour. A charter will be about $70 for one to five passengers, plus $12 for each additional passenger. You can also charter boats to Little Harbour, Treasure Cay and Green Turtle Cay, among other islands. Note the "Tips cheerfully accepted" signs in the ferries. A good **taxi**

service to contact in the Marsh Harbour area is Cay Russell's (☎ *367-2809 or 367-2202*).

The taxi from the Treasure Cay airport to the dock for ferries to Green Turtle Cay will cost about $8 per couple. Plan to pay about $9 per person for the brief ferry ride. Again, if you arrive after the last ferry your taxi driver will have to radio for a charter, which will run you considerably more.

MARSH HARBOUR

Most of the boaters on craft of all sizes streaming into the Abacos wind up at Marsh Harbour for rest, food and fuel. The town is also a center for chartering bare-boats (fully equipped yachts without crews), or boats with captains, crews or fishing guides. The Bahamas Yachting Service (BYS) does a brisk business among veteran sailors as well as novices, who can take a BYS sailing course. Trainees are never sent out alone until fully ready, and even then, fast boats are just a radio call away if trouble arises. Also try **Rich's Boat Rentals** (☎ *367-2742*). If you visit in late April or early May, you'll be just in time for the annual Penny Turtle Billfish Tournament, which is accompanied by all kinds of parties.

Nearly centrally located on the "mainland," Marsh Harbour is the Abacos' chief town. It claims the Out Islands' only traffic light. Twice a week, the mailboat from Nassau ties up, bringing passengers, replenishing stores and unloading materials for building, furnishing and merely carrying on life in the Abacos. A few shops have sprung up that are clearly geared to tourists. Next to A & K Liquor on Queen Elizabeth Drive, the main drag, you'll find **The Perfume Bar**, where prices for name-brand fragrances are generally much lower than in the U.S. Near the Conch Inn Hotel (pronounced "conk") and Lofty Fig Villas are **John Bull** and **Little Switzerland**, which also has a larger branch in a huge building down the road at the Great Abaco Beach Bazaar shopping center.

In addition to the hotels in Marsh Harbour, there's a time-sharing development called Abaco Towns. Along with the upscale Great Abaco Beach Hotel & Villas, this Mediterranean-style complex offers a touch of luxury in the midst of this mostly boating and fishing settlement. The 140 slips at **Boat Harbour Marina** (*VHF Channel 16;* ☎ *809/367-2736,* ☎ *305/359-2720 in Florida, or 800/468-4799; FAX 809/367-2819*), adjoining the Great Abaco Beach Hotel, draw yachts up to 125 feet long, with seven or eight foot drafts. Complete services are available for crews. Here **Harbour Lights** restaurant, specializing in Bahamian and American-style seafood, hangs over the edge of the water. The marina pool has a swim-up bar. **Penny's Pub** is for those who'd rather drink dry. Consider renting a Boston Whaler at the marina to spend a day visiting some of the Abacos' varied cays. Many people enjoy the cocktail and dinner cruises as well as the sightseeing trips and sails to deserted beaches. A night club featuring live entertainment keeps boaters occupied after dark.

Arrange to scuba dive through **Dive Abaco** *(P.O. Box 555, Marsh Harbour, Abaco, Bahamas;* ☎ *809/367-2014 or 809/367-2787),* based at the Conch Inn. If you'd like to take a sightseeing and/or snorkeling cruise to some of the nearby islands, contact **Albury's Ferry Service** *(*☎ *367-3147 or 365-6010).* Some trips leave from the ferry dock at The Crossing, a mile northeast of Boat Harbour Marina, and others from the 67-slip marina at the Conch Inn. This hotel makes a popular lunch stop for locals who drop in from various cays to conduct business in town.

Wally's, one of the Bahamas' most attractive restaurants, is a step down the road from the Conch Inn. Run by Wally Smith, the former owner of the Conch Inn, it is housed in a two-story building that resembles a small mansion. Shaded by an awning, the outdoor dining area faces the smooth front lawn and the marina. The snazzy interior, cooled by ceiling fans, is decked out in Haitian-influenced paintings by the country's renowned primitive painter Amos Ferguson. White peacock chairs sit on terra cotta tiles. Lunch fare ranges from burgers, buffalo chicken wings and fish and chips to conch fritters and escargot. Try the lemon mousse cake or the butterscotch blizzard cake for dessert. Wally's is open for lunch and drinks from Monday through Saturday. Live music accompanies dinner—served Monday night only, by reservation *(*☎ *367-2074)*—and Wednesday evening happy hours. The upscale boutique next door is open from Monday through Saturday.

Lunch and dinner are served daily except Sunday at nearby **Mangoes Restaurant**, which also has a boutique. Many people bypass the indoor dining room, decorated with potted plants, to sit on the breezy waterfront patio with its multi-colored captain's chairs and table cloths. Menu items include delicious popcorn shrimp, mozzarella sticks, conch chowder, seafood, sandwiches, salads and burgers. Popular for its Bahamian cooking, more modest **Cynthia's Kitchen** is in the center of town. The bar and dining room are informal, with hanging plants and plastic tablecloths. Try the curried goat or fried grouper. Other specialties are turtle steak, turtle pie, baked stuffed crabs and Cynthia's own johnny cakes. At **Mother Merl's**, between

Dundas Town and Murphy, about a 10-minute drive from Marsh Harbour, you might find wild boar, goat and turtle on the menu along with fish and chicken.

After dark, the main local hangouts are **The Jib Room**, across the water from the Conch Inn (you can get there by boat or over land); **Tiki Hut**, near the Conch Inn; **The Ranch**, also in Marsh Harbour and **The New Oasis** in Dundas Town.

MAN-O-WAR CAY

While you might see frigates (Man-O-War birds) gliding overhead, you won't find any crowds, liquor or police here. Residents take their religion even more seriously than in some other parts of the Bahamas, so be sure not to offend by walking around in your bathing suit or other skimpy attire. Like Spanish Wells in Eleuthera, the population of this island is almost exclusively white. It was settled in the 1820s by a sole couple, who came to be called Mammy Nellie and Pappy Ben. A poll conducted some hundred and fifty years later showed that 230 of the 235 residents of Man-O-War were descendants of this pair.

Here in the boat-building capital of the country, yachts and sailboats cluster in the harbor. The marina is bordered by gaily painted buildings, many housing boat yards. Residents note sadly that nowadays wooden boats are being replaced by those made of fiberglass. However, if you find one of the older artisans to talk to, he may tell you all about the good old days, when creating wooden boats was a craft very much in demand.

Along the dock, trees are hung with fish nets and buoys, like overgrown Christmas ornaments. In the shade of one such sea grape, you'll see the huge rocklike vertebrae of a killer whale. Nearby is **Albury's Harbour Store**, a grocery where you can overhear the local gossip. The prices here are generally better than those at groceries on neighboring Elbow Cay. Everyone seems to be an Albury on Man-O-War. As one young woman put it, "I know I can't marry anyone on this island."

In addition to bread and pies, **Albury's Bakery**, located in a private home, sells conch fritters. At **The Sail Shop**, on the waterfront at the northern end of town, sturdy handmade canvas bags come in all shapes, sizes and colors. While for generations sail making by hand has been in the families of the women who work here, they no longer carry on the tradition. As they sit behind sewing machines whipping up everything from pouches to overnight bags, they joke, "Call us the bag ladies. We don't make sails anymore—just S-A-L-E-S." A sign on the door at the edge of the harbor reads, "Fish-a-holic: A person obsessed with rods, reels, lures, and baits . . . who casts, trolls, and exaggerates."

To see sails being made or repaired, visit **Edwin's Boat Yard**. In the loft, you might happen upon a craftsperson sewing a portion of the canvas while the rest of the huge, unwieldy-looking cloth sprawls across the floor. Completing one sail can take up to a week. Along the dock, you'll see signs advertising half models—the glossy wooden miniature boats sold to be mounted flat on walls. You might be able to watch an artisan or two at work. Along with half models, **Joe's Studio**, decorated with old nautical gear, sells ceramics, watercolors, wind socks, jewelry, t-shirts and postcards, among other merchandise. At **Seaside Boutique**, custom-made clothing can be fashioned from Androsia, the bright batik cloth created on Andros. **Aunt Mady's Boutique** offers a variety of resort wear.

ELBOW CAY

Long slim Elbow Cay, a serene stretch of land, lies off Marsh Harbour. It is noted for its New England-esque Hope Town, its gorgeous empty beaches and its much-photographed red-and-white striped lighthouse. Some of them backed by sandy dunes, the island's long ivory shores are among the most picturesque in the Bahamas. In the early 1900s, Hope Town was the largest and wealthiest settlement in the Abacos. The main street, Queen's Highway, curls through Hope Town, following the island's configurations and passing pastel-trimmed clapboard houses with a profusion of purple and orange bougainvillea and other blossoms tumbling over stone and picket fences. Were it not for the palms and other tropical vegetation, Hope Town might be mistaken for a Cape Cod fishing village. The sea is never far from view, whether it is the pounding, crashing ocean, the calmer bay or the placid harbor with its bobbing forest of masted boats. Some travelers, especially serious boaters, have been so bitten by the Elbow Cay bug that they now return annually and rent private houses. Many of the largest and most impressive homes are owned by Americans, Canadians and Europeans.

Cars are restricted from the center of town, so bikers and pedestrians have the narrow paved roads (with names such as Lovers' Lane) to themselves. As they pass each other in the street, residents are quick to greet strangers. Visitors can spend some time browsing through the gift shops or chatting with locals. You'll learn interesting tidbits about the island's past and present. Margaret Sweeting, whose family runs both a grocery store and Benny's Place (housekeeping apartments) outside of town, remembers well the day Elbow Cay residents first got telephones. It was way back in...1988. The phones were turned on the night her daughter-in-law gave birth in Nassau, and Grandma Sweeting got to talk to the new mother in the hospital. Before the advent of telephones on Elbow Cay and other Out Islands, everyone communicated the way many still do: by VHF.

Most islanders are white, the descendants of British Loyalists. In their distinctive accent, *h*'s pop up in and disappear from words unexpectedly. You might run into the old man who looks for new faces in town so that he can point out the site of the Methodist church that was destroyed by fire. He delights in telling the story of its preacher, who "didn't know 'is hass from a 'ole in the ground." It seems that the minister gave his sermons while facing the window that overlooked the ocean. His congregation sat with their backs to the water. One day he saw a shipwreck and decided to claim the booty. He told the congregation to kneel and pray. He then jumped out of the window, intending to land on his jackass and take off for the ship down the beach. Instead, he fell into a hole. The old man says the preacher ended up claiming the loot anyway.

Stores in Hope Town are shut tight on Sundays, and the various churches are in full swing. You can stand on a corner and hear two different sermons at the same time. An outdoor Catholic service is held in waterfront Jarret Park Playground, next to the main dock (often called the post office dock, since it's overlooked by the P.O.). After parking their bicycles at the entrance, people crowd the benches in the shade of huge overhanging trees—and some even find perches in the branches. If you ask why the priest must stand in the hot sun while the congregation enjoys the shade, residents will answer, "So he won't talk so long." During the service, people rise one by one to read Biblical selections. A child or two often uses the swings and the priest may have to compete with a radio from a nearby house. Behind the white-robed clergyman, a group of boaters in skimpy bathing suits might disembark at the dock.

Down the street, the mouth-watering aroma of baking bread floats out of **Harbour's Edge** restaurant. Topped with wooden tables and benches, the deck here provides a perfect view of the candy-cane lighthouse and the boat-packed harbor. The gullywings (chicken wings), conch chowder, crawfish salad and fish sandwiches are all eagerly gobbled up. A pool table, juke box and satellite television entertain the young folks who pour in after dark, especially on Wednesdays (reggae night). Lunch and dinner are served daily except Tuesdays, when only the bar is open (in the evening). Note that this restaurant is strict about its hours: if you arrive just a few minutes after 2 p.m., when lunch ends, for instance, you won't be served anything but drinks.

Neighboring **Whispering Pines** specializes in Bahamian dishes, such as the usual conch, peas and rice, and chicken or fish and chips. But the menu might also include less common selections such as stir-fried beef and vegetables with rice. The South American wall hangings reflect the Ecuadorian origins of Tanny Key, the owner, who also works at **Native Touches Gift Shop**. Selling t-shirts and other beach- and sportswear, this nearby store takes credit cards. You can spend more money at **Edith's Straw Shop**, where hats and bags are handmade, or **Kemp's Souvenir Center**.

For delicious, freshly baked bread and pound cake, stop at **Vernon's**, the general store across the way. The indefatigable Vernon Malone is not only a grocer, baker, taxi driver, artist and minister, but he's also a descendant of Wyannie Malone, Elbow Cay's most celebrated historical figure. You can learn all about her role in the Abacos' past at the Hope Town museum bearing her name. Not far from town, **Bessie's Bakery** is the place to go for key lime pie. At **Albury's Fish Market** in Hope Town, people staying in rented houses can pick up crawfish, conch and fish filets. If you have a boat, your best bet for groceries is another **Albury's**, on nearby Man-O-War Cay, where the wide selection of merchandise is somewhat less expensive than on Elbow Cay.

Next door to Hope Town's stark white St. James Methodist Church is **Ebb Tide**, which sells everything from jewelry and books to Androsia (colorful batik clothing made on Andros). For a truly Bahamian breakfast, try waterfront **Cap'n Jacks**, which serves boiled fish and homemade bread on Sunday mornings and cornbeef and grits on Mondays. At other times you might be able to sample turtle burgers here, along with fish, chicken, conch and burgers.

The garden of the Wyannie Malone Museum is filled with greenery. Set within the low, stone-walls are coconut palms, hibiscus, Norfolk pine, crotons and sea grape, among other plants. After all this vegetation, it is startling to see an empty area here, Cholera Cemetery, which was closed during the 19th century after a cholera epidemic. Graves and headstones are no longer in evidence. A nearby park, sporting a gazebo and filled with flowers, overlooks the beach. This is a wonderfully tranquil setting for cooling out.

At first glance, Hope Town Harbour Lodge seems just another of the clapboard houses along Queen's Highway. Then you notice that one wing has three stories, probably making it the tallest building in the Out Islands. An informal poll among conch fritter addicts reveals that this is the best place in town for these Bahamian snacks. The Sunday champagne brunch here also receives high marks. At night, the dart board in the bar is often the center of attention among the lively young crowd. Across the road, near the swimming pool on the ocean side, is the hotel's early 19th century Butterfly House, often rented by families.

Club Soleil, a restaurant across the harbor from town, will pick up diners at the post office dock and ferry them over. You can arrange transportation through your hotel or at Vernon's store. Rudy Malone, who runs Club Soleil with his wife, Kitty, happens to be Vernon's brother. As a matter of fact, the driftwood wall sculpture of Hope Town that adorns the breezy, pine-panelled dining room was done by Vernon. Windows all around provide spectacular views of the harbor. The confit of duck, poached red snapper with dill and white wine sauce, and the steak with herb butter are all highly recommended. Bring your meal to a close with Bahamian, Jamaican, Spanish or Irish coffee. Club Soleil is closed on Mondays and serves only brunch on Sundays.

Rudy's Place and the dining room at **Abaco Inn**, both outside Hope Town, also provide complimentary transportation, from hotels and private homes. Abaco Inn is known for its multi-course gourmet meals. Many people renting private homes gather on the oceanview patio for cocktails before dinner. Serving dinner only, rustic wood-panelled Rudy's is closed on Sundays. Here the filling meals include conch fritters, soup (perhaps lima bean, potato or broccoli), salad, warm freshly baked bread (maybe cinnamon raisin) and dessert. Entrees might include New York strip steak, lamb chops with mint jelly and turtle steak sauteed with mushrooms. But the most popular choice is the crawfish, which is removed from its shell, lightly battered, fried, replaced and baked with Parmesan cheese. Wine is available from France, Germany, Portugal and the U.S. The night you dine, a child—the very serious son or daughter of one of the other workers—might be waiting tables. Rudy himself will periodically take a break from the kitchen to ensure that all is well in the dining room. A sign by the door reads, "All of our guests bring happiness—some by coming, others by going."

Near the Hope Town public dock, **Hope Town Dive Shop & Boat Rentals** (☎ *366-0029*), which also sells ice, will see to your aquatic needs. Other operations to try for boat rentals or fishing guides are **Island Marine** (☎ *366-0282 or FAX 809/366-0281*), **Day's Catch Charters** (☎ *366-0059*), and **Sea Horse Boat Rentals** (☎ *367-2513 or FAX 809/366-0189*). For exploring the island by land, rent bicycles in town or at Abaco Inn (where the use of bikes is gratis for guests). Be sure to take a ride or a walk outside town. Except for the occasional car and the distant motors of boats, the only sounds you'll hear in many areas will be birds conversing, the sudden scuttle of a curly-tailed lizard in the bushes or the buzzing of a stray fly.

Just north of the center of town, a sandy road, cushioned by pine needles, is bordered by calm waters on one side and private ocean-front homes high on a bluff on the other. You'll pass a tiny offshore island topped by a single house. Although the homes along the other side of this narrow strip of land obscure the view of the open ocean and the long white beach, you'll hear the crashing surf. Take a left where the road forks and you'll come to a small calm beach—if the tide is in, that is.

While Hope Town Harbour Lodge is right in town, the two other main accommodations, Abaco Inn and nearby Sea Spray Resort, are about two miles south in White Sound. At the southernmost tip of Elbow Cay, quiet palm-shaded Tahiti Beach yields all kinds of shells and sand dollars.

Many people enjoy the bike ride from Abaco Inn to town. Take the bumpy dirt road parallel to the beach, keeping the ocean to your right. Turn left at the corner by the two houses with a row of 11 palms out front. (If you see a "NJ Turnpike" sign in front of a house, you'll know you've gone too far—unless you don't mind taking the longer route.) Not far from Abaco Inn, you'll pass Terry's Auto Repair. Terry's wife, Wanda, prepares homecooked take-out meals for vacationers upon request (☎ *366-0069*).

The dirt road then curves to the right into a perpendicular paved road. Take the fifth right (back toward the sound of the ocean). You'll pass a small inlet on the left where a boat or two may be docked. The road curves left, now bordered by a low stone wall with bright fuschia and orange bougainvillea spilling over it. Then suddenly to your left, a spectacular view opens up of the red-and-white striped lighthouse and the boat-filled harbor. To your right is the harborside entrance to Hope Town Harbour Lodge, which looks down on the road from its lofty perch.

If you'd rather walk to town, take the shorter route (which is too rugged even for mountain bikes). Instead of turning onto the street with Sweeting's Grocery and Terry's Auto Repair, continue straight, and you'll come to the narrow path that eventually intersects with the paved road to town.

GREAT GUANA CAY

Another long, slender island off Marsh Harbour, Great Guana Cay remains a tranquil, unspoiled hideaway known to few outsiders. Cruise ships do stop here from time to time, but passengers see little of the island and islanders see little of passengers since they just spend a few hours at one of the gorgeous isolated beaches. Other visitors are overnight guests at the lone hotel and some come by while exploring nearby cays by boat. Through the hotel, scuba divers can arrange to dive with dolphins. Only about 100 people, many of them lobster fishermen, call this island home. Children go to school until they are 14. To continue their education, they must leave the island, but many don't.

The miniscule village is always quiet—except when the silence is pierced by the cry of a rooster. Here a hand-lettered sign echoes the sentiments of the island's warm, welcoming residents: "It's Better in the Bahamas, but . . . It's Gooder in Guana." There are no cars along the paved paths bordered by palm trees. Laundry flutters on clothes lines between small clapboard houses with picket fences. Browse through the handmade shell jewelry at **Pinder's Gift Shop**, a typical all-in-one Family Island store that also sells lobster, fish, t-shirts, fruit, books, and handles real estate and boat rentals. For ice, stop by **My Two Sons Liquor Store**. The menu at **Sand Dollar Cafe**, on the waterfront adjacent to **Guana Harbour Grocery**, includes hamburgers, sandwiches, fish and conch.

Walk up a path from the waterfront, and you'll come to a small graveyard with above-ground tombs decorated with flowers and colorful bows and ribbons. A tiny, weathered grave bears an inscription that reads, "Pearl Bethel, born April 23, 1920, Fell Asleep in Jesus July 2, 1920." Another path takes you across the island's narrow width, past the school with its bright mural, to the Atlantic. The long, wide ocean beach is stark white, backed by grassy dunes. Boulders stud the electric blue water here and there. Waves thrash the rocky outcroppings, burst into the air, then pour over them like waterfalls. Shaded by palms and casuarina pines, this is by far one of the nicest beaches in the Bahamas. However, unfortunately, it is marred in some areas by bottles and cans that have washed ashore from cruise ships or been left by beachgoers.

Guana Beach Resort & Marina, the island's only hotel, sits on a finger of land. To appreciate just how slim this peninsula is, take a walk along that path that begins near the far end of the bay beach. You'll stand on a rise high above the water, with the town and boats in the distance on one side and the beach on the other. Rocky in some places, cushiony in others, the path curls through woods dappled with sunlight, past palmettos, sea grape trees and bright orange mushrooms growing on fallen branches.

The hotel sends a boat to pick up arriving guests at the Mangoes Restaurant dock in Marsh Harbour. If you're not staying at the hotel, you can come over on the regular ferry, which usually leaves from Albury's dock.

TREASURE CAY

Despite its misleading name, Treasure Cay is on the mainland and is second to Marsh Harbour as an Abaco entry point. Like Marsh Harbour, it is easily reached from most of the Abacos. From the dock, a brief taxi ride from the airport, ferries depart for Green Turtle Cay or Spanish Cay. Treasure Cay, with its inviting coastline, is the out-island center for golf and tennis enthusiasts at Treasure Cay Beach Resort & Villas. The hotel here has been closed for some time, but the villas are available for rent. Facilities include an 18-hole golf course designed by Dick Wilson, a marina and swimming pools.

Treasure Cay was the first part of the Abacos to be settled after the Lucayan Indians were killed off by European explorers. Founded in the early 1780s, the town of Carleton was built by American colonists loyal to Britain. It stood near the northern end of Treasure Cay Beach. However, less than 90 days after the settlement was born, the 600 or so residents fell to fighting over when and how each person should work in the communal provisions store. Unable to come to an agreement, most of the population pulled up stakes, moving about 20 miles southeast, where they founded Marsh Harbour. Carleton eventually died out, after only a few years.

GREEN TURTLE CAY

Green Turtle Cay, northwest of Marsh Harbour, is one of the most charming islands in The Bahamas. Unless they arrive by boat, travelers fly in to Treasure Cay, then take a taxi to the nearby ferry. Like Hope Town on Elbow Cay, Green Turtle's tiny town of New Plymouth resembles areas of Cape Cod. During the 1800s, it was the most prosperous settlement in the Abacos. It brings to mind those British Loyalists who would not face the consequences of the American Revolution. It was to this island that the notorious pirate Vain the Great fled around 1717 after Woodes Rogers, the first royal governor, was sent to Nassau to wrest it from the buccaneers.

Although you can walk most places on the island, people usually get around by boat. When you arrive at the dock in New Plymouth, you'll be greeted by a row of small, handsome clapboard houses trimmed in pastel pinks, blues and greens. Bushy palms and tropical flowers decorate streets and front yards enclosed by white picket fences. Away from the waterfront, you'll see goats and roosters as you walk along narrow, paved roads and you might hear children spelling in unison in a one-room schoolhouse. Barclay's, the lone bank, opens only once a week. Lobsters trapped offshore have become a thriving local export business for American restaurants. If you're staying somewhere with kitchen facilities, this is a good place to buy fresh lobster for dinner.

At **Sea View Restaurant**, you can have a hearty, inexpensive Bahamian meal before strolling down to the beach. The casual, friendly restaurant has patrons' business cards, photographs of visitors, and dollar bills plastered on the walls. Another popular local restaurant is **Rooster's Rest**, where the Gully Rooster band plays on weekends. At **Laura's Kitchen**, which sells conch, fish, chicken and ice cream, you can order at the window, then eat on the breezy porch. Light meals are served between 9 a.m. and 3 p.m. at **Plymouth Rock Liquors & Cafe**, next to **Ocean Blue Gallery**. When in the mood for pastry, cool drinks, or local snacks, stop at **The Wrecking Tree Restaurant & Bar**, where a large casuarina grows up through the front porch. Some say this place was named because people used to sit in the shade of the tree and get "wrecked." Try the conch fritters. Speaking of getting wrecked, **Miss Emily's Blue Bee Bar**, on Victoria Street, is said to be the birthplace of the Goombay Smash, a potent rum-based fruit drink. However, this bar keeps irregular hours. The island's fanciest restaurants are found at **Bluff House** and the **Green Turtle Club** hotels, outside town. For t-shirts, try the **Loyalist Rose Shoppe** or the **Sand Dollar Shoppe**.

Visitors who like to be enveloped by history may stay at the restored New Plymouth Inn, a former private home dating back to the mid-19th century. The inn's lively restaurant is a popular spot. More history is found at the Albert Lowe Museum, which has a collection of hand-carved ships as well as information about the little island's early settlers, and at the Memorial Sculpture Garden.

 About a 15-minute walk from Bluff House and five from the Green Turtle Club, Coco Bay is one of the most beautiful crescents in the Bahamas. Shaded by casuarinas and lapped by calm waters, this long beach is often empty. The Green Turtle Club plans to build additional accommodations here. We hope they make the new structures as unobtrusive as possible. Farther along, the frothy waves thrash the island's Atlantic beach. The intense blue of the ocean here is set off by the stark white surf and sand. Unfortunately, however, in recent years this expansive ocean beach has become increasingly trash-strewn, with bottles and cans lying amid the pine needles at the edge of the sand. Pristine shores are found on nearby uninhabited islands such as Manjack Cay. Both Bluff House and the Green Turtle Club take guests there for picnics.

WALKER'S CAY AND GRAND CAY

Walker's Cay and Grand Cay are two tiny islands seemingly cast off by Abaco and left to drift into the Atlantic. Walker's Cay attracts fishermen who come in search of the abundant variety of marine life and boaters who pass through these small islands and others in the Bahamas chain. Most visitors stay at the lone hotel on Walker's Cay.

The vegetation here is markedly different from that of other Family Islands. You'll see few casuarinas, and many of the kind of gnarled old trees that are more common in the U.S. One surprise near the hotel is the ficus with its trunk growing around the trunk of a tall palmetto tree.

Take a guided tour of Aqualife, not far from the island's one hotel. This commercial operation produces tropical fish that will eventually end up in pet stores. The marine life, which comes mainly from the Pacific, is in various stages of development. The black fish with iridescent bright blue and purple stripes or orange and red tiger stripes are something to see. Swarming in black tanks, they look like thin neon lights flashing back and forth.

Most of the hotel's workers live across the water on Grand Cay, where everyone has a boat instead of a car. The popular **Island Club Bar and Restaurant**, also known as Rosie's, attracts visitors in their own boats for lunch and dinner, or transports them by water taxi. Rosie Curry owns the restaurant as well as a modest motel. Also on the island is the **Seaside Disco and Bar**, near a cut bordered by a tangle of mangroves. The bar's walls are decorated with the nicknames of such patrons as "Thatch," "Hitman Rev," "The Sea Wolf" and "Flash Dancers." When they want a good beach, the locals, again by boat, take off for nearby Whale Bay Island, another minuscule dot in the Atlantic.

PERSONAL FAVORITES

*Adventure: A trip to uninhabited **Manjack Cay**, near Green Turtle Cay, for a beach picnic.*

*Sports: **Sailing** anywhere in The Abacos.*

*Restaurants: **Club Soleil**, on Elbow Cay, for its harborfront locale. **Mangoes**, at the water's edge in Marsh Harbour, where locals and others from nearby cays mingle with visitors.*

*Hotels: **Abaco Inn**, on Elbow Cay, for its quiet beaches and gourmet food. **Green Turtle Club**, on Green Turtle Cay, for its gracious hosts. **Bluff House**, on Green Turtle Cay, for its rustic comfort.*

WHAT TO SEE AND DO

Sports

Serious divers go to Marsh Harbour, Walker's Cay, Elbow Cay, Green Turtle Cay and Treasure Cay. Anglers and boaters have the run of the cays, with rewarding deep-sea fishing and convenient marinas. While boats can be rented in most areas, Marsh Harbour is the main sailing center. Tennis buffs can choose among Marsh Harbour, Treasure Cay, Green Turtle Cay and the tonier Walker's Cay up north. Treasure Cay also has an 18-hole Dick Wilson-designed golf course. Windsurfing is available on Walker's Cay, Great Guana Cay, Elbow Cay and Treasure Cay.

Sea Kayakking

Ibis Tours, Boynton Beach, Florida; ☎ *800/525-9411* • One of the most exciting ways to see the Abacos is by kayak. This company offers eight-day excursions during which you paddle by day and at night sleep in cozy inns in handsome New England-like settlements. Bahamian specialities are on the dinner menus. You'll spend part of the day paddling around Abaco Sound. Then you can relax on the beach or wander through the picturesque streets of Loyalist villages. Groups are limited to eight people.

SAILING DESTINATIONS

Manjack Cay

North of Green Turtle Cay • Through Bluff House, the Green Turtle Club or on your own boat, take a day trip to this uninhabited island surrounded by some of The Bahamas' most beautiful sandy shores. The guide from Bluff House spears lobster, catches fish and then cooks it right on the pine-rimmed beach along with other lunch good-

ies. The guide at the Green Turtle Club also prepares a great meal on
the beach. There's plenty of time for swimming, jogging, relaxing and
drinking rum punch. Most visitors get a kick out of watching the baby
nurse sharks that appear when the guides clean the fish and throw the
entrails into the water.

Tilloo and Pelican Cays

South of Elbow Cay • Especially if you're based on Elbow Cay, excellent targets for a day's sail are pencil-thin Tilloo Cay and the tiny Pelican Cays, with their irresistible deserted beaches. The waters around
Tilloo Cay, packed with grouper and conch, are particularly good for
both fishing and swimming. In the Pelican Cays Land and Sea Park,
Sandy Cay Reef is one of the most colorful dive sites in the region.
The area is protected, so line fishing, spearfishing, crawfishing and
shelling are all taboo.

Art Colony at Little Harbour

South of Marsh Harbour, Great Abaco • At this small, picturesque
anchorage, you'll find the studio and home of the family of the late
Randolph Johnston who specialized in lost wax casting in bronze. His
creativity has been passed down to their son, Pete, who makes jewelry,
among other items. Look for the sign by the dock that tells when the
studio is open to visitors. Whether you stop by this art colony or not,
be sure to stroll over to the old lighthouse and the ocean side of the
narrow peninsula.

Local Shipbuilding

Man-O-War Cay • This cay was once one of the strongest contributors
to the Bahamian economy as a center for shipbuilding. Although that
industry has waned, some shipbuilding continues, and visitors may
watch craftsmen at work. A sunken ship of the Union Navy, the U.S.S.
Adirondack, lies off Man-O-War Cay. It was wrecked on a reef in the
middle 1800s and can now be explored by divers.

Sea and Land Preserve

Fowl Cay • North of Man-O-War Cay, Fowl Cay is a Bahamian government sea and land park reserve. Divers can explore undersea caves
and the shallow reefs that are also accessible to snorkelers.

GREEN TURTLE CAY

Albert Lowe Museum ★ ★

New Plymouth • This museum is housed in one of the village's historic
buildings. Exhibits go back to the early Loyalist settlers and include
much other Bahamian history. There is a collection of model ships
built by the late Albert Lowe, for whom the museum is named. In a
workshop at his nearby home, Vertrum Lowe, a son of Albert, carries
on his father's nautical craft. The artwork of another son, Alton Lowe,
one of the Bahamas' best- known artists, is on display at the museum,
and you can purchase prints of his paintings. Also on sale here are silk

scarves in hard-to-resist colors, Bahamian straw goods and books on local history.

Memorial Sculpture Garden

Across from New Plymouth Inn • Laid out in the pattern of the British flag, this garden honors residents of the Abacos, both living and dead, who have made historical contributions to the Bahamas. Busts sit on stone pedestals with plaques detailing each person's accomplishments. You'll learn about some of the American loyalists who came to the Bahamas from New England and the Carolinas, their descendants and the descendants of the people who were brought as slaves. You'll see everyone from Albert Lowe—whose ancestors were among New Plymouth's first European-American settlers—to Jeanne I. Thompson, a black Bahamian, a contemporary playwright and the country's second woman to practice law.

ELBOW CAY

Hope Town Lighthouse

Elbow Cay • Before the installation of the lighthouse in 1863, many of Hope Town's inhabitants made a good living luring ships toward shore to be wrecked on the treacherous reefs and rocks so that their cargoes could be salvaged for cash. To safeguard their livelihoods, residents tried in vain to destroy the lighthouse while it was being built. Today people can climb the 130-foot red-and-white striped tower for sweeping views of the harbor and town. If you can't hitch a ride across the harbor to the lighthouse, arrange a visit through Dave Malone's Dive Shop in Hope Town or Abaco Inn in White Sound. Or if you take the morning ferry from Marsh Harbour to Elbow Cay, ask about being dropped off, then picked up a little while later.

Wyannie Malone Museum and Garden

Hope Town, Elbow Cay • The museum is a tribute to the South Carolinian widow who founded Hope Town in 1783. It gives some interesting details of the cay's history. The garden displays indigenous plants and trees. Open 10 a.m. to noon.

Tahiti Beach ★★

Southern Elbow Cay • This curving sandy stretch got its name from its thick wall of palms. At low tide, the shelling can be excellent. Bonefishing is also rewarding in these shallow waters. Picnics are periodically held here, and some residents have chosen this site for wedding receptions. Unfortunately, at one end of the otherwise pristine beach, someone has built a house so large and rambling that it looks like a resort. However, you can round a bend and put this intrusion out of sight. Across the cut, you'll see uninhabited Tilloo Cay and the thrashing waves of the Atlantic in the distance.

The beach is a pleasant, though up and downhill, bicycle ride from Abaco Inn (about 20 minutes) or the closer Sea Spray Resort & Villas. You might have to walk the bike up and down a few of the small but very rocky rises. Along the way, you'll pass sea grape trees, fluffy long-needled pines and other varied roadside vegetation. Turn left when you come to a corner with a house on a bluff to your left. Go all the way to the end of this path, and you'll see the ocean crashing at Tilloo Cut in front of you. Turn right and follow that road past houses with barbed wire fences enclosing banana groves and pink and orange bougainvillea bushes. Walk through the dense palm grove to the beach. Since you'll be headed for the shore, which is public, ignore the "Private. No Trespassing" signs.

WHERE TO STAY

If you're interested in **renting a private home** on Elbow Cay, contact Malone Estates *(Hope Town, Elbow Cay, Abaco, Bahamas; ☎ 809/366-0100; or 809/366-0157 phone or FAX)*. Some houses have their own docks and laundry is often included in rates. For **beach houses or garden villas** in the Treasure Cay area, try PGF Management & Rentals *(P.O. Box TC 4186, Treasure Cay, Abaco, Bahamas; ☎ 809/367-2570, ext. 127)*. On Great Guana Cay, contact Edmond Pinder *(☎ 809/367-2207)* of Pinder's Cottages.

MARSH HARBOUR

EXPENSIVE

Great Abaco Beach Hotel   ☆☆☆

This modern hotel adjoins Boat Harbour Marina, with its extensive facilities. Guest rooms in the main building and the two-bedroom, two-bath villas all face the beach, backed by a palm grove, or the marina. Decorated in wicker and colorful prints, each bedroom has either two queen sized beds or one king. All units are air-conditioned, with satellite TV, telephones and sliding glass doors leading to balconies. Dressing areas with well-lit mirrors and built-in vanities add to the pleasure of a stay here. Tennis courts and swimming pools keep people active when not out on the ocean. In the attractive marina pool, you can swim under a bridge or float up to the bar for a drink. On weekends, there's live entertainment at Below Decks Lounge.

INEXPENSIVE

The Conch Inn   ☆☆

The entrance to the Conch Inn is lined with palms. Although this hotel is only 10 minutes from the airport, its most enthusiastic guests are the boaters who come to tie up, have a drink at the bar and join in the "wollyball" game that sometimes takes place in the pool. In addition to using its 67 slips, boaters who do not take rooms get everything from berths to baths as well as laundry services, mail and messages. The needs of guests are seen to under the watchful eyes of the managers, who are always nearby when needed. Most rooms, furnished in sunny yellows and apple greens, have small terraces overlooking the marina and its moored boats and, sometimes, a spectacular sunset. The pleasant dining room has a view of the harbor and its twinkling night lights. The homemade potato chips and the grouper are both delicious. Another good restaurant and several shops are right next door to the Conch Inn. The beach is about a 10-minute walk away.

Island Breezes Motel

Within walking distance of downtown Marsh Harbour, this small, comfortable facility has air-conditioned rooms with microwave ovens, television, refrigerators and ceiling fans. Meals are available at one of the nearby local eating places.

The Lofty Fig Villas

Conveniently located across the road from restaurants, shops and a marina, these housekeeping cottages surround a bean-shaped swimming pool. The smooth lawns are set off by bursts of bougainvillea and other attractive plantings. Each cottage, air conditioned and with ceiling fans, has a large screened-in patio, full kitchen and both a double and single bed. A 10-minute stroll will take you to the beach. Bicycles are available for rent.

Pelican Beach Villas

Five 2-bedroom, 2-bath villas are available at this beachfront resort. Hammocks and beach chairs are on the premises and boating can be arranged at nearby Rich's Rentals. The Jib Room at the Marsh Harbour marina, across the road, is good for inexpensive dining, and there are cookouts on Wednesday and Sunday evenings.

ELBOW CAY

MODERATE

Abaco Inn ★★★

At this small resort on a narrow strip of Elbow Cay, the ocean's froth-crested surf washes the beach on one side while the tranquil waters of White Sound bathe the other. Overlooking the ocean is a sunbleached gazebo and a salt-water swimming pool. Tucked away a bit up the shore, a secluded area is reserved for guests who enjoy bathing in the buff. Hammocks wide enough for two are strung outside the various cottages where rooms are located. In the six oceanview units, vacationers fall asleep to the sound of crashing surf. Completely renovated in 1991, the six smaller harborside rooms look out to pines and a sliver of water. While the cottages are rustically furnished, they are perfectly comfortable, with a homelike feel. All have books left behind by previous travelers. Some rooms are air-conditioned, while ceiling fans cool the air in others.

The focal point of Abaco Inn is the main building, where a stone fireplace commands the inner lounge. Before dinner, guests and vacationers renting private homes gather for cocktails here and at the bar on the screened-in harborview porch. Choices for the five-course evening meal might include cream of spinach soup; salad with raspberry vinaigrette dressing; warm, freshly baked Bahamian nut bread and chicken breast stuffed with mushrooms, onions, peppers and cheddar cheese. Chocolate peppermint silk, hot apple coconut crisp or key lime pie might be on the dessert menu. Calories can be burned off by riding the mountain bikes that are lent gratis to guests and rented to outsiders. Upon request, travelers can be driven by van to Hope Town, a couple of miles away. Those who rent boats or are sailing their own should be sure to visit nearby Shell Island, where the lovely beach is great for shelling.

Club Soleil Resort

Built by Rudy Malone and his Dutch wife Kitty, the owners of the popular neighboring restaurant by the same name, this hotel sits on the waterfront. Lunch is served on the deck surrounding the freshwater swimming pool. Guests are ferried across the harbor into town. They can walk to the beach from there. Boat rentals are also available.

Hope Town Hideaways

One of the newest establishments on Elbow Cay, this collection of brightly decorated villas overlooks the harbor and the center of town. Panelled in white-washed wood, each unit has a large modern kitchen with a long counter and stools, two bedrooms with queen-size beds and two baths. Daybeds are in the sunny living rooms, which, along with bedrooms, open onto spacious decks. A freshwater swimming pool is on the premises. Rooms are cooled by central air-conditioning and ceiling fans. Club Soleil Restaurant is right next door. For real pampering, you can have a cook. Ask about charter flights.

INEXPENSIVE

Hope Town Harbour Lodge ✩✩

Sandwiched between a gorgeous stretch of stark white beach and the harbor with its red-and-white striped lighthouse, this hotel is right in town. Perched on a bluff, it's a great vantage point for some of Elbow Cay's most appealing views. Originally from Boston, co-owner Mark Sullivan came to Hope Town Harbour Lodge as a chef in 1980. Ten years later, he married the woman who has owned the hotel since 1977, Laddie Wilhoyte Sullivan, who hails from San Francisco. Together they offer guests a welcome dose of personal attention. The lodge is known for its excellent dinners, served in the wood-panelled dining room off the bar and lounge. The Sunday champagne brunch is another popular meal here. Norris Smith, the young European-trained Bahamian chef, has been at the helm for years. At night, visitors and locals often play darts in the convivial bar.

Rooms are located in the main building, in cottages by the freshwater swimming pool and in nineteenth-century Butterfly House, one of the oldest surviving buildings in Hope Town. This historic two-story house with hardwood floors sports a living room, bedroom and full kitchen downstairs, and both a double and a single bed in the attic. The hotel's other guest rooms are plain but comfortable. Some have twin beds while others have queens or a double and a twin. The closets of those in the main wing are located in the bathrooms. Cross breezes usually make staying in rooms that aren't air-conditioned perfectly pleasant.

Sea Spray Resort

Here in White Sound, 3.5 miles from Hope Town, the oceanside and harborside cottages range from one-bedroom, one-bath to two-bedroom, two-bath. Grounds are handsomely landscaped. Built in 1989, oceanside Sea Mist Villa is the newest, with blond wood panelling, a modern kitchen with generous counter space, a dining area, two bedrooms, two full baths and a sunny living room with two day beds. Sea Grape is also especially nice. Although Sea Spray Villa was built around 1980, it was recently refurbished. All cottages have decks, barbecue pits, air-conditioned bedrooms and ceiling fans. Oceanside units, on a bluff overlooking the somewhat rocky beach, all have queen-sized beds. Maid service is provided.

Guests, as well as people staying elsewhere on Elbow Cay, can arrange to have meals catered by Belle Albury (☎ *366-0065*), the mother of owner Monty Albury, who lives on the property with his wife. Among Belle's specialties are cracked conch, pork chops, fish and all kinds of baked goods. The harborfront club house, where Monty and his father used to build boats, now houses a pool table. Docking is convenient for sailors, and 17- to 22-foot boats are rented here. Use of sunfish and windsurfers is free to guests, who can also take day sails with a captain. One free transfer is provided to and from Hope Town. Bikes can be rented at Abaco Inn, down the road a piece. A 20- to 30-minute hike will take guests to scenic Tahiti Beach. Sweeting's is the closest grocery store.

GREAT GUANA CAY

MODERATE

Guana Beach Resort & Marina

For total escape, book a room at this hotel on an unspoiled island near Marsh Harbour. It sits on a slender peninsula with the bay on one side and the harbor on the other. Instead of telephones, televisions, radios and cars, you'll find seven miles of virtually empty beaches, a freshwater swimming pool and hammocks strung between palms. The hotel deck is great for sunset watching. Vacationers spend their time sailing (Sunfish are complimentary to guests), fishing, snorkeling, scuba diving, shelling and simply soaking up sun. Rooms are all air-conditioned, with ceiling fans as well. The studio and two-bedroom villas, complete with kitchens, attract families. Neither these nor the individual rooms with screened-in patios and porches get much sunlight. But that's all the more reason to go out and explore the glorious surroundings. Gazebos with shady benches stand along the waterfront. Scuba divers should not pass up the opportunity to dive with dolphins. This adventure takes place three times a week. Fishing (even for lobster), sailing and snorkeling are easily arranged. A short walk through town will take you to the beautiful, long ocean beach.

The hotel picks up guests twice a day from Marsh Harbour at Mangoes Restaurant, a brief taxi ride from the airport. The last hotel boat usually departs the restaurant dock at 4:30 p.m. If you'll be arriving later than that, contact the hotel ahead of time to try to avoid having to charter a special ferry (which could run you about $70 for the half hour ride!). Some guests prefer to rent a boat in Marsh Harbour and sail over themselves. This way they have flexibility in island hopping. But note that during the winter, when the water is roughest, you'll need to rent at least a 21-foot powerboat.

GREEN TURTLE CAY

MODERATE

Green Turtle Club

Born as a yachtsman's hangout in the 1960s, Green Turtle Club now welcomes all kinds of travelers. After an extensive renovation, some rooms have been completely redone Colonial style, putting them among the most upscale in the Bahamas. Twenty-five thousand dollars was spent on each refurbished unit, and it shows: mahogany headboards and dressers; oriental throw rugs and vases; oak floors; wood-trimmed doors; bedspreads, dust ruffles and drapes imported from France; snazzy baths with dressing areas; and terra-cotta tiles on patios. Individual rooms, suites and villas with private docks are available. All have air conditioning, ceiling fans, clock radios and refrigerators or full kitchens.

In the bar/lounge in the clubhouse, yachting club flags hang from the ceiling beams and the walls are papered with dollar bills. During the days when commercial flights to the Out Islands were limited or nonexistent, private pilots, many of whom had flown in World War II, would write their names on dollars, paste them to the walls and say, "If I don't come back, have a drink on me." Other visitors have carried on this old wartime tradition (and taken it a bit further). While people gather in the lounge for cocktails, it is not unusual to see a man hoist a woman onto his shoulders so that she may stick a bill on the ceiling. Managers Bill and Donna Rossbach run Green Turtle Club as if they were entertaining friends in their home. There is one seating for dinner, and Donna escorts guests into the elegant dining room, table by candlelit table. The delicious food is beautifully presented. With live bands, the Wednesday night patio parties draw locals and visitors from all over the island.

The ocean beach is about a 10-minute walk from the clubhouse and the calmer beach at Coco Bay is about five minutes from the main part of the hotel. The reef just 50 yards off the hotel's shore makes for excellent snorkeling. Brendal's Dive Shop, which also rents bicycles, snorkeling gear and windsurfers, has a very good diving and snorkeling program. There is a large pool as well as tennis. Those who aren't in the mood for the long walk into town may take the complimentary boat ride. The hotel can arrange for guests to play golf at nearby Treasure Cay.

Bluff House Club & Marina

Many people make a habit of returning to this beautiful hotel perched high above a beach. The view of the water from the main house and pool deck is breathtaking. Some say the wooded trails and dirt paths bordered by flowering shrubs and plants remind them of summer camp. Especially since wooden boardwalks and stairs lead up and down throughout the hilly property, this is not the place for heels or for people who have trouble walking. There are suites, villas with full kitchens, and individual rooms. Over the years, Bluff House has expanded from eight guest rooms in the main house to more than 30 in various wings. All have private porches with views of the water. Some of the modern, air-conditioned units are duplexes. Appointments include wicker chairs, floral couches, ginger jar lamps, weathered wood paneling and wall-to-wall carpeting. The sunny clubhouse, overlooking the pool and the ocean, is decorated with tiles, paintings and framed posters. In the dining room, where guests get to know each other at large tables, many people ask to be seated at the huge round oak table in the center, with its high-backed chairs. The personal attention of the warm staff, the beautiful beach and the good food create many repeat guests. Daytime boat rides to the town of New Plymouth and evening sails into town for the weekly dance are free to those staying here. Tennis and rackets are also complimentary. The staff will arrange fishing, scuba and snorkeling excursions.

New Plymouth Inn

Staying at this old home with high ceilings and antique furniture may make you think you've slipped back in time. The 10 inviting guest rooms, all with private baths, have old-fashioned quilts on the beds, attractive floral wallpaper and handsome chairs and chests. Books line shelves in the hallway. A large octagonal Mexican brasero table sits in the center of the living room. Instead of coals in the center, you'll see fresh hibiscus. The shell of a giant turtle hangs on a wicker partition in the bar area. Paintings decorate the walls, and lanterns hang from the ceiling. The inn was once the home of Captain Billy Roberts, whose ghost is said to appear from time to time. But don't let that scare you away from this charming place. While New Plymouth is located in town, it has a pool, and beaches are not far. Guests can also arrange to go boating, diving and fishing.

WALKER'S CAY

MODERATE

Walker's Cay Hotel & Marina

Walker's Cay can be picked out from the air from among the cluster of islets off northern Abaco by its neat houses and the airstrip extending from its flank like a tentacle. The plane lands, follows the strip, makes a sharp turn to the right and you have arrived. If you've come in from the U.S., you can clear customs right here.

The 100-acre island has 62 hotel rooms and four villas, three of which are six-sided and look out to the sea. The other, Harbour House, high on a hill, sleeps six and has a jacuzzi on its broad deck and also looks out to sea with a vista including the 75-slip marina. Rooms are divided between the Coral and Hibiscus buildings, both of which are on the water, screened through lacy casuarinas and palms. There are no TV's or telephones, but newshounds will snap up complimentary copies of the *Miami Herald* and *USA Today*.

Although golf carts perform some of the heavier duties, an effortless stroll will take you to any point on the island. The main house has the office, dining room, game room, indoor-outdoor bar and shop. There are two swimming pools, one salt water, and lunch is served in the Lobster Trap, which looks out on the marina.

There is a sprinkling of children, but most guests come to fish for such game as marlin, wahoo, tuna, grouper and dolphin. The extensive facilities for boaters include dockage, ice and fuel, box lunches, airline reservations and long-term docking. Arrangements can also be made for scuba diving or snorkeling. Some guests enjoy being marooned with a box lunch and each other on an isolated beach of one of the nearby islets such as Seal Rock or Mermaid's Cay. Other cays in the cluster are Tom Brown's Cay, Sit Down and Jump Off Rock and Grand Cay. While strolling, guests encounter an interesting non-denominational chapel built by the widow of the island's former owner, Elon C. Edwards, who was fondly called "Mr. Ed." Carved wood statues stand at each side of the chapel's doorway.

SPANISH CAY

EXPENSIVE

The Inn at Spanish Cay

This tiny resort, on a three mile long private cay off north Abaco, stresses service, luxury and exclusivity. Guests arrive by boat, docking at the inn's marina, by chartered or private plane, landing on the resort's 5000 foot strip, or by ferry from Treasure Cay. European, Canadian and American vacationers come to enjoy the empty beaches and a selection of water sports and tennis. Accommodations consist of a garden suite, a one-bedroom/two-bath apartment, and a two-bedroom apartment, also with two baths. Service is a 24-hour affair and there are two waterside restaurants for meals. Larger accommodations or a private house can be rented upon request. In addition to dockage, boating supplies are available at the marina.

ACKLINS & CROOKED ISLAND

Together Acklins and Crooked Island comprise an almost 200-square-mile area and are about 223 miles southeast of Nassau. The narrow Crooked Island Passage, separating the two islands and sprinkled with tiny cays, is still an important sea lane on the southern route. Twice a week, planes visit Spring Point on Acklins and Colonel Hill on Crooked Island.

The islands are a point of interest for fishermen, boaters cruising the southern Bahamas and devoted divers, all of whom are attracted to the fishing and diving possibilities off Landrail Point on Crooked Island. Since the islands hardly swarm with tourists, those who do come can expect leisure and serenity at one of the few places of accommodation.

The known settlers of these islands were **Loyalists** who arrived toward the end of the eighteenth century. Soon almost 50 plantations had sprung up, with hundreds of slaves working the fields. But by the 1820s most of the plantations lay in ruins, the crops having been destroyed by blight.

Most activity is centered on the smaller, 70-square-mile Crooked Island. This is where visitors find the one resort, **Pittstown Point Landing**, and a few guest houses. The mailboat from Nassau makes the overnight trip twice a month. Small farming and fishing are the principal industries, and a fish processing plant is under development. There are few telephones and communication is mainly by CB and marine radio.

Crooked Island's capital is Colonel Hill, a small settlement with colorfully painted wood and cement buildings. In Church Grove stands tiny **Tiger Bar**, the first drinking establishment on the island. Every Friday night, dances are held at the **Bloom of the Valley** bar and pool hall, across the street from the **Hillside Grocery** store. There are other minute settlements, such as Cripple Hill, with about a dozen residents; Moss Town, with the houses clustered around the Anglican church; and, to the northeast, Landrail Point where nearly all the residents are Seventh-Day Adventists.

Beyond Landrail Point are several private, beachfront homes owned by Americans and other foreigners. At a salt pond, just outside of town, you'll see flamingos, tropical birds with long, thin tails, mocking birds, finches, wild canaries and humming birds. *The 33 miles of barrier reef off the islands make for excellent diving and snorkeling.* Boats are unnecessary for seeing the exciting coral formations and colorful fish. Masks and fins are all that are needed.

Pilots were the first to "discover" Crooked Island in the fifties and built some of the early beachfront homes. One American describes the island as "the kind of place where, if I lost my wallet, someone would look inside to see who it belonged to, then walk two miles to return it."

A government-provided "ferry" at the southeast tip of Crooked Island takes visitors across to Lovely Bay on Acklins. Driving from Pittstown Point Landing to the ferry takes about an hour and a quarter. *Hard woods such as mahogany and lignum vitae are found on Acklins, as well as the bark used to make Campari.* Many of the houses on the island have dirt-floored, separate kitchens. In some, a corn grinder, used for making one of the staples, grits, stands in the corner. Although weatherbeaten, some houses are painted startlingly bright shades of purple, green, blue and orange. Built in 1867 off Acklins' southern tip, the Castle Island Lighthouse guides ships through a passage that was once used by pirates escaping pursuit.

WHAT TO SEE AND DO

Bird Rock Lighthouse ★

Crooked Island Passage • If there were more visitors, the gleaming-white Bird Rock Lighthouse guarding Crooked Island Passage would

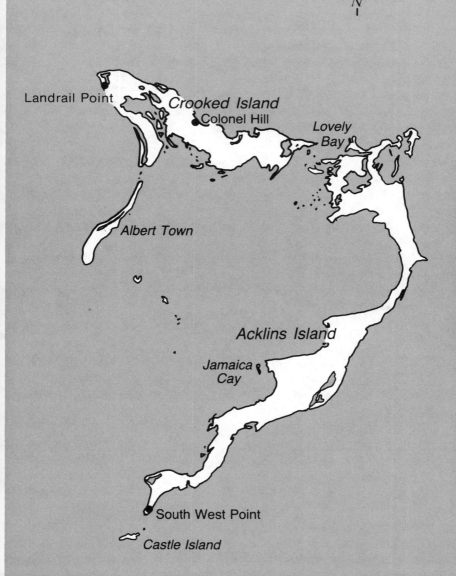

Acklins-Crooked Island

be as famed and photographed as the lighthouse at Hope Town in the Abacos. This is a popular nesting spot for ospreys.

Crooked Island Caves

Like many other islands in the Bahamas, Crooked Island is riddled with caves. These look like majestic, ancient cathedrals or medieval castles that have fallen into ruins. It is best to explore them with a Bahamian guide arranged through Pittstown Point Landing. Dark, narrow, low passageways suddenly widen into gaping chambers. Fingers of sunlight poke through holes high above. Clusters of harmless bats cling to the ceilings and begin squealing and crawling when flashlight beams hit them. No, you probably won't find drawings of the ancient Arawaks who once inhabited the caves. However, more recent visitors have certainly scratched their names into the stone.

Southwestern Beaches

Crooked Island • Accessible only by boat, these shores are some of the island's best. As you approach, schools of flying fish, resembling flocks of birds, jump out of the water and sail through the air before dipping back in. Snorkelers head for Shell Beach, where coral heads loom beneath the clear water and large slabs of coral rock lie along the coast. In some areas, the layered rock looks strangely like ancient crumbling stone steps. At Bathing Beach, the light turquoise water reveals an immense expanse of sandy ocean floor, completely free of rocks and seaweed. Look for the inland freshwater springs. The location may still be marked by a pile of stones on shore. Make arrangements at Pittstown Point Landing to cruise to these beaches.

French Wells

Crooked Island • It would be difficult to find a more serene part of the island. Flamingos often beach here, near a narrow passage lined with a jumble of mangroves. If you come by power boat, turn off the motor and listen to the quiet. You'll look through crystal water at barracudas and other fish. Sharks have been sighted in this area, so don't go swimming.

Marine Farm

North end of Crooked Island Passage • This is the ruin of a Bahamian fort. It was built by Britain to guard Crooked Island Passage against marauding pirates. Although rusted, markings on the cannons are well preserved.

Mayaguana   ★ ★

Across the Mayaguana Passage, and flanked by Acklins and Crooked Islands as well as Inagua • The 24-mile long island has few more than 400 inhabitants, who are almost completely out of touch with the capital at Nassau. The forests are rich in hardwoods, especially lignum vitae. The U.S. has established a missile-tracking station on the island. There are two acceptable harbors, inviting beaches and astounding vistas. Because there are no accommodations for tourists, Mayaguana is visited mainly by boaters. It remains quiet, undeveloped and undisturbed.

WHERE TO STAY

INEXPENSIVE

Pittstown Point Landing ☆☆☆

This hotel is 16 miles from the Colonel Hill airport. If there are no taxis, by asking at the airport you'll find a driver who'll charge from $25 to $40 for the trip to the hotel. The hotel has its own airstrip, and most guests arrive in their own private planes. The management will arrange for guests to be flown in from Florida, Nassau or George Town in Exuma. The rooms, with two double beds, bright baths and good reading lights, are comfortable but somewhat spartan. The bar, separated from the dining room by the kitchen, is built around what is said to be the first post office in the Bahamas. Guests get to know each other over meals, games, drinks, discussions about birds sighted during the day and, of course planes. Guests also get to know the staff. The cook often doubles as a waitress; the bartender might take a group on an excursion to the caves, or the assistant manager might take guests bonefishing. The gift shop, where the register is signed, sells Androsia batik resort wear as well as t-shirts, books, film and toilet articles. Things are casual, although house rules are outlined in a booklet found in your room. In regard to proper dinner attire, for example, it says, "Hair on the chest and low cleavage are great but distract the attention from things on your plate."

ANDROS

A boy plays with his toy sailboat off Andros.

Andros, 108 miles long, about 40 miles across at its widest point, and covering 2300 square miles, *is the largest of the Bahama islands.* It is interlaced with channels, bays, bights and inlets. These waterways—called creeks by locals but seeming more like bays, rivers and open sea to outsiders—divide the island into three main sections.

Running almost parallel to the east coast is the awesome 120-mile-long **Andros Barrier Reef**, *which is in the league of Australia's Great Barrier Reef and the one off Belize.* Multicolored marine life of all kinds is found in these waters. Ocean blue holes, fathomless freshwater columns of deep cobalt and ultramarine rising from the depths, are also offshore. **Benjamin's Blue Hole** is one that has attracted wide interest. In 1967 Dr. George Benjamin found stalactites and stalagmites 1200 feet under the sea. His conclusion was that The Bahamas are really the peaks of former mountains, since such formations never occur under water. Benjamin's Blue Hole and **Uncle Charley's Blue Hole** have been featured in the Jacques Cousteau television series on oceanic exploration. In addition, more than 100 inland holes have also been found on the island. Examples are **Captain Bill's**, near Andros Town and Evansville, not far from Nicholl's Town. *The island is also riddled with intricate underground caves such as those at Morgan's Bluff.*

Andros has the best farming land in the Bahamas as well as an abundance of plant life found nowhere else. It is said to be the home of nearly 50 kinds of **wild orchids**. A new species of peony, the white-petaled *P. mascula* subspecies *hellenica*, was recently discovered here, according to Niki Goulandris, a botanist and botanical painter.

GETTING AROUND

If on schedule, the mailboat stops weekly at Morgan's Bluff, Mastic Point, Stafford Creek, Fresh Creek and Mangrove Cay. The boat brings supplies to the various points and returns with deliveries and passengers. The arrival of the mailboat is a signal for a social occasion, with locals suspending their activities to see who and what are arriving and to catch up on bits of news and gossip.

Similar gatherings also take place at the four airports of Andros. They are located in the north at San Andros, near the center of the island at Andros Town, and down south on Mangrove Cay and in Congo Town.

FISHING AND HUNTING

Andros is known as the **bonefish** capital of the world. Marlins and tarpons are found in the surrounding waters as well as reef-seekers such as snapper, amberjack, yellowtail and grouper. Several fishing lodges are south of Fresh Creek. Three of the nicest are the upscale **Cargill Creek Fishing Lodge** and the **Andros Island Bonefishing Camp**, next door to each other near Cargill Creek, and **Charlie's Haven** in Behring Point. During the summer, land crabs crawl across the beaches to lay their eggs. Beachcombers can simply pick up the crabs and have one or two for dinner.

The forests are thick with pine, mahogany and other tropical trees. *These woods are an excellent habitat for quail, ducks, partridges, marsh hens and parrots, which are hunted by enthusiastic nimrods during the*

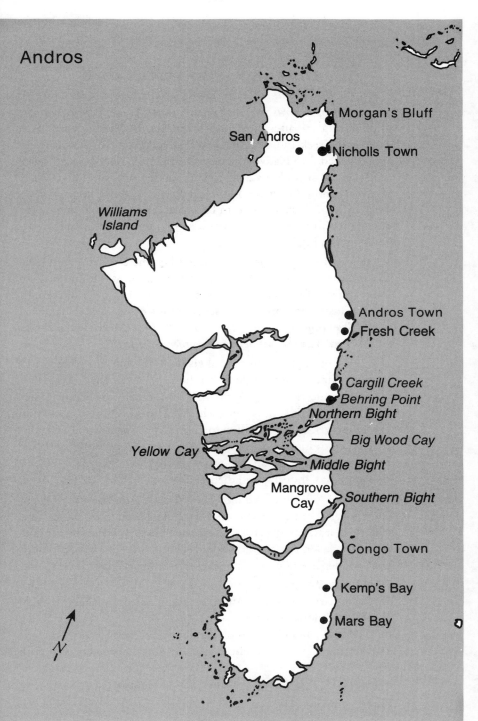

Andros

September through March season. In September and October, hunters in camouflage fatigues hunt white crown pigeons in the forests of South Andros.

HISTORY AND FOLKLORE

Andros, then populated by Lucayan Indians, is said to have been visited by the Spaniards in search of slave labor to work in Hispaniola. Both during and after the Seminole Wars in the United States, Seminole and Creek Indians, African slaves and escaped slaves who had intermarried with Native Americans fled Florida to northern Andros. They landed at Joulter Cays and later filtered south to the mainland at what is now Morgan's Bluff and Red Bay. Other former slaves, freed by the British, came from Exuma and Long Island on the other side of the Tongue of the Ocean, settled in southern Andros, and took up farming.

Later in the 19th century, **sponging** became a thriving and lucrative industry in Andros. This undersea organism was found in abundant supply off the mud flats of the southwest coast. Until then, the chief industry had been **ship wrecking** for often very valuable cargoes. *Sponging continued until the late 1930s, when an unknown blight killed only the sponges and no other marine life.*

Another profitable industry was **sisal** production, the plant used in rope making. It was introduced to the Bahamas in 1845. One of the largest producers was the Andros Fibre Company, owned by Joseph Chamberlain. His son, Neville, who later became British prime minister, supervised the plantation for a time. The shallow soil of Andros resisted cultivation and, about 1896, the enterprise was abandoned, throwing about 800 Bahamians out of work. By the early 1920s, the Bahamas' sisal industry had died out.

From the '60s until well into the '70s, the U.S. company Owens-Illinois harvested Andros timber for pulp production. To facilitate shipment, a system of crushed limestone roads was built by the company. The roads remain, now somewhat in disrepair, but that industry, too, departed, leaving a pocket of unemployment.

Sir Henry Morgan, the notorious pirate, is said to have established his headquarters in north Andros at the point now called Morgan's Bluff, which looks out toward the Berry Islands. According to legend, Morgan buried some of his ill-gotten treasure near the site. However, searches both serious and frivolous have uncovered nothing.

Another persistent legend tells tales of **chickcharnies**. These are impish, mischievous, red-eyed, feathered creatures with three toes and three fingers and a long, prehensile tail. Some say chickcharnies have the ability to turn their heads completely around. They are said to live in the pine and hardwood forests of Andros and are not found on any of the other islands.

If a wanderer happens upon a chickcharney and treats it well, then blessings and good fortune follow. However, if the chickcharney is mistreated, the wanderer can be struck by the direst misery, which can last a lifetime. Having done its mischief, the chickcharney scampers merrily off into the forest. Today, locals with a twinkle in their eyes warn each other of the wrath of mischievous chickcharnies and frighten naughty children into obedience.

Red Bay Village is said to be near the home of a primitive people who maintain old tribal traditions, still use bows and arrows and dwell in the forests. Although this belief persists, no evidence of such people has been found. Some believe that the legendary tribe are descendants of the mixed Africans and Seminoles who fled slavery and war in Florida.

NORTHERN ANDROS

In North Andros, the distinctive, unusually tall, straight pines look like telephone poles with trees stuck on top. *Most of the action in this area is in Nicholl's Town.* The residential road leading to the tiny town is filled with the sound of roosters crowing to each other. The small, colorfully painted wooden houses are overhung with palm fronds and the bright green leaves of banana trees. A 15-minute walk to town will take you past stores such as **Curry's Grocery** and **Wellie's Variety**, and the popular **Picaroon Restaurant** near the beach. Mr. and Ms. Henfield have run the restaurant, affectionately called Picaroonie's by locals, for over 25 years. They serve chicken, ribs and fish Bahamian style. Next door at the Henfield's gift shop, you can rent bicycles for about $12 a day.

Other good restaurants in town are **Hunter's**, with a bar and satellite television, and **Donna Lee's**. Both also have inexpensive guest rooms and often give parties on weekends to which everyone, including tourists, is invited. If you didn't rent a car at the airport or through the Andros Beach Hotel, you can rent one at Hunter's. **Pinewood Cafeteria** and **Paula's Inn** also serve homestyle food. About two miles south of Nicholl's Town, at Conch Sound, is a tiny settlement devoted to fishing and boat repair. It was once the site of a thriving local boat construction industry. The boats were then used primarily for spongers.

Not far from Nicholl's Town, in the Pleasant Harbour area, are nicely landscaped beachfront homes owned by foreigners. When the tide is low you can walk out to uninhabited Money Cay to collect colorful shells.

Some seven miles south of the San Andros airport is **The Bahamas Agricultural Research Centre**. Presently headed by Dr. Godfrey Springer, a Tuskegee Institute-trained veterinarian, BARC advises and assists local farmers in obtaining maximum production from their land. The center was established in 1973 through the cooperation of the U.S. Agency for International Development and the Bahamian government. Visitors are welcomed to the facility and given informative tours. At the center's large packing house hangar, vegetables such as potatoes, okra, cucumbers, cabbage, tomatoes and some grains are brought in for sorting, grading, packing and shipment to Nassau. Other products grown on Andros are papayas, cantaloupes, strawberries and a variety of citrus fruits. Another section of the center is devoted to breeding and raising improved strains of horses, cattle and other livestock such as sheep, hogs and poultry. Dr. Springer attests that there is no rabies in the Bahamas and that a rigid inspection program is in force for meats such as beef and mutton.

Andros supplies much of the nation's fresh water. The two-million gallon reservoir off Queen's Highway between Nicholl's Town and the San Andros airport produces more than six million gallons of potable water each day, a record for the Bahamas. Almost three million gallons of water are shipped by barge each day from the port at Morgan's Bluff to New Providence, just 20 miles across the channel. Because the deep Tongue of the Ocean divides the channel, barges are the only way of transporting fresh water across. One of the engineers says that bad weather sometimes interrupts water shipments and worries that continued development and growth in Nassau might soon overtax the supply.

ANDROS TOWN AND FRESH CREEK

Most visitors to Andros Town, south of Nicholl's Town, stay at **Small Hope Bay Lodge**. Before the lodge was built in 1960, this area had no roads, electricity or running water, and only one telephone. While this part of Andros has come a long way since then, it is still mainly undeveloped, with just a few small settlements here and there. If you go bike riding, you'll notice that people in cars will wave to you as they pass.

Many locals consider the beaches in Staniard Creek, about 10 miles north of Andros Town, the nicest around. **Prince Monroe's** is a popular restaurant here. **Androsia Batik Works**, which began in 1973 at Small Hope Bay Lodge, is at the edge of nearby Fresh Creek. This factory, which produces brightly colored resort wear and decorative batiks, has been a real boon to the island's economy. It is on the grounds of the former Lighthouse Club, a luxurious resort built by a Swedish millionaire in the '50s. Although the club has been torn down, another more modest hotel has risen in its place, on the shore of a wide creek where masted houseboats bob. In the old club's heyday, peacocks strolled through the attractive grounds.

Good local restaurants in Fresh Creek include **Papa Gay's** on the waterfront, which sells chicken in a bag, the dining room in tiny **Chickcharnie's Hotel**, **Skinny's Landmark Restaurant** and the somewhat more upscale **Golden Conch**. At midday, you'll see people clustered around cars and trucks selling home-cooked beef stew, peas and rice, cole slaw, potato salad and other local favorites. In this drowsy town where the quiet is punctured by crowing roosters, you'll also find stores such as **Turpi's Straw Market** and **Rosie's Gift Shop**, which sells t-shirts and other items.

The peaceful town of Calabash Bay is within walking distance of Small Hope Bay Lodge. On weekends, the Samson Center opens as a bar and disco, where many teenagers gather. On nights when the moon is full, the walk along the beach to Calabash Bay is especially pleasant. **Minnes' Diamond Bar** is one of the oldest bars in the area. Cyril Minnes, the owner, was nicknamed "Twenty-Four Hours" because he could almost always be seen sitting outside watching life happen. During the summer, there are church fairs practically every weekend to raise money for various causes.

On the way to the freshwater Captain Bill's Blue Hole from Small Hope Bay Lodge, you'll pass bushes that partially obscure "pothole" farms, where corn, cassava, pigeon peas, sugar cane and bananas are grown. These farms are called potholes because the soil has accumulated in small depressions in the land. You'll also pass the pretty settlement of Love Hill, where there are several churches, but no bars (usually it's one for one). Here **L & S** is a local restaurant owned by taxi driver/bartender Linwood Johnson, who often puts in appearances at the Cargill Creek Fishing Lodge. He claims his chicken or pigfeet souse, served for breakfast, will do wonders for a hangover. Also on the menu are cracked conch, peas and rice and baked goods such as benny cake (made from sesame seeds), peanut cake and coconut cake.

Divers appreciate the proximity of the Andros Barrier Reef to shore. Many are enthusiastic about the extensive dive programs offered by Small Hope Bay Lodge and the Andros Beach Hotel. So much marine life lies close to beaches that snorkelers get as excited as scuba divers.

A station of the Atlantic Undersea Testing and Evaluation Center (AUTEC) is located at Fresh Creek. This research station is jointly operated by the British and U.S. governments. It was established in 1966 as an antisubmarine research center and is protected from heavy ocean traffic by the offshore Tongue of the Ocean chasm.

CENTRAL AND SOUTHERN ANDROS

The central and southern parts of Andros are even less built up than the north. Towns, few and far between, are smaller and quieter. In Cargill Creek, about 30 miles south of Fresh Creek, **Green View** restaurant specializes in cracked conch, lobster and peas and rice. Not far from Cargill Creek Fishing Lodge and the tiny, quiet settlement of Behring Point, Bigwood Cay is the largest islet in Andros.

Fishing guides charge about $50 to drop a group of people off at the long, wide, pine-shaded beach here and pick them up later. **Manta rays** glide through the clear, shallow water, and you can wade out to **bonefish** just off shore. Turning the Atlantic a pale turquoise, the sandbar known as Bigwood Cay Flat stretches nearly as far as you can see. Then the water becomes deep blue where the ocean floor abruptly falls away.

Nearby Steamer Cay is one of the places where sponge fishermen do their thing. You'll see (and smell) the mounds of sponges in various stages of preparation. They are black as they lie on shore drying in the sun. Then they are anchored in clumps in the water and later dried again so that they turn a golden brown. When they are ready, the sponges are sold in Nassau. Visitors are surprised that no one worries about anyone stealing them as they lie unattended. This area is also popular for **lobster fishing** between August and May. With jagged coral and a tangle of mangroves at the water's edge, this beach is not good for swimming. South of Bigwood Cay, a few accommodations are found in Mangrove Cay and Congo Town.

A luxurious oasis, **Emerald Palms By the Sea** is a hotel in the Congo Town area. In the nearby settlement of Driggs Hill, try **Ezrena's** for local food. **Haylean's**, in High Rock, is another good place to eat when you're in the mood for fish, pork chops, cracked conch, peas and rice or other Bahamian specialties.

Adventure: Discovering inland and ocean **Blue Holes** *for swimming or admiring colorful marine life.*

Sports: **Bonefishing** *with a guide. Scuba diving along the* **Andros Barrier Reef***, the third largest in the world.*

Hotels: **Emerald Palms By the Sea***, near Congo Town, for its spectacular gourmet meals, remote location and tasteful decor.* **Small Hope Bay Lodge***, near Andros Town, for its friendly staff and outstanding scuba diving program.*

WHAT TO SEE AND DO

Sports

Small Hope Bay Lodge near Andros Town offers diving. For fishing and boating, the places to stay are the Cargill Creek Fishing Lodge and Andros Island Bonefishing Club, both near Cargill Creek; Charlie's Haven in Behring Point; and the Chickcharnie Hotel in Fresh Creek. Andros is in one of the world's most famous areas for bonefishing. For excellent guided fishing excursions in the Cargill Creek/Behring Point area, contact the North Bight Bonefishing Service, run by Andy Smith. (Write to him at *Behring Point, Andros, The Bahamas,* or *(809) 329-5261.*) Andy has long been a guide and has gone bonefishing for as long as he can remember. He'll take you to the best spots and teach you anything you don't already know. According to Andy, "You can fish all day and not see another boat. That's how many flats there are." High season for bonefishing is from September to June. The rest of the year Andy dives for conch and escorts the occasional fisherman.

Andros Barrier Reef ★★★

Off the east coast • At this natural wonder, the third largest reef in the world, divers can swim through caves and tunnels to get a close look at some spectacular marine life, including brilliantly colored (and friendly) fish and many kinds of coral and sponges. Small Hope Bay Lodge, outside Andros Town, specializes in diving excursions to a depth of from 10 feet on one side of the reef to 185 feet "over the wall," where the reef plunges into the 6000-foot Tongue of the Ocean.

Blue Holes and Inland Ocean Blue Holes ★★★

Points throughout the coast and island • Ocean blue holes, the 200 feet and more fresh water wonders arising from the briny deep, may be visited by either rented or tour boats. Some of these holes have been featured in a Jacques Cousteau TV program. Diving expeditions off Andros give visitors another way to see these majestic undersea phenomena in the waters surrounding the island. Inland ocean holes are tucked away in the woods throughout Andros. With steep, porous limestone walls that catch the dancing reflection of the sun on the water, Captain Bill's Blue Hole, near Small Hope Bay Lodge, is a tranquil place for a private swim. Many birds, including great blue herons, snowy egrets and hummingbirds, come through this area.

NICHOLL'S TOWN AREA

Morgan's Bluff ★

North Andros • This is a site where pirate Sir Henry Morgan's treasure is said to be buried. Visitors are not barred from seeking clues. At the Andros Beach Hotel, arrange to explore caves here.

ANDROS TOWN AND FRESH CREEK

Androsia Batik Works ★★

At the edge of Fresh Creek • Started by Rosi Birch, the former wife of the owner of Small Hope Bay Lodge, Androsia began in the early '70s with a staff of three who worked out of bathtubs on the lodge's property. The batik factory now employs about 70 people who design, dye and sew the colorful wall hangings and resort wear that are sold throughout the Bahamas. The clothing, for both men and women, ranges from shorts, jackets and dresses to bathing suits. Visit Androsia to see how the material is dyed.

Turnbull's Gut ★

Off Small Hope Bay Lodge • This is a coral and sun-filled underwater tunnel that opens onto a thrilling vertical drop to the depths, where divers encounter awesome undersea life.

The Barge ★

Off Small Hope Bay Lodge • This navy landing craft from World War II was sunk by the owner of Small Hope Bay Lodge to enhance underwater adventure for his guests. Curious fish join the divers in this protected area.

WHERE TO STAY

CENTRAL ANDROS

EXPENSIVE

Small Hope Bay Lodge ★★★

Outside Andros Town • Many guests have remarked that this family-run resort has the casual, convivial atmosphere of summer camp. *Leave your jackets, ties and evening wear at home when you come to this rustic beachfront lodge that specializes in diving.* Less than 15 minutes from shore is one of the world's longest barrier reefs, and snorkelers need only swim under the dock to see some of the most exciting marine life around. Small Hope Bay Lodge was the first resort in the Bahamas to make diving the main attraction. Nondivers and nonsnorkelers don't have to miss the wonderful underwater displays. Expert dive masters will teach them how to snorkel or dive—at no cost—and will allow them to learn at their own pace. Because the reef is so extensive, dive masters are always finding new sites for visitors to explore.

The lodge's cabins (which aren't particularly soundproof) are spread out along an expansive beach shaded by tall coconut palms. Some have picture windows. All are cooled by ceiling fans and are colorfully decorated with wall hangings, pillows and curtains made of the distinctive batik cloth created at the Androsia factory, begun by the former wife of the lodge's owner. Families with children often request the cabins with two rooms and a shared bath. No room keys are provided, but you can lock up your valuables in the office. Hammocks wide enough for two are strategically located throughout the grounds so that guests can stretch out while gazing at some of the best views. This is probably not the kind of place where you'd expect to find a hot tub, but one is right on the beach. You can even arrange to have a massage. Complimentary bicycles are available for trips to nearby settlements or Captain Bill's Blue Hole, a secluded inland body of fresh water about five miles away. Bonefishing, birdwatching, shell collecting, examining unusual species of wild orchids, finding plants used in bush medicine and shopping at the "batik boutique" are some of the ways guests spend their time when not diving. Cocktails, along with conch fritters that go quickly, are served every evening before dinner.

Young children, who are well taken care of while their parents are off diving, eat in the game room off the main dining room. On barbecue nights, meals are served on the waterfront by the outdoor bar. After dinner, there might be an impromptu party or a showing of underwater slides in the lounge, with its overstuffed pillows and gaping fireplace. Or a staff member might simply give guests directions to the disco in nearby Calabash Bay. The lodge runs a charter air service between Andros Town and Fort Lauderdale.

Cargill Creek Fishing Lodge ★ ★ ★

About 30 miles south of Fresh Creek • "This place is too nice to be called a lodge," one guest told us. Owned by a Nassau businessman, this upscale waterfront resort opened in December 1989. Within its first year, the lodge already had repeat guests. The vast majority of people who stay here are avid bonefishermen (yes, *men*), but reef fishing for grouper, snapper, barracuda and jacks, and deep-sea fishing for marlin, tuna, sailfish, wahoo and dolphin are excellent as well. While there is no real beach (there's an artificially created sandbar just across the channel), the small pool is fine for cooling off. All of the appealing rooms and cottages are air-conditioned, with televisions, double beds and very chic baths. Fans hang from the high, sloping wooden ceilings that are set off by exposed beams. The attractive A-frame dining room is paneled in honey-colored wood and has a tile floor. Overhanging the water, the adjoining bar/lounge gives guests the feeling of being on a moving ship. Every afternoon when the fishing boats return, guests gather on the waterfront patio for cocktails and hors d'oeuvres.

Cookouts are hosted on Saturdays. Located between the towns of Cargill Creek and Behring Point, this lodge is about 30 miles from the airport.

MODERATE

Lighthouse Yacht Club & Marina

Andros Town • While the one-story E-shaped main building resembles a motel or a school from the outside, the interior has more character. Cooled by ceiling fans and air conditioning, guest rooms, which contain refrigerators, are decorated with marbled tile and reproductions of Federal furniture. Most windows face the marina, the jumping off point for fishing excursions. Rooms have little privacy since walkways pass right by patios. The swimming pool is outside the "villas," which are actually just larger rooms (in separate buildings) with two double beds instead of one queen. With terra cotta tiled floors, a high wooden ceiling and picture windows that gaze out to the marina, the dining room is quite pleasant. Look for Bahamian favorites, such as steamed conch, grouper fingers and peas and rice for dinner. Breakfast and lunch are also served here. A beach is a five-minute stroll around the lighthouse that gave the hotel its name. Also within walking distance are neighboring Androsia, the batik factory and Fresh Creek, with its local restaurants, across the bridge. Scuba diving can be arranged through Small Hope Bay Lodge, about a 15 minute drive.

INEXPENSIVE

Andros Island Bonefishing Camp

About 30 miles south of Fresh Creek • Next door to the Cargill Creek Fishing Lodge, this seaside club is more rustic and low profile. There is no beach, but guests don't seem to mind, since they spend their days out on the water. Off the homelike lounge, the expansive oceanfront deck with heavy wooden chairs is a wonderful place for relaxing. On the grounds, hammocks hang between trees. Although the rooms aren't air-conditioned, they are modern and comfortable, with ceiling fans.

CONGO TOWN AREA

MODERATE

Emerald Palms by-the-Sea

Driggs Hill • One of the Bahamas' most attractive—and remote—hideaways, Emerald Palms rests on a beach fringed with palms and casuarinas. Hammocks are strung between trees. There's also a swimming pool. In the lobby, wicker sofas, pine bookcases with books and magazines and a discreet TV set invite relaxation. Many guests gather here for drinks before dinner. White tiles cover the floors of guest rooms, which are furnished with wicker and pale pine. The TV is housed in a pine armoire. Four-poster beds are festooned with filmy mosquito netting, and duvet covers are embroidered on white lace.

From each room, French doors lead out to a small patio with Adirondack chairs with footrests. Bicycles are available and guides for bonefishing excursions can be arranged. Honeymooners and others looking for complete escape find Emerald Palms by-the-Sea ideal.

THE BERRY ISLANDS

The 12 square miles of the Berry Islands are a series of small cays, most of them privately owned, just north of Andros and New Providence. Some have colorful names such as Cockroach Cay, Crab Cay and Goat Cay. Bebe Rebozo, remembered from the Nixon years, bought a home on Cat Cay. There's a private bird sanctuary on Bond's Cay and a private airfield on Hog Cay. The remnants of a farming community, established for freed slaves, can still be found on Whale Cay. Sponge fishermen live on many of the smaller islands. Sailors and fishing enthusiasts enjoy cruising around this area.

Chub Cay, the southernmost part of the Berry Islands, is just across the channel from Andros. This resort—which has hosted Bill Cosby and Quincy Jones—is called the **Chub Cay Club**, and sports a 76-slip marina, full boating services and a commissary. Beyond fishing, boating, scuba diving, relaxing on beautiful beaches and playing tennis (but only if you are a member of the resort's club or make special arrangements with the manager), there is little to do on Chub Cay. Every week, the Nassau mailboat docks at this island, which is home to the main airport.

Another airport is found on Great Harbour Cay in the north, where the Berry Island's population (of little more than 500) is concentrated. At seven miles long and 1.5 miles wide, this is the largest chunk of the archipelago. After aggressive developers got hold of it, Great Harbour Cay began attracting the international wealthy. Where the monied set goes, golf seems to follow. The island's clubhouse sits on a rise overlooking the carpetlike fairways with the sea as a background. Douglas Fairbanks, Jr. was once chairman of the development company's board. His presence drew film people and jet setters eager to catch a glimpse of and be part of the new "in" place.

WHERE TO STAY

EXPENSIVE

Great Harbour Yacht Club

For those with a taste for luxury and the wherewithal to indulge it, this tiny cay in the Berry Islands might be just the place. Your accommodation might be a villa on the ocean, a house on the eight-mile white sand beach, or an apartment overlooking the private, 80-slip, full service marina. These upscale living quarters vary according to location, number of rooms needed, the number of people using the rooms and special amenities. Dining is available at the resort's Beach Club, The Wharf or the elegant Tamboo Dinner Club. For a change of pace, Bahamian style meals can be had in town at local spots such as Beulah's Bridge Inn, The Chicken Shack, Wayside Inn, Graveyard Bar and Grill and the Backside Lounge. Bicycles and motor bikes are available locally as well as diving and snorkeling expeditions and small boat rentals. For the more ambitious and well-heeled, both power and sailing yachts may be rented bare or with a full crew and chef. Those with their own boats can use the marina for food, fuel, equipment, ice, laundry and private showers. The exclusive Great Harbour Yacht Club welcomes memberships and members receive a 25 percent discount on dockage rates. Bone, bottom, permit and deep sea fishing, and the necessary guides can all be arranged at daily rates. Guests wanting a respite from the sea can make use of the nine-hole golf course. *Tropical Diversions Air* flies guests in from Fort Lauderdale on executive class planes, with convenient wet bars.

MODERATE

The Chub Cay Club

The beachfront rooms, one of the restaurants and some of the other facilities are reserved for members of this expansive fishing and boating retreat. Members also get first priority on the tennis courts. However, nonmembers will certainly enjoy themselves in this tranquil, picturesque setting. Guest rooms, though plain, are perfectly comfortable, with TV and pots for making coffee or tea. Since most visitors spend their days out in their boats, this resort is the perfect place to find complete peace and quiet. The calmer of the two beaches is long and wide, and vacationers often have it to themselves. It is lined with bungalows for members as well as attractive private vacation homes. The other beach, where the frothy surf trims the electric blue water, is even more unpeopled. You'll find this one at the end of a sun-dappled, casuarina-shaded path cushioned with pine needles.

The members' pool overlooks the more placid beach, while the palm-shaded pool for nonmembers is near the marina. But no one seems to

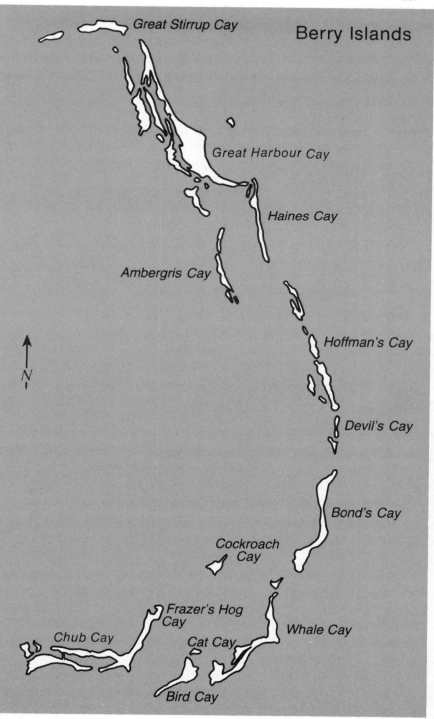

Berry Islands

Great Stirrup Cay

Great Harbour Cay

Haines Cay

Ambergris Cay

Hoffman's Cay

Devil's Cay

N

Bond's Cay

Cockroach Cay

Frazer's Hog Cay

Chub Cay

Cat Cay

Whale Cay

Bird Cay

mind when nonmembers decide to take a dip in the private pool. The dive shop offers scuba lessons as well as trips for experienced divers. Nearby are the t-shirt-packed gift shop, the commisary and nonmembers' bar and dining room. The restaurant serves three meals a day, with selections including broiled fish with grits for breakfast, lobster salad and grouper fingers for lunch, and grilled lamb chops, chicken creole and peas and rice for dinner. At night, those who don't turn in early play pool and dominoes, dance and talk up a storm with the hotel workers who frequent the bar in the staff housing area. Through the resort, arrangements are made for charter flights between the Chub Cay Club and Nassau or Florida.

THE BIMINIS

Queen's Highway is the place to shop on North Bimini.

Many avid anglers consider the Biminis the place for serious big-game fishing. These islands are definitely *not* for those in search of exceptional hotels or fine dining. Both visitors and residents seem more reserved than on other Out Islands. Some say this difference stems from the island's proximity to the U.S. and its relatively long history of American tourism. Beginning just 50 miles east of Miami, the Biminis are closer to the U.S. than the rest of the Bahamas. Yet, with only a handful of small fishing-oriented hotels, Bimini could hardly be considered overdeveloped. Hook-shaped North Bimini, where the action is centered, is trimmed by seven miles of mostly empty sandy shores on one side while marinas and docks line the other. Fringed with tall grasses accented with purple flowers, the beach is shaded by palms and pines. Like long fingers groping for the water's edge, vines reach out along the sand. Although there's an airport on nearly deserted South Bimini, most travelers arrive with a splash—by seaplane from Miami—on North Bimini. It drops them off right in Alice Town, the capital.

The ocean is in view from just about all points along narrow North Bimini. Visitors can ride rented scooters or take taxis to the most picturesque beaches, which are found in the north. King's Road runs along one side of the island and Queen's Road claims the other. The story goes that the names of the roads are exchanged periodically depending on whether a male or female monarch is in power in England, with the larger road honoring the current ruler. Most hotels are within walking distance of the seaplane landing in Alice Town, but vacationers with heavy luggage can board minibuses.

Across the road from the Bimini Big Game Fishing Club in Alice Town is the **Bimini Breeze** restaurant, which serves lunch and dinner. The Bahamian food at this neat, sparkling eatery is hearty and tasty. Always lining the bar, a lively, vocal group of local philosophers provides diversion for diners. Other hangouts along the main road are **Diandrea's Inn**, the dining room of a hotel; **Captain Bob's**, which whips up breakfast and box lunches for fishermen; and **Fisherman's Paradise**, which serves all three meals. **The Wee Hours Club** is nearby. At the **Anchorage Restaurant** at Bimini Blue Water Resort, views of the multihued ocean are served up along with cracked conch, lobster salad, peas and rice and conch chowder. About three miles north of Alice Town, the paved road parallel to the beach ends, turning into a pine-needle cushioned dirt road. Leaning toward each other, the wispy branches of evergreens create a canopy overhead. Bimini is known for its white bread, freshly baked with a touch of sweetness. Bailey Town, where **Pritchard's** sells the best fresh bread around, and Porgy Bay are quiet settlements north of the capital.

BIMINI LORE

Folklore and legends, an integral part of the heritage of the Biminis, are happily shared with vacationers. Ponce de Leon visited the islands during his fruitless quest for the Fountain of Youth. A spot said to be the fountain, near Bimini's only airport, on South Bimini, is invariably pointed out to newcomers. *During U.S. Prohibition, the Biminis were a refuge for bootleggers and rumrunners who took advantage of the islands' closeness to Florida.* They used the cays and inlets as

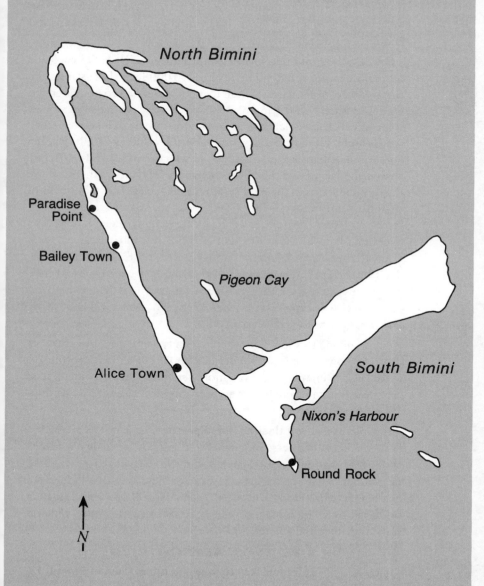

The Biminis

shelters while they eluded their pursuers, as their piratical predecessors had.

Samuel Brady, a black man from Florida, was a member of one of the first five families to settle in Bimini in 1835. His wife and children had been sold and he had been left alone. Through the Underground Railroad, he escaped St. Augustine, Florida, and wound up in Bimini. He eventually made his living through ship wrecking and became a modest landowner. Brady died in 1914.

Off Paradise Point on North Bimini, a group of large **flat rocks** lie on the ocean floor. Extending for about 1000 feet, these slabs seem to have been either part of a wall that collapsed or a road that ended up under water. Low flying planes can see these symmetrical stones, some of which are as large as 16 square feet. Made of limestone, they are thought to have been submerged for 6000 to 10,000 years. Some archaeologists think these rocks, which appear hand-hewn, are an ancient sacred site, like Stonehenge in England. Others believe they are remnants of the road system of the fabled Lost Continent of Atlantis. Centuries ago, Europeans spoke of Atlantis, a large Mediterranean island. Its powerful rulers, according to legend, held sway over that island as well as Egypt in North Africa and Tuscany in what is now Italy. Since that time, Atlantis has disappeared from maps. Today's historians and scientists feel that the lost Atlantis could have existed anywhere from the Mediterranean to The Bahamas.... *While the story behind these rocks is intriguing, they aren't worth a special trip, since not much can be seen.*

Ask someone to show you where **Memory Ledge** is. Some say that if you lie down here face up, you'll be hit with flashbacks of your life as well as of Bimini's past. Even more eerie, the **Devil's Triangle** is an area near Bimini where planes and seacraft have disappeared without a trace.

If you'd like to visit **Healing Hole Springs**, whose waters are said to have medicinal powers, inquire about a guide at Brown's Hotel. We're told that only a few islanders know how to get there. Located near bonefish flats, the clear fresh water of these springs is hidden beneath a layer of muddy salt water. Your boat will pass through a cut bordered by gnarled mangroves before reaching this spot, which is some nine feet in diameter.

THE TWO AMERICANS

Two Americans, **Ernest Hemingway** and **Adam Clayton Powell, Jr.**, have put their stamps on the Biminis. Well known for hunting in Africa and Idaho, and fishing in Key West, Florida, Ernest Hemingway also left an impression on Bimini. He was an avid fisherman spent his time away from the water at the bar of the Compleat Angler Hotel. He was one of its first guests after it opened in 1935. At one time he lived in a cottage called Blue Marlin, which is now part of Bimini Blue Water Resort. *The lobby of the Compleat Angler Hotel is filled with Hemingway memorabilia,* and there is a rentable guest room where sections of *To Have and Have Not* are said to have been written. According to oldtimers, Hemingway had a standing offer of $100 for any Biminite who could beat him at boxing.

Adam Clayton Powell, Jr., the New York congressman, could be found in Alice Town's **End of the World Bar**, where he was a favorite among residents who admired him as the black man who, with satire, wit and good humor, could tell off white Americans. With sand on its floor and walls covered with grafitti and business cards, the waterfront End of the World Bar still stands. Powell, too, fished enthusiastically. Every December, Bimini holds the Adam Clayton Powell Memorial Fishing Tournament.

Powell, in exile from the United States except for weekends, won the hearts of Bimini locals with his humor and his concern for their welfare. His deep interest in education for young people brought a Ford Foundation grant to provide learning programs for Bimini's schools. When hurricane "Betsy" hit Bimini, Powell refused President Lyndon Johnson's offer of evacuation and rode out the storm on high ground with the rest of Bimini's people. In the entryway of Brown's Hotel, you'll see a marble plaque in memory of Congressman Powell, "for his outstanding contribution to Big Game Fishing in the Commonwealth of the Bahamas." It was donated by the Bimini Progressive Sporting Club in 1972.

PERSONAL FAVORITES

Sports: **Deep-Sea Fishing**

Hotel: **Bimini Blue Water Resort**, for its comfortable rooms and its good restaurant where you're likely to overhear tall tales from guests who fish.

WHAT TO SEE AND DO

Sports

Deep-sea fishing records are held by many who have fished Bimini waters. The walls of the Bimini Hall of Fame are covered with photographs of fishermen displaying their catches. Veteran fishermen wax ecstatic about the seas swarming with giant tuna, tarpon, dolphin,

snapper, bonefish, amberjack, bluefish, white and blue marlin, sword-
fish, sailfish, bonito, mackeral, barracuda, grouper and shark. Bonefish flats are also found in the Biminis. Make fishing and boating
arrangements through the Big Game Fishing Club & Hotel, Bimini
Blue Water Ltd., Brown's Marina or Weech's Bimini Dock. Brown's
Hotel also has a dive program.

For diving, contact Bimini Undersea Adventures or Brown's Hotel.
Tennis Courts are at the Bimini Big Game Fishing Club.

Hemingway Memorabilia
Compleat Angler Hotel, Alice Town • The lobby of the Compleat
Angler Hotel has a display of mementos associated with Ernest Hem-
ingway, including manuscripts, photographs and paintings.

Hall of Fame
Diandrea's Inn, Alice Town • Proud anglers from around the world
pose in photographs displaying their prize-winning catches in this
fisherman's hall of fame. Some of the beaming exhibitors are celebrities.

The Sapona
Between South Bimini and Cat Cay • During the first World War, the
automobile magnate Henry Ford built a large, concrete ship, the
Sapona. No longer his during Prohibition, it was anchored off South
Bimini for a private club much used by rumrunners. In 1929, it was
wrecked and blown toward shore during a hurricane. Now sitting
upright in 15 feet of water, it is a reminder of the Bimini's adventurous past.

WHERE TO STAY

MODERATE

Bimini Big Game Fishing Club
This hotel, with 35 rooms, 12 cottages and two penthouses, is the
largest in the Biminis. It is operated by Bacardi International, the rum
people, and is headquarters for serious sport and game fishermen. This
is where they find comfort after their boats are tied up in the hotel's
marina. The marina accommodates up to 100 boats. There are also a
swimming pool, tennis court, three bars and two dining rooms. The
Fisherman's Wharf restaurant has an attentive maitre d' and colorful
murals of local life. Local specialties are served in the Bahamian
Kitchen, which overlooks the marina. Guest rooms, which come with
TVs, have tiled floors, area rugs and some rattan pieces painted a cool,
celadon green. Sports people are grateful for the outof-the way, built-
in racks for boating, fishing and scuba gear. The beach is a few steps
away.

Bimini Blue Water Resort ★★
Nicely landscaped, with a picket fence out front, this 12-room estab-

lishment has a welcoming dining room and bar. It has its own beach and two pools. *Most rooms overlook the sea and sunset views can be spectacular.* Now accommodating guests of the hotel, Blue Marlin cottage is one of the places where Ernest Hemingway stayed during his frequent writing and fishing visits to the Biminis. Hanging over the stone working fireplace in the living/dining room is—what else?—a blue marlin. This spacious, wood-panelled room is also decorated with other fish and huge fish tails. With a kitchen, three bedrooms and three bathrooms, this cottage also sports a large front patio. Bimini Blue Water Marina shares management and facilities with the Compleat Angler next door.

INEXPENSIVE

The Compleat Angler Hotel   ☆☆

With its rich dark pine walls and 13 cozy rooms, this three-story balconied building resembles an overgrown private home. At the entrance, a huge almond tree shades a courtyard that doubles as an outdoor bar. Ernest Hemingway certainly seemed to feel at home here. Opening onto a balcony, the small room where he stayed is sometimes rented to visitors. Downstairs, the bar where he drank is fashioned from prohibition-era rum barrels. Walls are hung with U.S. license plates, yachting flags, nautical items such as a time-worn rudder and old photographs. Shots include Hemingway with the 500-pound remains of a blue marlin that was attacked by a shark, and the writer on Bimini dock firing his machine gun. Excerpts from his novels, such as *The Old Man and the Sea* and *Islands in the Stream* (much of which took place on Bimini) are also on display.

For years, most of the after-dark action on Bimini has revolved around the Compleat Angler. This friendly hotel seems to be the great equalizer. American college students whooping it up during Spring Break, middle-aged yachties, fishing fanatics and partying island residents all get busy on the dance floor to the live calypso band (three to seven nights a week, depending on the season). Sometimes manager Ossie Brown, a Biminite whose family owns the hotel, plays percussion and sings lead vocals. His father, Harcourt Brown, bought the historic Compleat Angler in 1973, the year the Bahamas won its independence from Britain. The Browns also run the neighboring Bimini Blue Water Resort.

Diandrea's Inn   ☆

The rooms in the original part of this small hostelry all have color televisions. Some have double beds and others, twin. The one-room "suite" with two double beds, is huge and the cottage has cooking facilities. There is a front porch and a sunny, outside reception area. With more modern rooms, the 30-room addition has a bar, dining room, and disco.

Seacrest

This small hotel has 10 rooms, all with television. Each room has a single and a double bed. Some can be adjoining and are good for families. There is neither a pool nor a restaurant, but the beach is across the road and good, local restaurants are nearby. Ask about dive packages.

Admiral Hotel   ☆

Farthest from the Alice Town seaport, the Admiral Hotel is in residential Bailey Town. Reached by taxi or minibus, the 24 rooms have television, air conditioning, and two double beds. A favorite with vacationing Bahamians, the hotel offers doubles, suites and efficiencies.

CAT ISLAND

The Hermitage is a miniature abbey on Mount Alvernia, Cat Island.

Across the sound from the Exumas, Cat Island has the highest elevation of all The Bahamas. Like many Bahamian islands, it is long and thin. At 50 miles in length, it varies from one to four miles across. Despite its natural beauty and near pristine beaches, Cat Island is not a major stop on the tourist path. It is a good island for mingling with residents, walking trips and bicycling. The one airport is at Arthur's Town, in the north, but small planes fly into airstrips at or near the different resorts.

During the 1700's, Cat Island was known as San Salvador, the contemporary name for the Bahamian island to the southeast that is thought by many historians to be the first place Columbus visited in the Americas. So, because of its old name, *some Cat Islanders believe that their home is really the original Columbus landing point.* More than a few grumbled that, with all the hoopla of 1992 cinquecentennial celebrations, they were being beaten out of their birthright. Thus, a bit of rivalry developed between Cat Island and neighboring San Salvador, and a few pranks resulted. In 1990, a foreign landscape architect was on her way to San Salvador. When the plane made its first stop, on Cat Island, the flight attendant announced, "Welcome to Arthur's Town, San Salvador." Believing that she had reached her destination, the architect climbed off and before she realized her mistake, the plane had taken off! To make matters worse, Bahamasair had only two flights a week in and out of Cat Island.

Atop the island's 206-foot Mount Alvernia is the Hermitage, built by Father Jerome Hawes, a revered Catholic missionary who died in 1956. As in many such communities, his untiring efforts did not succeed in wiping out century-old religious practices such as obeah, a mixture of African and Caribbean ritual.

There are still the remains of colonial plantations on the island. One, built by the slaves of a loyalist from the colonies, Colonel Andrew Deveaux, lies in ruins near Port Howe.

Cat Island is slow-paced, far removed from the frenetic tourism of Nassau and Freeport. That is, unless it's Regatta Time (August) when the population (around 4000) doubles. Some people have no electricity, cook outside and draw water from wells, just as their ancestors did centuries before them. Since there's no bank on this island, locals can bank at the post office. You might see people sitting on their front steps while they burn coconut halves in their yards to convince mosquitoes to go elsewhere. Cat Island's residents live by limited farming and fishing. Young people tend to seek more lucrative ways of making a living on other islands or in the U.S. One of the island's native sons, the actor-director Sidney Poitier, did just that, leaving Arthur's Town as a youth.

As with other Bahamian islands, there are stories of pirates having come this way. But unlike other islands, treasure was actually found here. This discovery gave rise to a belief that there is still more awaiting discovery somewhere on land or sunken offshore.

For good local food in New Bight, **The Bridge Inn**, also known for its lively parties, serves three meals a day. Mutton, souse, grouper, stew fish and steamed conch are a few of the selections you might

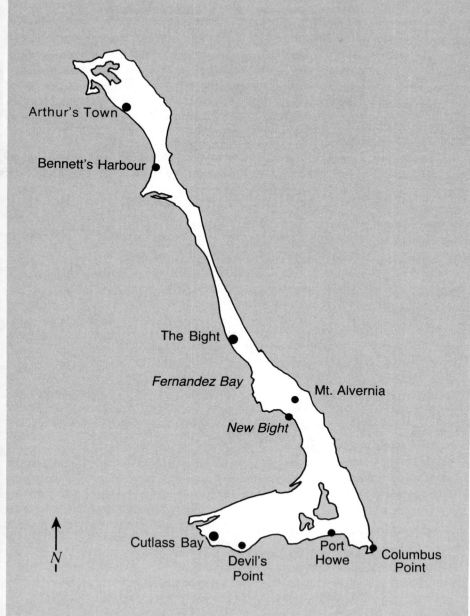

Cat Island

Arthur's Town

Bennett's Harbour

The Bight

Fernandez Bay

Mt. Alvernia

New Bight

Cutlass Bay

Devil's Point

Port Howe

Columbus Point

N

find on the menu. More homestyle cuisine is served at **The Pilot Harbour Restaurant and Lounge**, owned by a local pilot.

PERSONAL FAVORITES

Adventure: *Climbing to* **The Hermitage**, *the highest point in the Bahamas.*

Hotel: **Fernandez Bay Village**, *for its rustic, horseshoe beachfront setting and open-air bathrooms.*

WHAT TO SEE AND DO

The Hermitage   ★★

Town of New Bight • This structure, at the 206-foot pinnacle of Mount Alvernia, is a small abbey with a miniature cloister and a round corner tower, all of gray native stone. The Hermitage commands a sweeping view of Cat Island, taking in the Bight as well as Fernandez Bay to the north. It is reached by turning off the main road at New Bight and following the dirt road to the foot of the rise. Here, you'll have to abandon your car or bike. A free-standing arch marks the beginning of the foot path up the hill. Rubber-soled shoes are recommended for the tricky climb to the top (about a 15-minute hike). Where he could, Father Jerome Hawes, who built the abbey, carved steps into the existing stone and also carved stations of the cross along the way. Just to the right of the main road leading up to Mount Alvernia, standing like a forgotten movie set, is the ruined stone facade of a structure from the Armbrister Plantation.

Deveaux Plantation   ★

Town of Port Howe • This plantation was constructed for Colonel Andrew Deveaux by his slaves when he settled on Cat Island after leaving the Colonies. It is reputed to have been beautifully furnished and the scene of much entertainment, but is now in ruins.

Armbrister Plantation   ★

Near Port Howe • This is another reminder of colonial life in The Bahamas. Crumbling stone fences and the remains of walls are all that is left of this plantation.

WHERE TO STAY

EXPENSIVE

Fernandez Bay Village   ★★

The Bight • Charming, rustic and laid back, this resort is on a curving stretch of dreamed-of beach, fringed with feathery casuarinas. You'll almost have the beach to yourself. A charter plane will pick you up in Nassau or elsewhere, if you so arrange, and fly you to the island. From Nassau, flying time is just under an hour. The "village" consists of eight houses and two cottages. The houses, constructed of native stone, have window-walls opening to individual terraces facing out to the sea. A special feature of the villas is the open-air bathrooms, which, surrounded by tropical vegetation and protected from viewers, are open to the outdoors with sky overhead. Some of the villas are duplexes with cathedral ceilings and overhead fans.

Sailing, waterskiing, fishing and snorkeling are available and there are complimentary bikes and rental cars for those who want to visit nearby settlements or landmarks, such as Mount Alvernia. Books are found in the lounge area and in villas for those who prefer to curl up in the shade. Radio, television and newspapers are out. This is the place for total escape. Guests become a congenial group, which gathers for pre-meal drinks using the honor system to sign for what they take or are served. The home-cooked food is ample and delicious. A hefty dose of will power is needed to resist the slabs of fresh bread, which turn up toasted at breakfast. Many guests are repeaters who swear by this resort and pray that Fernandez Bay Village remains an unspoiled secret. Be sure to pack a flashlight for getting around at night.

ELEUTHERA

Harbour Island, Eleuthera, is known for its New England-like architecture.

Some visitors say that Eleuthera, among the most developed Out Islands, is the most beautiful part of the Bahamas. It certainly competes with New Providence and Grand Bahama for some of the more upscale resorts. This island was host to the first Bahamian settlers, sometimes called the Eleutherian Adventurers, who came from Bermuda in search of religious freedom. Spanish Wells, Harbour Island and Current are tiny islands just offshore.

About five miles at its widest point, the island is a long, thin arc, curling southward from New Providence for 110 miles toward Cat

Island and the cays of the Exumas. Despite a coral and limestone surface, which might seem forbidding to farmers, Eleuthera is the agricultural center of the Bahamas. In the late 1800s, it dominated the pineapple market with its luscious fruit of a special sweetness without a tart aftertaste.

Like most of the other Out Islands, Eleuthera has few large trees. Its thin but rich soil crust bears mainly small trees and shrubs. Along its main north-south road, you are seldom able to see beyond the hedgerows to the rocky fields where the island's rich crop of fruits and vegetables grow. You can drive for miles between towns. Beautiful, deserted and endless beaches, some palm-shaded and with pink sands, border Eleuthera. Rough coral caves are found throughout the island, with one of the largest at Hatchet Bay, located in the north.

Some of Eleuthera's most arresting attractions are under water. Awesome ocean holes and inland blue holes (seemingly bottomless landlocked salt-water tidal pools) are a constant surprise, where fish in all their tropical splendor swim to the surface to be fed by visitors. The Devil's Backbone off the northern coast is a spine of reefs that in the past caused many shipwrecks that still lie below the surface awaiting exploration by divers. A Civil War train that was being transported by barge to Cuba sits wrecked in the middle of the Devil's Backbone. The Union locomotive came to grief during an 1865 storm and its rusted remains now lie among coral. An old steamship, the *Cienfuegos*, is nearby. It went down in 1895, though all passengers survived. The treacherous Devil's Backbone has claimed still other victims that remain visible to divers, including the freighters *Vanaheim* and *Carnarvon*. Current Cut, between Eleuthera and the cays off Current island, is rich in undersea life, which can be seen over 50 feet down. Six Shilling Channel, separating Eleuthera from New Providence, is a coral reef system among the cays of Current Cut. Underwater photographers have captured magnificent views of exotic creatures making for the depths of Tongue of the Ocean to the south.

The island's three airports are in North Eleuthera, Governor's Harbour and Rock Sound. In addition to Bahamasair flights from Nassau, there are also direct flights from Miami to all three airports. Nassau mail boats make weekly trips to various points throughout Eleuthera.

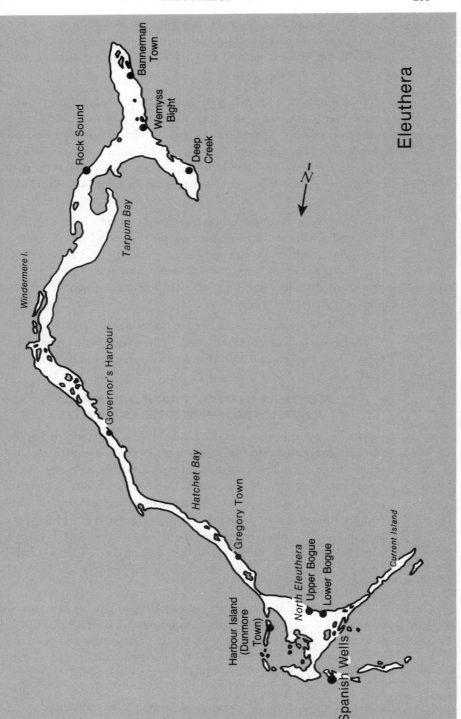

Eleuthera

Eleuthera now participates in the **People-to-People** program. For information, contact the Ministry of Tourism in Governor's Harbour, ☎ *(809)332-2142*, and give at least four day's notice.

A LITTLE HISTORY

When Captain William Sayles and 70 other Englishmen came south from Bermuda in search of religious freedom in 1649, they settled on Cigatoo, as the Arawaks (whom they replaced) called the island. They were joined by New England Puritans, also in search of religious freedom. The island had been called Alabaster, but the new colonizers called it Eleutheria, basing it on the Greek word for freedom.

The early New England settlers continued contact with their fellow Puritans back home. In 1650, for example, a rare and valuable wood found on Eleuthera was shipped back to New England to be sold to raise funds for the new Harvard College. This was in payment for provisions that the New Englanders had previously sent the hard-pressed settlers.

By 1831 white settlers had been outnumbered three to one by 12,000 enslaved and free black people. Three years later, Queen Victoria issued the proclamation that set slaves free throughout the islands.

ROCK SOUND, TARPUM BAY, AND WINDERMERE ISLAND

Rock Sound, it is said, was once called "Wreck Sound." It has replaced Governor's Harbour as the island's leading settlement. Its small village has a liquor store, a grocer's and very little else. For a hearty home-style meal cooked by Kathleen Culmer, wife of the proprietor, stop at family-operated **Sammy's Place** in Rock Sound. This comfortable, spotless restaurant attracts tourists and out-of-towners as well as locals. Although some resorts use a Rock Sound mailing address, they are all really outside town. Near the Rock Sound airport, look out for the house-sized, shady banyan tree, its tentacle-like shoots dripping from its branches.

With a thriving, if minute, art colony, Tarpum Bay is just north of Rock Sound. Here transplanted Americans Mal Flanders and his wife, Kay, paint tropical seascapes, scenes of island life and portraits of its people. You're welcome to stop by their studio. Also in Tarpum Bay another artist, MacMillan Hughes, has erected with his own hands what he calls "The Castle." This odd, elevated structure, poised at an intersection, defies description. After climbing the entrance steps, you'll see sculpture, paintings and drawings by this bearded, expatriate Scotsman who will take you on a personal tour.

A bridge connects five-mile-long Windermere Island with the mainland. A favorite hideaway for the affluent, this sliver of land has played host to Prince Charles and Princess Diana, in happier days, as well as other notables. The Windermere Island Club (now-closed) was the island's only hotel, but there are also many spectacular villas for rent. The main road is overhung with tall pines whose branches form a shady roof. Set back from the road are many private houses with names such as Cherokee, Dolphin House and Beaumaris. Most of these luxury homes are owned by foreigners. Chances are you'll pass by at least one more being built.

The former omelet chef at the Windermere Island Club operates her own restaurant outside of nearby Savannah Sound. Called **Big Sally's**, it is on the mainland not far from the bridge to Windermere, and it serves up hearty local dishes.

It is said that major expansion is planned for the Winding Bay/ Half Sound area near Rock Sound and the all-inclusive Club Eleuthera hotel, which caters exclusively to vacationers from Italy.

SOUTH ELEUTHERA

South of Rock Sound, Eleuthera has settlements such as Bannerman Town, Wemyss Bight and Deep Creek, which shelter local populations where children are seen in uniform colors of their various schools, and tourists pass through as sightseers. At Powell Point, on the island's southern tip, is the Cape Eleuthera Yacht Club which, although not in full operation as a resort, does have limited facilities for boaters.

GOVERNOR'S HARBOUR

Governor's Harbour, at Eleuthera's center, away from the ocean on the bay side of the island, is thought to be one of the earliest settlements and seat of government. While this picturesque town with well-restored homes—some of them guesthouses—may seem quiet now, for many years it was an active port. Family-oriented Club Med is here on a long broad beach. The town's few other accommodations are small and family-run.

With beautiful, wide, pink beaches (tinted by powdered coral and shells), hilly Governor's Habour is considered a real find by most visitors. Tourists, few and far between, are often unhappy to run into each other. In town, attractive pink and white government buildings face the water near a much used basketball court by a long, narrow cemetery. Many streets are shaded with tall palms and pines. The waterfront, with its handsome Victorian houses, is one of the nicest places to spend time, especially at sunset. A leisurely walk along the shore will take you across a bridge to Cupid's Cay.

Ask someone to show you Twin Coves, a secluded private estate that welcomes visitors who want to relax or snorkel at the quiet northshore beach. You'll drive through a lush, wonderfully landscaped palm grove.

Across from the **Governor's Harbour Bakery**, **The Blue Room** (☎ *332-2736)* serves good conch and other seafood as well as chicken. **Picchio** (☎ *332-2455)* is in an atmospheric building that was built as a home in the mid-nineteenth century. The menu might include baby lamb chops and pasta with conch. **Ronnie's Hi-D-Way** is a restaurant and bar where parties often take place on weekends. Many visitors and locals spend their evenings at the bar at the **Buccaneer Club**. The outdoor cafe at the Buccaneer is a pleasant place to have an inexpensive lunch. The swivel chairs around the umbrella-covered tables are made from old wooden casks. **Mate 'n Jenny's** (☎ *332-2504)*, a bar and restaurant in Palmetto Point, about five miles outside Governor's Harbour, specializes in Bahamian pizza and is another local hangout in the evening.

Rodney Pinder, the former maitre d' at the Windermere Island Club, runs his own restaurant near Palmetto Point. Called **La Rastic** (☎ *332-1164)*, it specializes in home-style Bahamian dishes including mutton, cracked conch, grouper and pork chops. He does not serve alcohol, but you can bring your own bottle. **Sandy Beach Inn** (☎ *332-1008)*, a stone's throw from Mate 'n Jenny's, is known for its generous portions of grouper, conch and crawfish. The huge tail of a 500-pound marlin adorns a wall. The bartender dares you to ask for a drink for which his bar does not have the ingredients.

HATCHET BAY

At Hatchet Bay, to the north, there is an old plantation where prize Angus cattle were once raised. Instead of cattle, poultry and dairy products comprise its present output. At Shark Hole, these hungry fish devour the unused chicken parts thrown into the Atlantic several times a day. Locals now live in the homes built by employees of the once prosperous plantation.

GREGORY TOWN

Gregory Town is the pineapple capital of the island. If you go beyond the shrubs along the main road, you'll see fields of the fruit. Pineapple rum is a favorite among visitors as well as locals. Eleuthera's highest hill, near the Cave and Glass Window, which will give you a wonderful panoramic view of the area, is also here. Near some houses, you'll notice outdoor ovens for baking bread. For a fresh-baked treat, stop at **Thompson's Bakery**. The Thompson's take guests in their home for about $40 a night per person, including two meals. This town caters to young surfers, many of whom are convinced that its beaches have some of the best waves around.

HARBOUR ISLAND

Once visitors see this breathtaking oasis, called "Briland" (with a long *i*) by residents, many return year after year. Its shores, where sands are tinted pink by crushed coral and shells, have some of Eleuthera's most beautiful beaches. This island easily boasts the best group of hotels in the Bahamas, from Canadian-owned, antiquefilled Ocean View to modest, locally owned Tingum Village, known for its good homestyle food. All with fewer than 50 rooms, the island's accommodations are perfect for travelers seeking personal attention and distinctive decor. Along the east coast and cupped by greenery, several of these small hotels, secluded from each other, are perched on a bluff above the three-mile pink sand beach. Others hug the harbor, where friendly wild dolphins sometimes allow themselves to be stroked by swimmers.

Not even two square miles, Harbour Island can be explored on foot. Dunmore Town, its charming settlement, is one of the Bahamian villages with New England-style architecture. Located on the harbor side of the island, the town is named for Lord Dunmore, who built Nassau's Fincastle and Charlotte forts. Overhung with orange, purple and pink bougainvillea, white picket fences enclose brightly painted clapboard houses with gingerbread trim. Dangling in front of shuttered windows, wind chimes tinkle on porches.

The late afternoon sun on the striking wooden buildings along Bay Street, the main drag, is a spectacular sight. Most of these homes are owned by Americans and Canadians, and some are available as vacation rentals. Streets are shaded by fig trees, coconut palms and wispy tropical pines. On Sundays, people dressed to kill stand in clusters outside churches before and after services. Two of the Bahamas' oldest churches are found in Dunmore Town: St. John's, the oldest Anglican house of worship, erected in the mid-eighteenth century, and Wesley Methodist, built around 1846. Titus Hole, a harborside cave, is said to have served as the island's first jail.

Those who don't hoof it around the island ride bicycles, scooters or golf carts. All these can be rented at various hotels or along Bay Street. Big Red (☎ *333-2045*), the bartender at Coral Sands hotel since 1974, rents boats in addition to wheels. He also drops off and picks up vacationers on nearby islands for the day or afternoon (about $20 per person). Man Island is the best for snorkeling, and there are plenty of beaches there for couples to be alone together. Most hotels will pack picnic lunches and make other arrangements for deserted island trips. Groups of four or more will find it less expensive to rent their own boats (a 13-foot Boston whaler for about $60, for instance) and hit several islands.

Anglers looking for an excellent bonefishing guide could hardly do better than Bonefish Joe. Considered the best of the best, he's always in demand, so write to him (Joe Cleary, Harbour Island, The Bahamas) well in advance of your trip. Snorkeling excursions can be arranged through most accommodations. Valentine's Yacht Club & Inn and Romora Bay Club hotels are the centers for scuba diving.

At **Miss Mae Tea Room and Fine Things**, on Dunmore Street, the sign and shutters are handpainted with flowers that mirror the real blossoms out front. Here you'll find J & M Davidson leather belts and bags, Haitian paintings, colorful boxes with designs done by hand and silver jewelry from Bali. Merchandise is displayed on antique chests. In addition to selling gourmet foods such as French wine vinegar and Italian olive oil, Miss Mae serves muffins, sandwiches of deli meats and cheeses, and, of course, tea. Patrons can dine on the patio in the back. **Island Treasures**, nearby, sells jewelry, t-shirts and mugs, among other items.

Androsia Bahamas, on King Street, carries clothing made from the bright batik cloth created on the island of Andros. **Sugar Mill,** on Bay Street, stocks music boxes in the shape of Harbour Island cottages, one-of-a-kind toothbrushes and ceramic teddy bears and wall hangings. Next door, the front porch of **The Harbour Lounge** (☎ *333-2031)*is the place to be for fabulous sunset views as well as people-watching. Lunch, afternoon cocktails and dinner are popular among visitors. At night, a very local crowd gathers at the bar. Along the water across the street, some vendors sell straw goods, fruit, and vegetables while others rent bicycles.

Picaroon Landing (☎ *333-2241)* welcomes guests for cocktails and sunset watching every day except Sunday. This handsome harborfront building dates back to about 1800. Sit outside on the verandah or inside, where there is a lounge and gallery. Walls are hung with etchings of old island scenes with amusing stories, 1950s record albums by Harbour Islanders and 19th-century photographs. You'll also find books on the history of the island. The bar opens at 5 p.m.

Bahama Bayside Cafe (☎ *333-2174*), on Bay Street, serves three island-style meals daily. Across the street, the harborfront open-air shelter known as The Tent is a gathering spot for "lazy people," the local term for those who spend their days hanging out, playing dominoes, drinking and relaxing.

More restaurants are found outside of town, where roosters do their jerky march through yards and horses graze in small fields. Family-run **Angela's Starfish Restaurant** (☎ *333-2253*) is one of the best places for Bahamian-style fish, chicken, cracked conch, pork chops and peas and rice. Go easy on the hot sauce. You can sit outside on the palm-shaded grassy lawn overlooking the water and mainland Eleuthera. At night, tables are lit by tiny bulbs hidden in conch shells. Inside, where the decor of the casual dining room is nautical, a sign requests that patrons refrain from swearing and wearing bare-backed clothing.

Open 8 a.m. to 5:30 p.m., **Arthur's Bakery & Cafe**, at the corner of Dunmore and Crown streets, is a great place to stop for a light breakfast. The sticky buns are delicious. **Gusty's Restaurant & Bar**, with its pool room, often hosts fashion shows. On the other side of the island, roadside tables sit outside **Three Sisters Native Food** (☎ *333-2078*), where meals are served by reservation only. Adjoining a house where laundry often flutters on clothes lines, this restaurant also has an inside dining room. At the eastern end of this street is the tree-lined entrance to **Runaway Hill**, a hotel with one of the island's best dining rooms. More excellent gourmet creations are served at neighboring **Dunmore Beach Club.** Nonguests are welcome to make dinner reservations at these hotels, if there's room.

On Harbour Island, nightlife wakes up on weekends. Locals usually bar hop. Each person seems to have his or her personal route, but most folks end up at the same place—the hot club of the moment. The Funk Gang, the local band that for years commanded Friday and Saturday nights from George's Night Club, has moved to its own **Seagrapes Club** next door. A rake 'n' scrape (music played with a saw, washboard, cowbell, conch shell and maracas) might be happening at the harborside bar at **Valentine's Yacht Club & Inn**. Also popular with tourists as well as locals, **Willie's Tavern**, built in 1948, is the island's oldest nightclub. Patrons entertain themselves with the pool table, juke box, bar and TV, where videos are constantly playing. Palm fronds, t-shirts, and posters are plastered on walls while flags from various countries decorate the ceiling.

The pool room at the **Vic-Hum Club** is another popular night spot. If you're lucky, owner Humphrey Percentie (whose family also owns Tingum Village hotel) will show you "the world's largest coconut," which measures 33 inches around.

Active until around the 1970s, the old airstrip near Romora Bay Club hotel is no longer used. Today travelers take the 10-minute ferry ride from Three Island Dock, which is a brief taxi ride from the North Eleuthera airport. Ferries go back and forth all day. Once they reach Dunmore Town, most visitors must take another taxi to their hotel or vacation rental home. Young boys wait at the docks to transport luggage between the cabs and ferries. It can be annoying to have them quickly unload your bags, carry them a mere two feet to or from the boat and then expect tips. However, keep in mind that there are few other opportunities for children to earn money here. We always remind ourselves, "At least they're working."

SPANISH WELLS

This pretty cay floats off the northern coast and makes a good sailing destination. If it weren't for the tropical vegetation and all the satellite dishes outside the brightly painted homes, visitors might think they were in a quiet suburb somewhere in the U.S. The island is known for its booming crawfish (or spiny lobster) business, which, at least in part, is responsible for the extremely high standard of living here. Many boys quit school at fourteen to spend most of every August through March underwater. The lobster industry is so lucrative that it is not uncommon for a man barely in his twenties to purchase a $100,000 house—paying most of the money upfront!

In a predominantly black country, Spanish Wells is also unusual in that its population is virtually all white. Some say that this is because the original settlers opposed slavery and agreed not to bring slaves to the island. Others relate stories of residents trying to make sure that Bahamians of African descent do nothing more than work in Spanish Wells. A few black people have made this their home in recent years. However, it is commonly understood, as it has always been, that most are expected to be off the island by nightfall. Race even played a role in shaping the island's present religious climate. During the 1950s, when members of the sole church invited a visiting black minister to preach, the congregation split, establishing other houses of worship.

Whether visitors are black or white, they notice that residents are not especially friendly, at least not at first. After all, with a flourishing economy, they really don't need tourism. They can afford to take their time deciding whether or not to mingle with outsiders. Blond hair and blue eyes prevail, and islanders look as if they all come from one big family. That is not surprising, since most of them *are* related. Outsiders whisper about the genetic problems—a high incidence of physical birth defects and mental retardation—that have resulted from relying on such a small gene pool.

Spanish explorers are said to have used the island as a final point to take on fresh water before beginning the long, arduous voyage back to Europe. The wells had to be dug carefully, only to a certain depth. Beyond that, salt water would be struck, spoiling the cargo. Spanish Wells was one of the islands that the 17th-century Eleutherian Adventurers and 18th-century British Loyalists dropped in on. After years of fishing, farming, shipbuilding and even pirating, lobster fishing took off with a vengeance in the 1970s.

CURRENT

Another tiny cay worth sailing to at Eleuthera's north tip, Current is reputed to be the island's oldest settlement. The story goes that a group of North American Indians were exiled to Current after a "massacre" of white settlers on Cape Cod. Today, there is no trace of exiled Indians, and Current's present inhabitants are mainly black.

PERSONAL FAVORITES

Sights: **Harbour Island**, *for its picturesque gingerbread cottages, historic churches and pink sand beaches.*

Restaurants: **Angela's Starfish**, *on Harbour Island, for its homestyle cooking.* **Miss Mae Tea Room and Fine Things**, *on Harbour Island, for its eclectic collection of art and artifacts, and its gourmet snacks.*

Hotels: **Runaway Hill**, *on Harbour Island, where personal touches and the glorious pink sand beaches make this inn a standout.* **Ocean View**, *on Harbour Island, where each cozy guestroom resembles a small folk art gallery.* **Cotton Bay Club**, *at Rock Sound, for its championship golf course, curving beach, endless pampering and varied dining areas.*

WHAT TO SEE AND DO

Sports

Diving expeditions may be arranged on Harbour Island through the Romora Bay Club or Valentine's Yacht Club; in Rock Sound, through the Winding Bay Dive Center; and on Spanish Wells, through the Spanish Wells Beach Resort and the Harbour Club. The best fishing here is from April to August. For fishing and boating on Harbour Island, contact the Coral Sands Hotel, Romora Bay or Valentine's; near Rock Sound, the Cotton Bay Club, and on Spanish Wells, Sawyers Marina or Spanish Wells Beach Resort. Eleuthera's golf course is at the Cotton Bay Club near Rock Sound. Tennis courts are in Governor's Harbour, Rock Sound, Harbour Island and Spanish Wells.

UPPER BOGUE AREA

Glass Window

Just south of Upper Bogue, at a spot where the island is almost divided, this windowlike formation was created by erosion from the sea and the wind. It provides a spectacular view both east and west, from the ocean to the bay. The deep blue of the ocean's water on one side of the island contrasts with the bright turquoise of the more shallow water on the other.

BRIDGE POINT AREA

Preacher's Cave

Shipwrecked settlers, the Eleutherian Adventurers, sought shelter in this cave in northern Eleuthera. A rocky pulpit formation gives a churchlike feeling, which generated the cave's name.

HARBOUR ISLAND

Historic Churches

St. John's Anglican Church on Harbour Island dates from the 1700s and is the oldest in The Bahamas. Wesley Methodist, built in 1845, is the largest of that denomination in The Bahamas. You'll find a surprising number of other churches for such a small island. Near Wesley Methodist Church is flower-filled St. Catherine's Cemetery.

GREGORY TOWN

Gregory Town Plantation

This ancient plantation is a reminder of Eleuthera's days of leadership in pineapple production. One of its current products is pineapple rum, which visitors may sample and even take home for a treat.

HATCHET BAY

Hatchet Bay Plantation

This plantation was once the center for raising prize Angus cattle. Its present output is poultry and dairy products.

Hatchet Bay Cave

A giant fig tree marks the entrance to this cave. The tree was supposedly planted by pirates. The cave itself is more than a mile long and harmless bats live in its interior. Because there are no guards, visitors are warned against exploration without the company of an islander who knows his or her way about the cave.

TARPUM BAY

Ocean Hole

Among several "holes" on the island, this one, just north of Rock

Sound and also called "blue hole," is just east of the main road, and teems with a variety of tropical fish eager to be fed.

WHERE TO STAY

HARBOUR ISLAND

Note that most hotels here close during September, October and early November and that there are no telephones or televisions in most guest rooms. For details about renting private homes, contact Tip Top Real Estate Sales & Rentals (☎ *809/333-2251*).

EXPENSIVE

Dunmore Beach Club

White wicker couches and peacock chairs, floral cushions, potted and hanging plants, pastel-patterned throw rugs and white-washed blond wood panelling make guests want to linger in the lounge of this lovely hotel. The fireplace is flanked by bookcases. Partially done puzzles wait to be tackled on card tables. As in many Out Island hotels, guests keep track of the drinks they make at the adjoining honesty bar. All three meals are included in the rates. Dunmore Beach Club has an excellent reputation for innovative gourmet cuisine. Men are required to wear jackets and ties for the evening meal, served in an attractive room with a built-in wine cabinet. The set menu changes daily. Among the house specialties are salmon mousse, spinach soup, caesar salad, paella, cornish game hen with herbed rice stuffing, duck in sour orange sauce, banana crepes, mai tai pie and chocolate souffle with brandied creme. Nonguests are welcome for dinner when there is space. A lattice gazebo overlooks the beach, down below. The nine-acre grounds, with an archway created by palms, ficus and other greenery, also contain a tennis court. Some guest units have sitting areas, while others have separate sitting rooms with daybeds. Half the rooms come with king-sized beds. All are woodpanelled and have patios, refrigerators, ceiling fans and air conditioning.

Romora Bay Club

Caged parrots chatter near the entrance to this harborside hotel. Lush greenery and colorful flowers are all over the property. Trees bear papayas, sour oranges, lemons, sugar apples and almonds. Pathways wend their way through shady foliage, and hammocks invite relaxation. A breezy bar hangs over the harbor. Nearby, steps from a sunning deck lead down to the water for swimming. Patios are decked out with cast-iron garden furniture. Set off by a stone fireplace, the indoor bar/lounge, with its black-and-white tile floor and bleached wood ceiling, has tables and chairs set up for various games.

Covered with a tortoise shell-like wood veneer, the large table in the center of the dining room seats ten. It was rescued from a shipwreck. For those who'd like to search for more underwater treasures, dive packages are available. The beach is a five-minute walk away. Once a week, guests are taken to a deserted island for a picnic. Some of the rooms and suites are time-share units. All have patios and air conditioning, and many contain ceiling fans. Most are decorated with rattan, glass-topped tables and white-tiled floors. The kitchens in some are convenient for families. A couple of units even have Murphy beds. Because of their scenic location, the deluxe harborside rooms are booked well in advance.

Rock House ★★

Perched on a cliff overlooking the harbor, Rock House was built in 1947. The highlight of the inn is the bold Rousseau-inspired mural in the dining room, which is decorated in wicker and rattan. Men are required to wear jackets at dinner. Lunch and breakfast are often served amid the flower beds of the courtyard. Five of the six rooms have private patios, and all are cooled by ceiling fans. Some are air-conditioned. The handsome tile floors were laid when the house was originally built. Some rooms are decorated with four-poster rattan beds. Some have bathtubs, while others have stall showers. Scuba diving and deep sea, reef and bonefishing can all be arranged. The beach is about a five-minute walk away. A two-night minimum stay is required.

MODERATE

Ocean View ★★★

If you're looking for a small hotel that exudes character, this is it. Many agree that among Harbour Island's wealth of extremely attractive accommodations, Ocean View gets top billing. The centerpiece of the large living/dining room is an inlaid wooden table imported from France, which sits atop a tiled floor. Antique chairs and couches create a comfortable sitting area by the fireplace. Guests are welcome to borrow the books here. Framed watercolors and other paintings decorate walls and unusual statues and knickknacks sit on sideboards and tables. In the bar, weathered brass instruments hang next to the colorful Haitian-inspired work of Amos Ferguson, one of the Bahamas' best known artists. Jazz is likely to be played on the stereo, and there's a piano in the living room. Even the kitchen, by the dining area, is attractively decorated, with blue and white china hung on walls and cookbooks neatly on shelves. Off the bar, flower-trimmed patios provide stunning ocean views.

The decor of the nine guest rooms makes up for their small size. They all have air conditioning and ceiling fans, but the similarity ends here. Each done in a distinctive theme and color scheme, they sport antique chairs and chests, and old tile floors with intricate designs. Antique etchings hang on some walls, while old straw hats adorn others. They share a patio that faces the water. The pink sand beach is at the base of the bluff on which the hotel sits. Ocean View attracts many Europeans. Pip Simmons, the Canadian owner, also runs Miss Mae's boutique and teahouse in town.

Coral Sands ☆☆☆

Many repeat guests wouldn't stay anywhere else and quite a few staff members have been here for years. The friendly, personal attention provided by owners Sharon and Brett King has everything to do with the popularity of this beachfront hotel. Hammocks are strung throughout the grounds and large umbrellas provide shade on the long pink beach. Palms rustle above the elevated oceanfront bar. Breakfast and dinner are served on the breezy patio, where live bands entertain on weekends. Selections might include lobster goombay (in a parmesan and cream sauce with onions on toast), beef tenderloin, fried grouper and chocolate souffles. Lunch is served on a breezy, broad deck high above the beach. The view of the pinkish sand and the ocean is fabulous from here.

Individually decorated, rooms in the main building have a homey feel. Oceanfront suites are found in a separate building. Casually done with bright captain's chairs and ginger jar lamps, they have large patios, walk-in closets and living areas with day beds. The watercolors in most rooms were painted by Kimberly Nelson King, one of the three daughters of the owners. The tennis court is lit for night play. Sail boats and row boats are available. Other watersports are easily arranged as well. A pool table, cards, and various games are in the TV lounge. Talk to Big Red, one of the bartenders, about renting bikes, motor scooters and boats. Babysitting is available through the front desk.

Runaway Hill ★★★

Staying at this partially Bahamian-owned inn overlooking the pink sand beach is like visiting old friends. The homey atmosphere is a pleasant reminder that Runaway Hill was built as a private house. The dining room/lounge is furnished in wicker, and black and white tiles pave the floor. People from other hotels often stop by for drinks and the excellent meals served on the veranda. (Reservations are essential.) Each day, the handwritten menu appears on an old brass music stand by the entrance. Nearby, a large totem pole-like stylized statue of a pelican stands by an antique table with beautifully carved legs.

The personal attention of co-owners and managers Carol and Roger Becht is always apparent. They make sure that guests are informed of any social events taking place on the island. Parties and even weddings have been held on the broad pool deck overlooking the ocean. Hammocks are strung nearby. All rooms are air-conditioned and have ceiling fans. Three of the most popular are in the main house. One of these is huge, with beautiful, pink, patterned ceramic floor tiles, white wicker furniture and a large bath with two sinks. Rooms all have paperback books, which guests are welcome to exchange for those they've brought. When checking out, some vacationers book their favorite room for the following year.

Valentine's Yacht Club & Inn

Scuba diving and boating are the main draws at this harborside yacht club. A nautical theme is strong in the public rooms. Portholes decorate the wood-panelled wall that separates the pleasant lounge from the bar, which opens to the pool patio. Grounds are landscaped with crotons, palms and giant succulents. The comfortable but plainly furnished poolside and gardenside guest rooms are all air-conditioned, with ceiling fans. The 10 in the two-story gardenside building are the largest. A tennis court is on the premises. Across the road, lunch and dinner are served at the waterfront Reach Grill. At the harbor's edge, the open-air Reach Bar and the Reach Up (a second-story deck with wonderful sunset views) are popular evening hangouts. Live calypso bands appear here periodically.

INEXPENSIVE

Tingum Village

Best known as the home of **Ma Ruby's Restaurant**, this family-run accommodation is a good choice if you're on a limited budget. You'll dine on a breezy open-air patio, adjacent to the lively bar, with views of a palm-shaded grassy lawn. Entrees might be conch burgers, stewed grouper, chicken or steak. If you're going to be having dinner here, be sure to let Ma Ruby know by 6 p.m. The twelve comfortable guest rooms, with both ceiling fans and air conditioning, are located in three buildings. Two units share a central kitchen. The beach is not far.

GREGORY TOWN

MODERATE

Oleander Gardens

These white, red-roofed villas are perched on the shore overlooking the beach. Each attractively furnished villa has two bedrooms, two baths, a living room, a dining area, a kitchen and two terraces. Tennis, fishing and watersports are available.

The Cove Eleuthera

Set on 28 acres, this 24-room resort sits on a secluded beach where you can snorkel right off shore. There's also a swimming pool. The rooms are villa style with rattan furnishings and ceramic tile. Each is air-conditioned and has its own covered porch. Hammocks are available for lazing, tennis for the athletic, and strolling about the grounds for the energetic. The menu, which varies daily, is American and Bahamian. Mountain bikes are available for rent.

GOVERNOR'S HARBOUR

MODERATE

Club Med Eleuthera

Because this all-inclusive resort is child-oriented, ranging from toddlers to pre-teens, accompanied by parents and often grandparents, there is a constant, shrill vibration that prevails until bedtime. The parents, knee-deep in little ones, seem to love it and the kids are ecstatic. There are activites to please both children and adults, with escape programs for parents and day-care fun for toddlers away in a compound of their own.

Older children participate in programs—perhaps a circus or a musical presentation—that also include staff and that everyone enjoys in an evening show held in the vast open-sided auditorium. The staff creates ingenious scenery and costumes. In addition to the show, there is individual and line dancing, and singing, into which all are drawn. During the day, transport is provided to boating and other water-sports at a special marina where guests water-ski, snorkel and scuba dive under the guidance of qualified staff. The beautiful beach echoes the length of the resort, where little offshore islets seem to mark its limits.

Club Med Eleutherea is spread over abundant acreage. Your salmon and mauve painted guest buildings could be a distance from the central hub that includes the front desk, the large dining room, the bar, shops and the auditorium. So, if you'd rather be closer, clarify your location when you make your reservation. Although not luxurious, rooms are quite comfortable, with tiled floors and marble baths with showers. All rooms have safes into which guests can program their personal, six digit combinations.

After being directed to a table by a staff member, vacationers dine buffet style in the two-level dining room. Selections are endless—a variety of ice cream, beverage selections, salads and entrees. This is a good place to meet fellow guests and hear languages spoken from around the world.

If you are not using a Club Med taxi, the fare from the Governor's Harbour airport to this sprawling resort is about $21. However, most vacationers are picked up and greeted enthusiastically by members of the club's young, energetic and smiling staff. Most of the young people seem to be pre-career folks enjoying Club Med life before entering the real world. Departure is also an event. Baggage is collected and stacked out front where there is a mosaic trident logo, and staff, many of whom are now friends of travelers, come out to say goodbye and help load guests and their luggage into the line of taxis that leave in convoy for the airport.

INEXPENSIVE

Cigatoo Inn ☆☆

An attractive, family-run hotel, Cigatoo sports a pool, tennis court and a bar and restaurant where locals often stop for drinks. Guest rooms, with terraces surrounded by flowering plants, are small but comfortable. All the rooms have TV and refrigerators. Families with young children can arrange for baby-sitting. A short walk will take you to a broad, pink sand beach shared by Club Med. Guests are quickly drawn into the life of the town. One of the best things about the Cigatoo is the lively, warm and congenial atmosphere.

Tuckaway Motel

This pleasant guest house in a residential neighborhood is run by Carmen and Richard Rolle, who live across the street. All the rooms in the various cottages are air-conditioned, with refrigerators and shady front porches. A crib is available should a young one turn up. All the front yards are alive with colorful vegetation. Guests will be able to pick pineapple and other fruit when the plants mature. An unspectacular beach is a two-minute walk away. For a better, pink sand beach on the north shore, a 20-minute walk is required.

Laughing Bird Apartments

These four studio and one-bedroom units are sometimes referred to as "Nurse Jean's apartments," since this Bahamian nurse owns them with her English husband, Daniel Davies, an architect. Town is nearby. Although there's a neighboring beach, you'll find much nicer sandy shores a short walk away. Maid service is available at a small extra charge.

ROCK SOUND AREA

EXPENSIVE

Cotton Bay Club   ★★★★

This resort, now managed by Sofitel, was developed as a retreat for millionaires. It continues to be one of the finest in The Bahamas. From the road its 450 acres are reached by a winding driveway shaded by palms and Norfolk pines. The pink cottages have stair-stepped roofs like those used in Bermuda for catching rainwater. The rooms, most with outdoor terraces, are tastefully furnished with rattan, and have ceiling fans, white-tile floors and shutters at tall windows. The baths all have useful grab bars, and there are safe-deposit boxes in the closets. The pristine white-sand beach arcs off in each direction against a coastline of palms and casuarinas. There is an 18-hole Robert Trent Jones golf course and tennis courts. The grounds are landscaped with lush tropical plantings dominated by huge aloes. The dining room goes mainly unused because most dining takes place outside, beside the pool, under tall palms that lean protectively. There is a singer each night during season and, on buffet nights, a live band. Guests are expected to dress for dinner. As they check out, many make reservations for the following year.

INEXPENSIVE

Ingraham's Beach Inn

By the shore in Tarpum Bay, this two-storey building houses eight guest rooms and four 1-1/2 room apartments. The air-conditioned units face the beach. The dining room serves hearty meals.

Hilton's Haven

This 10-room guest house is run by a former public health nurse, celebrated for her past contributions to the nation's health and her present hospitality. Although her service is not as lavish as Rock Sound's larger resorts, it is much more personal.

THE EXUMAS

A pirate's treasure is said to be buried in this peaceful cove on Great Exuma.

The Exumas are a chain of 365 cays stretching for 100 miles from New Providence and Eleuthera to Long Island. These islands and the surrounding waters are one of the Bahamas' most memorable sights from the air. Strung out in a long line, the Exumas look like stepping stones. In the ocean around them, a giant hand seems to have done a whimsical finger painting, leaving swirls of teal, jade, turquoise and electric royal blue.

Great Exuma and Little Exuma, joined by a bridge, are the two largest islands in this chain. Up north, the gorgeous, peaceful Exuma

Cays Land and Sea Park comprises some 177 square miles of islands and marine life. Much of the aquatic underworld here is clearly visible from three to ten feet down.

A wonderfully drowsy ambience pervades the Exumas. Fishing and farming are the occupations of most of the nearly 4000 residents. Great Exumians are proud to say that unlike many other Bahamian islands, which import most of their produce, this island grows some 80 percent of its fruits and vegetables.

FISHING AND SAILING

The water is so shallow in some places that the artful ripples of the sandy ocean floor can be seen as you fly in. You can even spot the best bonefishing flats from above: just look for places where the water is milky (or "muddy," as Bahamians say). In some regions, bonefishing is excellent right off the beach. George Town (the capital) on Great Exuma hosts the Bonefish Bonanza Fishing Tournaments in October/November. Wahoo, dolphin, bluefin tuna, king mackerel and blue and white marlin are also plentiful in these islands.

Along with fishing, sailing could hardly be better in the Exumas. Each April, the Out Island Regatta at George Town draws Bahamians from all islands and many living abroad, as well as foreign visitors. With tall sails swelled by the wind, the locally built wooden work boats race each other for three days. Yachts, dinghies, Sunfish and windsurfers compete in the annual George Town Cruising Regatta in March.

FRIENDLY GREETINGS

If you're staying at one of the hotels about a mile outside George Town, you might have trouble walking into town. No, the road is fine. In fact, the views of the aqua and peacock blue waters between the pines and palms are magnificent. The problem is that folks in the Exumas are just too friendly. Motorists—even bicyclists—can't seem to pass strollers without stopping to offer them rides. And it's not just that residents don't want you to work up a sweat while they ease by on wheels. It's that Exumians love to chat. When they see strangers, they like to find out where you're from and make sure you know about that weekend's hot spot.

CHANGES AHEAD

The Exumas may be largely undiscovered now. However, you'd better hurry if you want a taste of the main island without busy, fancy hotels and splashy night life. A Ritz Carlton hotel, a golf course, and a casino (the first in the Out Islands) are being built at the Bahama Club resort in northwest Great Exuma. While many lo-

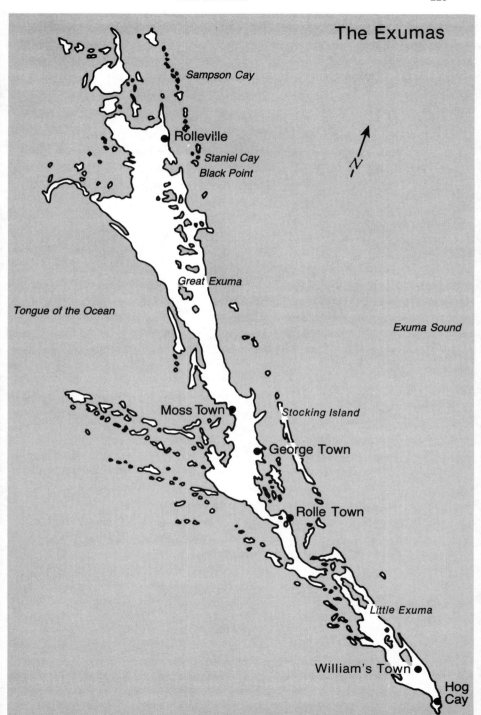

cals look forward to the additional jobs, not everyone is pleased about this major change. Some people are especially opposed to the casino, which, they say, will "bring in too much undesirables."

YEARS PAST

Lucayan Indians were probably the first people to call the Exumas home. During the 1500s, they were wiped out by Spanish explorers and other European adventurers. The islands' salt pans had proved quite lucrative by the 1600s, and many newcomers were lured from foreign shores. Pirates did well for themselves by attacking the ships of salt merchants. Yet, as ruthless as these buccaneers were, life was even worse on nearby New Providence island, where other pirates and tyranical Spaniards were running the show. Many residents escaped New Providence to the relative calm of Great Exuma.

A group of loyalists, upset by Britain's defeat in the Revolutionary War, also found refuge in the Exumas in 1783. Cotton fields blossomed for a while here along with the salt industry. (Today you can still come across wild cotton descended from seeds planted in past centuries.) The free labor provided by enslaved men and women brought in from Africa and the West Indies bolstered the wealth of English planters. But insects started destroying the cotton and neighboring islands were able to produce salt far more profitably than the Exumas. With the sag in the economy, most European land owners packed up and went home. Lacking in similar resources, the Africans and their descendants stayed in the Exumas and struggled to work the land.

Don't be surprised if four of the first five people you meet in the Exumas all share the surname Rolle. This is the legacy of Lord John Rolle, one of the Bahamas' largest landowers. He enslaved more than 300 people to work the hundreds of acres that had been granted him by the British Crown. After they were freed, those he had enslaved to work his plantations took his name.

Today Rolles abound in the Exumas. It's a wonder anyone can keep track of who they can and can't marry! Some say that Lord Rolle freed those who worked his land, then generously gave them the real estate. Others are convinced that after they were emancipated by the United Kingdom in 1834, they simply appropriated the land themselves. Whatever the true story is, these fertile acres have been passed down through generations of Rolles and cannot be sold to outsiders.

GETTING AROUND

Veteran boaters say that the Exumas offer some of the world's best sailing. There are so many uninhabited, beachfringed islands with tranquil anchorages. In fact, the water is the only way to reach some of the most stunning areas, such as the Exuma Cays Land and Sea Park. If you don't sail to the Park from your home base, you can fly to George Town, then sail from there (about a two-day leisurely trip), or charter a plane to Staniel Cay and arrange for a guide to sail you from there. For details about crewed yacht charters, contact **The Moorings** (☎ *800/437-7880*) on Stocking Island, across from George Town.

The Exumas' international airport is at Moss Town, about nine miles west of George Town. A taxi ride to one of the hotels in or near town runs about $24 for two people. George Town, where the Exumas' action is centered, can easily be explored on foot. The Coconut Cove Hotel and the neighboring Peace & Plenty Beach Inn both provide complimentary shuttle buses to restaurants in town, about a mile away, for their guests.

When you're ready to see more of Great and Little Exuma, take a taxi tour or rent a car or a moped. One of the islands' most pleasant guides is taxi driver-restaurateur-farmer Kermit Rolle. His enjoyable, informative taxi tours run from $60 to $140 for up to four people (☎ *345- 6038*). Your hotel can give you recommendations for other good tour guides, or you can check out the bulletin board outside Club Peace & Plenty in George Town.

Rental cars range from $55 to $70 per day, with more economical weekly rates. They are available through hotels, such as Club Peace & Plenty (☎ *336-2551*) and Two Turtles Inn (☎ *336-2545*), or Exuma Transport (☎ *336-2101*). Mopeds run about $35 per day and pedal bikes $10 at Two Turtles. However, Bahamians don't recommend that vacationers rent mopeds, since most visitors will be new to both these motorized bikes and to driving on the left.

Staniel Cay is a brief charter flight from George Town or Nassau. Solomon Robinson (☎ *809/355-2012*) and John Chamberlain (☎ *809/355-2011*) are two experienced charter pilots based on Staniel Cay. Taxi service is free to the Staniel Cay Yacht Club, which is within walking distance of the airport if your bags aren't heavy. However, most guests reach this island by sea, either on their own boats or by charter.

GEORGE TOWN

Most of the Exumas' few hotels are clustered in George Town. A long narrow stip of land rimmed with luscious beaches, Stocking Island lies just across Elizabeth Harbour. **Club Peace & Plenty**, which faces Stocking Island and provides the ferry to its sandy shores, could be considered the hub of Great Exuma. Locals and visitors can always be found socializing at this hotel's pool bar or in the indoor bar that was used as a kitchen during slavery days. And the legendary Saturday night parties here are always packed.

Nearby, handsome **St. Andrew's Anglican Church** perches on a rise. Walk up the hill to the gravesites in the back and you'll have a sweeping view of Lake Victoria. Boats rest along its banks. There's a narrow inlet to the harbor. Down below, the lake's pier is a quiet place to sit. While the water sloshes against the dock, you'll gaze back to St. Andrew's, high on the bluff. Bright green mangrove bushes, with their skeletal leg-like roots, decorate the circumference of the lake.

Next door to Club Peace & Plenty, the pink, white-columned **Government Administration building** sits at the harbor's edge. It houses the post office, police station and Ministry of Education. Enormous fig trees sprout at the fork in the road, near the public library. Under the shade of the expansive ceiling-like branches, vendors sell all kinds of straw goods, t-shirts and jewelry. In the morning, you can even get freshly prepared breakfast here.

N & D's Fruits & Vegetables, run by talkative Denzella Rolle Nixon, opens earlier and closes later than most other stores in town. Along with fresh produce, this store sells everything from conch fritters and hot dogs to toilet articles and clothing.

Kidd Cove, a bay by the Regatta Point inn, was named for the pirate Captain Kidd. A treasure is said to be buried somewhere in this pretty inlet. As you stroll toward the other side of Lake Victoria, you'll pass chickens in the front yards of small cottages, an ice cream parlor, Mom-and-Pop variety stores, several restaurants and bars and tiny Baptist, Catholic and God of Prophecy churches.

Some days, vendors sell fresh conch on the side of the road or by the lake. You'll come to a table piled high with the large beige pink-lipped shells. You can watch the fisherman prepare conch salad (raw marinated conch with vegetables), scorched conch (raw marinated strips), and pieces of the mollusk for people to cook at home. He'll hammer a shell, deftly cut out the dark brown sea animal and quickly skin it, exposing white flesh. If a vendor doesn't sell all his catch by the end of a given day, he keeps the remaining conchs alive by tying them together and putting them back in the water overnight.

DINING SPOTS

George Town and its environs offer a selection of good restaurants, most of which feature Bahamian cuisine. Note that some of those that are outside hotels are closed or have limited hours on Sundays.

If you're in the mood for a casual dinner with some upscale flourishes, book a table at the **Coconut Cove Hotel** (☎ *336-2659)* overlooking the beach and Elizabeth Harbour. Your meal might include crab fritters or blackened conch followed by Bahamian lobster tail or chicken breast with green pepper sauce. Those who still have room for dessert should consider the *crème brulée* or banana *flambé*.

Celebrated for its turtle steak, **Eddie's Edgewater** (☎ *336-2050)* is a brief stroll from Club Peace & Plenty to the far side of Lake Victoria. Other popular dinner selections are "peas soup with dumplings," broiled grouper, and steamed chicken. For breakfast, try the boiled fish, corned beef and eggs or stewed fish. Lunch might be pork chops with macaroni and cheese or okra soup with fried snapper and peas and rice. On weekend evenings, the bar here can be quite busy.

At the round-about in town, **Tino's Lounge** (☎ *336-2838)*, a truly local spot, is open for breakfast, lunch and dinner. In this tiny establishment, with only about five tables, walls are adorned with maps, posters of basketball players and family graduation photos. Order cracked conch, and you'll probably be able to hear the cook pounding it (to tenderize it) in the kitchen. Snapper, mutton and chicken, served with heaping mounds of peas and rice, are also on the menu.

The Towne Cafe & Bakery (☎ *336-2194)* makes a good breakfast stop. If you don't have enough of an appetite for the pancakes, "boil fish" (cooked with onions and pepper) and grits, or the chicken souse (a poultry stew) with mildly sweet Johnny cake, then try some pastry. The fresh donuts, bran muffins and coffee cake are delicious. This cheerful restaurant, which is open from 7 a.m. to 5 p.m., is decorated with household items from a bygone era. Irons that were heated by hot coals are on display. A grindstone once used for sharpening machetes stands in a corner. The hollowed tree trunks nearby held coffee beans that were ground with an iron pestle.

Veronica Marshall, the owner, seems to enjoy telling patrons about the old corn mill and the baskets hanging above it on the wall. She might show you how her grandparents taught her to pour the dry corn into the funnel, grind it several times to get the right texture, then "riddle" (sift) the grits in a flat round basket. Proper riddling requires a dance-like motion that involves a circular movement of both the torso and hips.

Three meals a day are served at **Sam's Place** (☎ *336-2579)*, at the water's edge. The elevated dining room has dramatic views of the water. George Towners flock to the Tuesday and Friday night barbecues at the Sunshine Bar at **Two Turtles hotel** (☎ *336-2545)*.

Near the airport, about 10 miles from George Town, **Iva Bowe's Central Highway Inn** (☎ *345-7014)* is a good choice for lunch when you're touring the island. Many people are partial to the cracked conch here. The shrimp scampi and the crawfish salad are also done well.

Around Mt. Thompson, **Three Sisters Club** is another good place to stop for a cool drink or a meal while you're exploring Great Exuma. When you step out back to the gorgeous beach, you'll see the trio of siblings that gave the restaurant its name—three huge rocks in the water. Note that this dining spot is not to be confused with a nearby hotel, which has been closed off and on, that gave itself a similar name.

Kermit's Airport Lounge *(☎ 345-0002)* is a huge, modern, high-ceilinged, wood-panelled affair. However, despite its physical attributes, we were quite disappointed when we showed up famished before a flight one recent afternoon and found that the only food left was sandwiches.

A better bet, when you're driving to the far northwest of Great Exuma, is to make a reservation at **Kermit's Hilltop Tavern** *(☎ 345-6006)* in Rolleville, the westernmost settlement. Dating back to 1956, this bar/restaurant is the focal point of Emancipation Day (in August), which is celebrated with a vengeance in Rolleville. The fruit and vegetables served here come fresh—very fresh—from the farm of owner Kermit Rolle. He tells the story of the day he was on the farm and heard a request for a reservation at his restaurant over his car VHF radio. He said to the caller, "By the way, you've reached me on a farm. So I'm going to pick your vegetables right now." Try the pan fried grouper, minced crawfish, steamed conch, or curried mutton.

In remote Barraterre ("Barry Tarry"), you'll find the nautical **Fisherman's Inn** restaurant and nightclub. It is particularly busy on weekends. On your way to visit the Shark Lady of the Exumas in Little Exuma, southeast of George Town, have lunch at **La Shante**; but check its hours, which can be irregular, before setting out.

AFTER DARK

Saturday nights find much of George Town at the poolside bash at **Club Peace & Plenty**, where a live band keeps the dance floor busy. Afterwards, those who still have the energy head to nearby waterside **Cousins** for after-hours partying.

The bar at **Tino's Lounge** draws a late-night crowd. While it officially closes at midight, its doors don't actually shut until the last person leaves.

THE OUT ISLAND REGATTA

Each April, Great Exuma closes down for a week. Fellow Bahamians, cruising yachtsmen, boaters, visitors and landlubbers all make their way to George Town to watch and take part in the festivities surrounding the annual Out Island Regatta. The festivities include a parade and a variety of other special events, as the hand-crafted work sloops, owned and operated by Bahamians, compete out in Elizabeth Harbour. The regatta signals non-stop eating, drinking and all-round partying. Accommodations are difficult to come by for outsiders and some make their reservations a year or so in advance.

Food stalls are set up along the waterfront selling fresh pineapples, grilled chicken, fish and conch in all its incarnations. Reggae throbs from the stalls and long lost friends greet each other with embraces and bottles of beer. Domino-playing men slap the tiles on card tables with sharp clicks. Pulsing drums, clanking cowbells, blaring horns and shrill whistles accompany a Junkanoo band down the center of the street.

Like birds lined on telephone wires, people sit on the low walls in front of the administration building to watch the passing line of honking cars decorated with colored streamers. Children in their Sunday best sit on hoods or poke their smiling faces from sun roofs. When the Police band performs in Regatta Park, everyone surges onto the steps of the Exuma Supplies building and nearby footholds for a better view. Members of the band, in sparkling white tunics, wide red belts, hats with red bands and black trousers with red side stripes, move children and their elders to dance to the beat.

BEYOND GEORGE TOWN

To see the sights in the most leisurely, enjoyable fashion, it's best to spend part of one day driving southeast of George Town to Little Exuma, then another day going northwest on Great Exuma.

SOUTHEAST OF GEORGE TOWN

You'll follow the main road, bordered by nothing more than bushes and wispy trees bent by the wind. The first settlement you'll come to will be **Rolle Town**, lush with banana trees, palms and flowering bushes. On a rise near the entrance to this village is an old-style Bahamian house with a crumbling shingle roof and peeling wooden shutters and doors. In sharp contrast, the modern neighboring house is said to belong to the uncle of American television actress Esther Rolle, whose family came from Exuma.

Just past these homes, the elevated road affords views of two opposite coasts of Great Exuma. On one side, Elizabeth Harbour, striped with aqua and navy, is studded with small islands. On the other, grassy expanses of land give way to water in a variety of other shades of blue. A flourishing path will take you down a slope to a clearing with the 18th-century Rolle Town Tombs.

In this area and back on the main road are a variety of fruit trees, among them tamarind, sugar apple, soursop, mango, breadfruit and guava. Hartswell, a small community with brightly painted houses, is the birthplace of the commissioner responsible for having the road built from one end of Exuma to the other. In the old days, when people used to walk long distances, the roadside wells that you will still see today had buckets so that pedestrians could stop for drinks.

Near the end of Great Exuma, a dark pea-green pond spreads itself on the right side of the road and the bright turquoise Atlantic is on the left.

The Peace & Plenty Bonefish Lodge sits at the shore, near the long drawbridge joining Great Exuma and Little Exuma. Before the bridge was built, people would drive their vehicles onto a plank-like ferry attached to a pulley. Drivers would have to help the ferryman pull themselves and their cars across the water. If the wind was strong, it could take half a day to get to the other side.

Little Exuma is much less developed than its sister island. Named for the old mode of transport from Great Exuma, the first settlement is called The Ferry. Spend a few moments here with Gloria Patience, **The Shark Lady of the Exumas**, at her home-boutique-museum. A sign outside her house claims that this is the spot where the Tropic of Cancer cuts through the island, marking the separation of the tropics from the temperate zone.

The abandoned Sand Dollar Beach Club is on **Pretty Molly Bay**, rimmed with sea grapes, palms and casuarinas. According to one legend, a beautiful young woman named Molly was enslaved on a nearby plantation. Melancholy about her barren life and a future of continued servitude, she drowned herself here one moonlit night. Some say that if you look carefully, you might catch a glimpse of Molly, who is said to roam the beach by moonlight. Many black Bahamians swear by this legend and dismiss another version in which Molly is a young white woman who was transformed into a mermaid and sits on a rock in the bay combing her hair with the aid of lunar illumination.

When you reach **Williamstown**, you'll see the sprawling pinkish salt pond that once brought great wealth to these islands. The tall pillar on a rise across the road once served as a marker so that mariners could find the salt flats. If you climb the hill, you'll look down on a pleasant curve of beach with rocky outcroppings. A ship is wrecked just offshore. Full of food and clothing, this boat recently met its end while on its way to Haiti to aid victims of that country's civil unrest.

There is little agriculture in Little Exuma. Fishing is the mainstay of the economy here. Known for its crawfishing, Williamstown also boasts **Mom's Bakery**. Once you get a whiff of warm coconut tarts, marble cakes and whole wheat bread, you'll find it hard to resist a visit. The rum cake and banana bread are the bestsellers, but Mom (whose real name is Doris Rahming) also does a brisk business with her cinnamon-raisin bread, key lime pie and mildly sweet Bahamian white bread. Mom earned her nickname by having nine children, 26 grandchildren and 3 greatgrands (at last count). If you don't make it to Little Exuma, don't worry. Almost every day, Mom loads her bus with freshly baked goodies, drives to George Town and sells her treats across from Exuma Market.

NORTHWEST OF GEORGE TOWN

Off a beautiful stretch of beach, the **Three Sisters Rocks** pose in a row against the horizon. Locals say that this trio appeared after three sisters drowned. You'll notice that each of the boulders has a smaller rock near it. Some say that each rock has a "child" who stays close by.

Farmer's Hill is verdant with banana trees and palms. Turn up the hill toward the telecommunications building dwarfed by an immense satellite dish, past the Baptist church. You'll gaze down on the picturesque town and on Ocean Bight, a huge, sparkling white sandy cove that is great for swimming and snorkeling. This is where **The Bahama Club** resort is being built, with its luxury hotel, casino and golf course.

Small old-style houses, painted fading pastels or bright greens, yellows and blues, are shaded by tall palms in **Steventon**. In this quiet settlement, you might see old women braiding palm fronds as they sit in the doorways of their homes. They "plait" sections, then send them to Nassau to be sewn into baskets, mats, bags and other straw goods.

When enslaved Africans and West Indians from other islands were brought to Exuma, many landed in Rolleville, at Great Exuma's far northwest. So **Emancipation Day** means a lot to people here. A mini regatta is part of the extensive annual celebration on the first Monday of August. Locally made boats sail in Rolleville Harbour, and food stands draw crowds to sample conch fritters, guava duff, "peas soup and dumpling" and other local favorites. The drink of choice is coconut water and gin.

With a fabulous view of the harbor from its rooftop patio, Kermit's Hilltop Tavern is the center of the festivities. In front of this restaurant, a cannon points to the water. Brought from England, it was among the heavy artillery put on Gun Hill to protect the entrance to the harbor from enemies who never came. Enslaved men were responsible for hauling the cannons up the hill and installing them there. Over the years, they were removed one by one, many used as ballast on boats. When there was only one left, Kermit Rolle, now the owner of the Hilltop Tavern that bears his name, overheard an American hotelier talking about stealing it during the night. Kermit quickly got together a crew of strong men who lugged the cannon to the tavern. When the hotelier stopped by for a drink on his way to snatch the one remaining weapon, he saw it here. Dismayed, he offered to buy it, but Kermit's father told him "It's part of our history. It's not for sale."

STANIEL CAY

Whether you sail here or fly in by charter from George Town or Nassau, Staniel Cay is well worth some time. This tiny, friendly island with quiet beaches is a great home base for visiting some of the Exumas' prettiest cays, including those in the Exuma Cays Land and Sea Park. If you're not on a boat, there are only two places to stay, both in the island's sole village. For fishing and exploring, you can arrange to rent a boat through the **Staniel Cay Yacht Club**.

Almost everything on the island is within walking distance. Hand-lettered signs nailed to trees point visitors toward the "Straw Shop on Your Right, East of Church," the "pink supermarket," the "blue grocery store" and even to one of the local pilots. Sure, houses have satellite dishes here. But a woman pulling a bucket of water from a roadside well is just as common a sight.

South Staniel Cay, connected by a bridge, has a completely different feel. This is because many Americans and other foreigners have built modern, upscale homes. The large splashy house just across the bridge is one of the few homes there owned by a Bahamian. (He also owns the general store next door.)

For many years, **Happy People Marina** was known as the spot for the liveliest night life. These days, however, the newer **Club Thunderball**, on a bluff overlooking the water, has moved into first place.

PERSONAL FAVORITES

Adventure:
Volunteering (perhaps rescuing a stranded boat or clearing a path to a historic Loyalist ruin) at the Exuma Cays Land and Sea Park.

Taking a sea kayak camping trip with Ibis Tours.

Hotel:
Club Peace and Plenty, *where townspeople gather to gossip, exchange news and chat with visitors.*

WHAT TO SEE AND DO

Sports

Both the **Coconut Cove Hotel** and **Club Peace & Plenty** in George Town offer dive packages. Scuba excursions and PADI-certified instruction can also be arranged directly through **Exuma Fantasea** (☎ *336-3483*). This company rents boats and leads snorkeling trips as well. Fishing trips and another good snorkeling excursion are arranged by **Cooper's Charter Services** (☎ *336-2711*). Before arrival, anglers can also contact the **Peace & Plenty Bonefish Lodge** (☎ *345-5559*) at the southern tip of Great Exuma. Bonefishing can be great right off the beach in front of the Coconut Cove Hotel. On Staniel Cay, make arrangements for boat rentals and watersports at the Staniel Cay Yacht Club or Happy People Marina.

NORTHERN EXUMA CAYS

Sea Kayaking   ★★★

Ibis Tours, Boynton Beach, Florida; ☎ *800/525-9411* • Groups of eight paddlers explore the northern Exuma cays in sea kayaks by day and camp out on remote beaches by night. This eight-day adventure is spent mainly within the Exuma Cays Land and Sea Park. Sails are hoisted when the wind cooperates as the kayaks glide from island to island. The small size of these boats allows paddlers into awesome sea caves and other areas that larger vessels couldn't enter. Each day, there is plenty of time to swim, snorkel, wander on terra firma or simply relax. The cost includes all equipment, food and a guide. You need not have tried kayaking before to enjoy this experience.

Exuma Land and Sea Park

Northern Exuma Cays • Accessible only by water, this sprawling government-protected land and sea park begins north of Staniel Cay. From here it is about an hour ride in a 24- or 26-foot powerboat. Designated a National Park in 1958, this area was chosen because of its variety of landmasses (from limestone to mangrove) and its diversity of marine life. Fishing or taking anything else from the park is strictly prohibited. Even removing shells is not allowed. (Stop by the headquarters on Warderick Wells for the list of park rules.)

Some 22 miles long and eight miles wide, this preserve is full of empty beaches, fantastic dive and snorkeling sites, ruins of Loyalist settlements and marked hiking trails. Animal lovers will be awed by the tropic birds, osprey, bananaquits, terns, large iguanas, hawksbill turtles, huge groupers, benign lemon sharks, crawfish and all kinds of other land and sea life. The park boasts one of the largest stands of rare pillar coral in the Bahamas.

For marked nature trails, head to Hall's Pond, Hawksbill Cay or Warderick Wells, one of the most beautiful islands in the Bahamas. Both here and on Hawksbill Cay, you can hike to the remains of buildings left by 18th-century Americans loyal to the British Crown. The park's Warderick Wells office and home of the warden sits on a rise above a stunning beach-rimmed bay. Endless shades of blue shimmer in stripes across the water, set off by bright green palmettos and other thick vegetation along the shore. Booklets about the park are available here, along with t-shirts and other items. You'll also find a book exchange and reference library.

Another very special place is Shroud Cay. Climb the hill and you'll gaze down on beaches on one side and expanses of verdant mangroves on the other. Be sure to spend some time at "Camp Driftwood." The strong current in this natural whirlpool will whip you past a rocky outcropping, around the corner to a powder-soft sandy beach.

Many visitors are surprised to learn that some privately owned islands are within the borders of the park. A couple have vacation villas for rent, some of which are quite upscale. However, development of these islands is kept to a minimum.

Although the park is overseen by the government, it is sustained by volunteers and donations. Groups of foreign students come several times a year to work on different projects. Anyone is welcome to volunteer. You can do anything from picking up trash that washes ashore from ships to rebuilding a shelter. No matter what your expertise or pleasure, there is bound to be something for you to do. Consider clearing trails, electrical work, computer data entry, carpentry, plumbing, scuba diving to install or maintain moorings or helping with searches and rescues. Along with money, the park is also in need of donations of equipment, particularly VHF and CB radios, batteries, solar panels and medical supplies.

Thunderball Grotto

Off Staniel Cay • No matter what else you do while you're in the area, be sure to save some time for snorkeling or diving in this magnificent cave. In a rocky islet facing the Staniel Cay Yacht Club, it was used as a setting for two James Bond movies as well as the film "Splash." Pouring through holes in the cathedral-like ceiling of the central cavern, shimmering columns of sunlight pierce the clear water. Yellowtail snapper, parrotfish, queen angels and trumpetfish flash back and forth against backdrops in different versions of blue. Like paint splashed against a canvas, underwater rocks in the various caverns are decorated with orange, lime green and maroon sealife.

Never go into the grotto alone. The safest time to snorkel in is at slack tide, when the water is low but is neither moving in nor moving out. At high tide, when the water reaches the lower ceilings of some of the entrances, you should only dive in. The water never gets as high as the towering ceiling of the central cavern, so there is always air there; however, in order to swim there when the tide is high, you might have to hold your breath a dangerously long time.

GREAT EXUMA AREA

Stocking Island

Across from George Town • This long, narrow island, with three hills in the center, is in the sound off George Town. Club Peace & Plenty provides the ferry there (free to hotel guests; $8 round trip for others) for isolated sunbathing. It's easy to find a secluded spot here for skinny-dipping. The boat will drop you off on the calm bay side, where red and black starfish float at the water's edge and a huge sandbar stretches out for half a football field. Try bonefishing right off the dock. Follow a path by the Peace and Plenty "Beach Club" (really a snack bar) across the narrow island to the ocean side, where the water is rougher and rockier in places. You'll find all kinds of shells in deserted coves. For a small fee, you may be able to talk the man who brings you here into taking a detour to Sand Dollar Beach at the southern end of the island. Here you can walk to the end of another sandbar, then swim to Elizabeth Island. And, of course, you'll have no trouble finding sand dollars. Divers should check out 400-foot-deep **Mystery Cave**.

St. Andrew's Church

George Town • St. Andrew's Anglican Church, with its graveyard, sits on a rise near Government House. At its rear is Lake Victoria. The church dates from 1802, and was erected for early settlers of British background.

The Hermitage

Jimmy Hill, down a narrow road off Queen's Highway • It's probably best to let a Bahamian show you the way to the crumbling tombs at the Hermitage, about eight miles from George Town. Dating back to the 1800s, the three tombs of slavemasters lie next to the grave of one of their servants.

Rolle Town Tombs

Rolle Town • Follow the path toward a cluster of palms and Elizabeth Harbour. You'll come to a clearing with three tombs, one small, one medium, one large. The biggest is shaped like a double bed with a headboard and footboard. Carved on a marble plaque, the inscription reads, "Within this tomb lie interred the body of Ann M. Kay the wife of Alexander M. Kay who departed this life the 8th of November 1792 aged 26 years and their infant child." Ann M. Kay was the wife of an overseer during slavery. Fruit trees, such as tamarind, soursop and sugar apple, flourish in this area.

LITTLE EXUMA

Patience House/The Shark Lady of the Exumas

The Ferry • Gloria Patience, a white-haired septuagenarian whose family came from Ireland and Scotland, is more commonly known as The Shark Lady of the Exumas. She has earned her nickname over decades of snaring makos, lemon tips, hammerheads and others—most weighing hundreds of pounds—and hauling them into her boat herself. More than 2000 sharks have fallen prey to this strong old woman. She tells us that she uses every part of the shark. The meat is eaten or buried for fertilizer, and she makes earrings and necklaces from the spines and teeth. The jaw bones are turned into wall hangings or coffee table conversation pieces.

Born in 1917, she traveled around the world, then returned to the Bahamas to raise nine children. She later moved to Little Exuma and began earning a living catching sharks. Today her home-boutique-museum is cluttered with a tangle of shark jewelry, coral, sea fans, antique china, nineteenth century glassware, driftwood, old sea bottles and paintings by her Scottish husband. You'll also find tiny sand dollars that have been dipped in gold and fashioned into earrings.

Williamstown Salt Marsh

Little Exuma • The site and other traces of Exuma's once-thriving salt industry are still apparent at Williamstown. The best way to view the salt pond is to climb the rise to the single concrete column overlooking the flats. With the sea at your back, the entire marsh is visible.

WHERE TO STAY

MODERATE

Staniel Cay Yacht Club

It took a decade, but in 1994 owner Joe Hocher finally won a lawsuit against his partner (for mismanagement of funds). Now flying solo, Hocher is in the process of renovating this rustic yacht club that sprawls along the water's edge in a dramatic setting. Perched on stilts along a rocky bank, cottages gaze out to sea and the neighboring sandy cove. Thunderball Grotto, one of the most beautiful diving and snorkeling sites in the Bahamas, is just offshore. In its heyday, this yacht club drew notables such as Malcolm Forbes. However, while the owners duked it out, the club deteriorated. With Hocher now in residence and at the helm, we have no doubt that it will soon surpass its former glory. Rates include all meals and a boat for guests who stay more than three nights.

Happy People Marina

As soon as you meet owners Theaziel and Kenneth Rolle, you'll understand how this unasuming yacht club got its name. Some of the rooms are undergoing renovation, but those that are available are brightly decorated, with ceiling fans and full baths. The best views of the water are from rooms on the second story. Here there's a spacious deck for sunning. Between the two piers, you'll find a petite beach, protected by a small scenic island topped with low vegetation. If you'd like to try Theaziel's grouper, conch, pork chops or peas and rice, make meal reservations in advance. Although there's a pool table in the restaurant/lounge, note that the electricity is often turned off during the day, so you may not have much light.

GREAT EXUMA

EXPENSIVE

Peace & Plenty Bonefish Lodge

Scheduled to open by mid-1995 • This small resort for dyed-in-the-wool bonefish enthusiasts overlooks the bridge that connects Great Exuma with Little Exuma. About 10 miles southeast of George Town, it offers eight guest rooms on the second story, with soaring 30-foot ceilings and screened porches with views of a blue hole and the ocean. Downstairs, the dining room is gearing up for a rib-sticking and memorable menu. Along with a bar and game room, guests will find fly-tying facilities and state-of-the-art fishing skiffs. Certified guides are available.

MODERATE

Club Peace & Plenty   ★ ★ ★

This is where all of George Town gathers for drinks, to swap gossip, to see who's in town and to catch up on the latest. It was once a sponge market and private home. Two rooms that served as a kitchen during slavery have been converted into the indoor bar. Visitors are treated like locals and are soon adopted into the little George Town community. A popular breakfast specialty is grits and boiled fish. Try the pumpkin soup for dinner. Rooms are large and have wonderful views of the bay. Entertainment at night includes parties by the pool. Twice a day, guests are taken by ferry to the beaches on Stocking Island, where there's an unobtrusive snack bar, and on snorkeling trips. For details about about photography workshop packages, call ☎ *800/466-1464 or FAX 216/928-9124.* Club Peace & Plenty also offers packages that feature bonefishing for both experts and novices and eco-diving.

Peace & Plenty Beach Inn ★★★

About a mile north of George Town, this 16-room hotel is the baby sister of its namesake. It sits directly on the sandy shore. The upscale rooms, with marble baths, have balconies facing the sea. Facilities include a swimming pool.

Coconut Cove ★★★

About a mile from George Town and next door to Peace & Plenty Beach Inn, this nine-room beachfront hotel exudes character. At the entrance, a footbridge spans a tropical pond with a waterfall. Lattice-work trims the waterside bar and restaurant. The upscale guest rooms are furnished with bathrobes, irons and boards, mini bars and both ceiling fans and high-tech remote control air-conditioners. Honeymooners and other loving couples enjoy staying in the suite, which sports a hot tub on its private deck, and a marble bathroom. Guests report that bonefishing is excellent from the beach. On evenings when dinner is not served here, the hotel provides complimentary transportation to George Town dining places.

INEXPENSIVE

Regatta Point ★★

Just past the public dock where the mail boat comes in, this accommodation sits on a 1.5-acre cay connected to the mainland by a bridge. The atmosphere in the five attractive apartments, decorated with summery wicker, is homelike. Rooms are large, including the full kitchens, and ceilings are high. Cross breezes blow through the many windows. There is no air conditioning, but ceiling fans usually suffice. Surrounded by water on three sides, this accommodation serves as a great vantage point for viewing the April Out Island Regatta. The broad wooden deck on the second floor of one of the two buildings has a wraparound view of Elizabeth Harbour and Kidd Cove. There are two small beaches that appeal to children, who amuse themselves with lizards, fish and cats instead of television. Most guests rent Boston whalers from Exuma Fantasea. If you rent a boat you can park it at the cove here. Although the heart of town is within sight, Regatta Point is in a quiet corner.

Two Turtles Inn   ☆

A cannon guards the entrance to this stone building. Conveniently located in the center of town, Two Turtles is the site of lively Tuesday and Friday night barbecues. Palm trees shade tables by the patio bar and by the restaurant. Three of the twelve guest units have kitchenettes. Car and moped rentals are available here and room rates include continental breakfast. Ask about scuba or bonefishing packages, fishing expeditions and boat charters.

PRIVATE ISLANDS

With vacation accommodations that range from rustic to five-star, small private islands are found throughout the Bahamas. They are perfect for people who want a real escape from the demands of their lives back home. Some of the nicest are in and around the Exumas Cays Land and Sea Park, in the northern Exumas:

If you and some friends or family are feeling extravagant and have always dreamed of having a secluded island almost all to yourselves, consider the luxurious main house and two cottages on **Cistern Cay** (☎ *809/326-7875)*. About eleven staff members, including several housekeepers and a butler, will cater to all your needs and desires. Along with seven beaches, you'll have the use of Windsurfers, jet skis, sailboats, motor boats, waterskis, scuba and snorkeling gear and other watersports equipment as well as a guide for deepsea fishing and bonefishing. You can even try underwater photography. Among the indoor exercise equipment are a Lifecycle and a stair climber. Meals (prepared by a gourmet chef), liquor and gratuities are also included in the rates ($38,000 per week for up to 10 adults and a few children). If that price tag is too rich for your blood, ask about **Soldier Cay**, **Dennis Cay** and **Wild Tamarind Cay**, other nearby islands with vacation facilities.

Bonefishing, scuba diving and snorkeling are all excellent around **Compass Cay** *(contact Petrat Travel Inc, 8515 Fondren, suite 206, Houston, TX 77074; ☎ 713/981-5306 or 800/253-5306)*. A beautiful crescent beach hugs the east side of the island. On a ridge overlooking a tranquil harbor (with boat dockage) in the west, the three-bedroom, one-bath rental house sleeps six or more. The rate is about $1500 per week.

More developed but still quite peaceful, **Sampson Cay Club & Marina** *(☎ 809/355-2034)* has full docking facilities (with fuel, oil, water, groceries and liquor available, along with Boston Whalers for rent). You'll need reservations to dine at the bar/restaurant. Two of the three cottages are right on the beach. Rates begin at about $95 per night.

INAGUA

Children pass an old-style Bahamian house in Matthew Town, Inagua.

If you're in Nassau or Freeport and mention that you're going to Inagua, people smile. Suddenly, they see you in a new light: You're no longer a run-of-the-mill tourist, but a real traveler, or explorer, someone who's interested in getting to know the country beyond its glitz and glitter. The most southerly part of the Bahamas, Great Inagua thrusts southward toward the Windward Passage and northern Haiti. It is the third largest of the nation's islands. Matthew Town, where the airport is located and the Nassau mailboat puts in once a week, is the only real settlement. There are just two flights a week between here and Nassau. Most of the 1200 or so residents are employed by the Morton Bahamas Salt Company, which collects and dries the sea salt before shipping it to the U.S. for processing. When you first catch a glimpse of the towering pyramids of sodium sparkling in the sun, you may think you're looking at snow-covered hills. Little Inagua, to the northeast, is uninhabited—that is, except for a few wild donkeys. Inagua has nothing to offer scuba divers or golfers, and good beaches are scarce. However, for bird lovers, deep-sea fishing enthusiasts (with their own boats) and those seeking complete tranquility and many opportunities to sit around chatting with easy-going locals, this island can be just the ticket.

COLORFUL WILDLIFE

In the interior, Lake Windsor attracts the world's largest colony of flamingos (known as "fillamingoes" by some residents). In surrounding Inagua National Park, protected by the Bahamas National Trust, more than 200 species of birds flutter around. Among them are roseate spoonbills, herons, egrets and hummingbirds. Visitors may camp out in cabins at the park. Green turtles and wild boars, cows and donkeys are also found roaming unhampered on and around the island. Residents tell a variety of stories explaining how the donkeys got to Inagua. According to some, they were brought by Henri Cristophe, the 19th-century Haitian revolutionary leader who crowned himself king and escaped to this island. Cristophe needed these beasts of burden to tote the gold he took from Haiti. He is said to have hidden his loot in a cave in Inagua's dense forest, and to this day, no one has been able to find it. Eugene O'Neill, the noted American playwright, drew upon this page from history for his play *The Emperor Jones.*

EXPLORING INAGUA

Until World War II, some 5000 people lived on Inagua. Mass emigration during the hard times that followed the war caused the population to shrink dramatically. While some young people have returned after being educated in Nassau, the U.S. or Canada, and some older folk have moved back home, the island is hardly booming. Along the quiet roads that are often empty of people, scrawny dogs are always barking, roosters crowing and goats munching whatever they can find. The former movie house on waterfront Gregory Street, the main avenue, is now used for local talent shows, rehearsals of Inagua's gospel group and a customs office. The profusion of satellite dishes on the island put the cinema out of business. On the main drag, one building stands out among the modest shops and the homes that range from forlorn to fancy: Topped by a clock

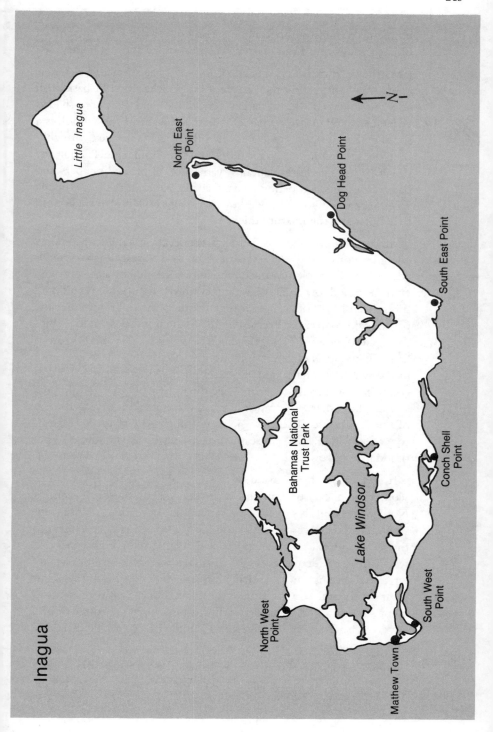

Inagua

tower and fronted by a row of palm trees, the seaside Bahamas Government Administration Building also houses the Commissioner's office, the customs headquarters, the post office and the library.

Matthew Town is very proud of its one professional-level tennis court. At night, young men battle it out on the flood-lit basketball court in Pigeon Park, the large recreational field. The tree-shaded vegetable stand at the corner of Albert Street, near the school, is a social gathering spot, especially when the street is flooded with children decked out in their pink and gray school uniforms. Piled in the tiny wooden stand are plantains, yams, jars of pickled peppers and bags of peanuts and benny seeds. Called sesame in the U.S., benny seeds are turned into benny cakes after being boiled with sugar until they burst and the mixture thickens.

Much of the town's coast is rocky. Especially at sunset, the craggy configurations add to the dramatic vista. The closest beach to hotels is a miniscule but picturesque sandy pocket cupped by slate-gray layered rocks and low cliffs. Walking toward the lighthouse, you'll find this peaceful cove off a short, rugged path to the right, just after the paved main road ends. Erected in 1870, the lighthouse guides ships using the Windward Passage channel between Inagua and Hispaniola, the island of Haiti and the Dominican Republic. The keepers live in the two octagonal wooden houses encircled by verandas. Unless you need the exercise or want to see the intricate workings and huge lens up close, there isn't much point in walking all the way to the top of the lighthouse. The view yields nothing more than the island's rocky coast and its flat landscape broken only by the buildings of petite Matthew Town.

To get to beaches outside of town, you'll need to rent a motor scooter or a car, or befriend a resident. Farquharson Beach, at Northwest Point, is popular for picnics and snorkeling. Cruise ships stop at Inagua once a month, and local guides bring passengers to the sandy shore. In the shade of a small palm grove, brightly painted truck tires provide places to sit. This area was once a settlement of white Bahamians who eventually intermarried with black Inaguans. Near the beach, you'll see the crumbling stone shell of the settlement's waterfront Anglican church. Around the bend, Alfred Sound is a good fishing spot. The Bahamas National Trust Turtle Hatchery is also in this area.

Topps, a bar and restaurant on Astwood Street near the school, packs them in for lunch and dinner. At family-style tables, people dine on chicken and chips, fish and chips, cracked conch, peas and rice, fried plantain, potato salad and lobster. Foreign currency scrawled with names has been plastered on the ceiling by residents and travelers. Sometimes the juke box and the satellite TV compete for patrons' attention. At spacious **Cozy Corner**, you might be served by a woman in bright yellow and green plastic curlers. The wall behind the bar is covered with bills signed by patrons from various countries, as in Topps. A handwritten sign reads "Credit is only allowed if 85 and accompanied by both parents. Leave swearing outside. Keep feet off chairs and stools." Try the curried chicken, plantain and smothered cabbage. The more sedate **Main House**, off Gregory Street in an inn owned by the Morton Bahamas Salt Company, serves three meals a day. The breeze rustles the lacy curtains at the windows in the small dining room. Tables are dressed in crisp linens, some days madras plaids, other times pastels. For breakfast, locals enjoy the chicken souse, but visitors tend to stick to eggs, bacon and toast. Inagua's nights wake up on weekends. Periodically, popularity swings back and forth among **Cozy Corner**, the **Hide Out Cafe** (with its pool hall and large dance hall), the **Afterwork Bar & Restaurant** and **Traveller's Rest** (about nine miles out of town).

WHAT TO SEE AND DO

PERSONAL FAVORITE

Adventure: Driving through salt flats to see the flamingo colony in Inagua National Park.

Inagua National Park

Interior • Maintained by the Bahamas National Trust, this 287-square-mile land-and-sea park takes up more than half the island (some 550 square miles in size). This is where you'll find Inagua's famed (bright) pink flamingos, some of which are sent to join the trained bird act in Nassau's Ardastra Gardens. You'll see the greatest number of flamingos (sometimes hundreds in one flock) and get close up views when the birds are nesting, usually from the end of February or early March through May or June. The 23-mile drive to the National Park camp, where the birds nest, takes about an hour from Matthew Town. Built by the salt company, dirt roads crisscross Lake Windsor, dividing it into huge geometric segments. The name was changed from Lake Rosa (pink in Spanish) to honor the Duke of Windsor, who served as governor of the Bahamas. However, pink remains an apt description of the shallow, placid water that clearly reflects the fluffy white clouds. The pronounced rosy hue comes from the salt in the water. Where dry land was once flooded, sticks and the naked branches of trees protrude from the lake. Other areas are scat-

tered with rocks or bordered by jungled vegetation. You may be lucky
enough to spot wild donkeys, who will keep their distance while snort-
ing at you.

Although Prince Phillip only came to the park's peaceful camp for a
day, some visitors spend the night or several days here in the heart of
the nesting region. The two very basic cabins sleep about 14 people
between them. Sheets and mattresses are provided, but we recommend bringing your own sleeping bag. There are also a cooking shed,
a dining shelter and two showers (1000 gallons of fresh water is always
kept on hand). Around March or April, about six weeks after the birds
hatch, a big party is held the night before the nest count. After feast-
ing on stewed fish and barbecued ribs and chicken, the group that
stays overnight counts nearly 10,000 nests each year. During these
months, the camp can sometimes be reached only by boat. Cost: $50
for one to four people to visit flamingo colony, plus tip for the driver.

Morton Bahamas Salt Company

Outside Matthew Town • At Morton's largest solar salt plant, you'll
learn something about the business that is the foundation of Inagua's
economy. There's a blueish-pink tint to the large, flat bodies of water.
The color is determined by the concentration of brine. At the edges of
the water, the buildup of salt sparkles like snow speckled with dia-
monds. The ponds resemble frozen lakes at the early stages of the
spring thaw. Most impressive are the mountains of salt you'll also see
outside, especially when a worker is at the top of one of these white
hills picking debris out of the sodium crystals. Morton Bahamas sells
its salt to fisheries, chemical plants, highway maintenance groups and
water softener companies. Arrange visits through the Ministry of
Tourism or the Family Island Promotion Board before arrival.

WHERE TO STAY

INEXPENSIVE

Main House

Off Gregory St.• Owned by the Morton Bahamas Salt Co., this well
kept inn is right behind the company's grocery and liquor stores. The
handsome wooden building is enclosed by a picket fence. Two of the
five neat, air-conditioned rooms come with two double beds and a private bath each, while the others have two twins and shared (very modern) baths. The upstairs sitting room (with a TV and phone), the
lounge downstairs (off the dining room) and the balcony are all pleasant places to relax.

Kirk and Eleanor's Walk-Inn

Gregory St.• Owned by the Walkines, who live in the adjacent building, this family-run guesthouse has five rooms. The two smallest share
a bath. The two largest come with double beds, while the others have
twins. Although you'll find clothing racks instead of closets, rooms are

air-conditioned and equipped with TVs. The carved wooden doors and railings add a special touch to this cinderblock guest house. If you happen to stumble out back, you might see clothes fluttering on the line one day and wild boar meat and conch hung up to dry the next.

Ford's Inagua Inn ☆

Victoria St., off Prison St. • One block from Gregory Street, the main thoroughfare, this two-story cinderblock guest house opened in 1969. It is run by Leon Ford and his wife Maude, an elderly couple. Originally from Inagua, Mr. Ford spent two decades on the police force in Detroit, Michigan, his wife's hometown. Each year from March through July, they close their five-room accommodation while they go to the U.S. The brightly painted, sunny rooms share modern baths. Upstairs is a comfortable, homelike sitting room with TV, desk, hardwood floor and balcony tiled in terra-cotta. Although the Fords sometimes serve breakfast, they no longer offer other meals. In the dining/sitting room downstairs, they proudly show off the many postcards they've received from former guests from around the world.

LONG ISLAND

Vegetation flourishes along the coast of Stella Maris, Long Island.

A narrow sliver of land with its top pointing northwest toward the Exuma Cays, Long Island is said to stretch anywhere from 60 to 100 miles. Curiously, there seems to be some question about its length, but no dispute about its being long. It is a little more than a mile wide and, at some of its hilly points, you can see the Atlantic to the east crashing against the craggy rocks and, to the west, the calmer blue waters of Exuma Sound. The hills almost reach the height of Cat Island's highest and, on the ocean side, sharp, jagged coral cliffs drop steeply to the sand-bordered beaches below. The Tropic of Cancer slashes through the island's northern quarter.

This island has some of the most beautiful and deserted beaches in the Bahamas. Some seasoned travelers call the beach at Cape Santa Maria one of the world's best. Located at the northwest tip of the island, it is a three-mile cove of cerulean water and deep, powdery white sand. Other fine beaches dot the coast, and ardent swimmers and sun lovers can stumble upon one after another.

Diving, snorkeling and shelling are ideally suited to the waters and beaches fringing the island. Be sure to visit Cape Santa Maria Beach, just north of Stella Maris. The water, in brilliant contrast to the stark white shore, is an amazing shade of neon turquoise. The soft sand is extremely fine. This is one of the most spectacular beaches in the Bahamas—and the competition is tough. Scuba divers have an almost limitless list of interesting sites including a blue hole and an undersea visit to a colony of tame groupers. A local guidebook lists almost 30 different dive sites. Fishing is another island attraction, and guides take visitors to places teeming with the kind of fish and fishing they seek, whether from land, inland or offshore. Stella Maris Inn at the north of the island arranges both diving and fishing expeditions.

Long Island was a stopping-off point for Columbus on his voyage to the "New World." He called it Fernandina after Ferdinand, the Spanish king. North of Stella Maris, a monument stands in his honor on a cliff at the water's edge. The island is riddled with ominous caves and mysterious ocean holes. The Stella Maris Inn has fashioned one of these grottos into an attractive entertainment setting—a party cave.

At the south of the island, near Clarence Town, the Diamond Crystal Salt Company operates a solar evaporation plant that provides some local employment. Many settlements such as Simms, Deal and others were named for leading families. The people of Long Island fish and farm on land considered fertile compared to the other islands. Some of their houses bear a kind of hex sign painted near the roof line. Religion plays an important role in their lives. In addition to well-attended local church services, traveling, revivalist-type preachers visit up and down the island and obeah, a variation of religious practices from West Africa, is still in evidence.

Father Jerome, the priest who built The Hermitage at the highest point on Cat Island, is also responsible for several churches on this island. One of the oldest in the Bahamas, a gleaming white, Spanish-style structure, is at Clarence Town on southern Long Island. Examples of early native architecture are evident in a sprinkling of the square stone houses with wood rafters and pyramidal, thatched

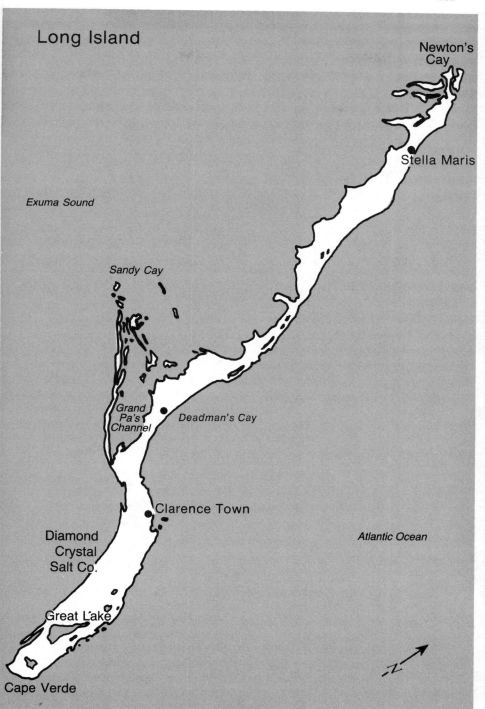

roofs. Many of the older buildings stand in ruins, but the basic design is reflected in later but similar styles built of cinder block.

Two airports serve the island, one at Stella Maris in the north and the other at Deadman's Cay, almost central. A highway, Government Road, runs the island's length.

Clarence Town receives the Nassau mailboat once a week. The boat puts in at Stella Maris or Deadman's Cay once or twice a week. Because of weather conditions and other hazards, the schedule is not always strictly adhered to. Cars can be rented at Stella Maris or at the **Thompson Bay Inn**, which is also a good place for fresh seafood and other inexpensive meals.

A BIT OF HISTORY

The ruins of the Adderley plantation stand at the northern end of the island, not far from the Stella Maris Inn. The remains of three roofless buildings still stand, with a tall stone chimney much in evidence. Large, hand-hewn stones are strewn about, and traces of stone fences can still be seen. Many stout cedar frames clinging to some windows and doors are still intact and give off their fragrant scent.

Near the plantation is the Adderley slave burial ground. It is off the beach near a stand of tall trees, but difficult to get to because of the thick, scratchy underbrush. Once through, however, the mounds of graves can be seen, but they are slowly disappearing from erosion and neglect.

The original Adderley apparently fled the United States with his slaves at the end of the Revolution. He established a cotton plantation and also did subsistence farming. He is said to have been prosperous in his new home. According to his black descendants, Adderley committed suicide upon discovering that his favorite son had formed a liaison with one of the female slaves. The liaison continued, nevertheless. By the time abolition came to the Bahamas, white Adderleys were hard to come by. Many Adderleys and Taylors still live on the island, and the name is a common one throughout the Bahamas.

Mrs. Adderley, the late matriarch and great-grandmother of present-day island Adderleys and Taylors, lived to the age of 130. She never once traveled by boat, automobile or airplane. She felt that the Lord had provided feet as the means of transport and there was no need for artificial, man-made devices. As the oldest living person on the island (and probably in the Bahamas), she was selected to be guest of honor and ribbon cutter at the gala opening of the tennis courts at Stella Maris Inn. The ceremony was attended by local officials and dignitaries as well as representatives from Nassau. Mrs. Adderley's descendants, who live in nearby towns such as Burnt Ground, Clinton and Seymour, will proudly relate the story.

WHAT TO SEE AND DO

PERSONAL FAVORITE

*Adventure: **Scuba Diving** (safely) with sharks.*

Sports

The Stella Maris Inn has a very good diving program with one of the best dive masters in the Bahamas. The adventurous go to a reef where they swim among black-tip, lemon and bull sharks. (According to the instructor, who even pets the sharks, people who fear sharks don't know much about them.) Rum Cay is also a popular diving site. Some say the best diving in the Bahamas is between Long Island and Conception Island. Fishing, boating and tennis are available at Stella Maris.

Dunmore's Cave ★

Deadman's Cay • There is convincing evidence that Arawak Indians used these caves and that, later, pirates made use of them for cargo storage as well as for hiding places.

Dunmore Plantation ★

Deadman's Cay • Lord Dunmore, an early Bahamian governor, had large landholdings here. His estate, commanding a view of the sea, is in ruins, but gateposts remain to mark the entrance to his mansion.

Deadman's Cay Caves ★

Deadman's Cay • These fascinating caves have never been completely explored and continue to reveal new findings. They have stalactites and stalagmites, and Indian drawings are found on the walls. One of the caves has a tunnel that leads out to the ocean.

Father Jerome's Churches ★

Clarence Town • The Catholic missionary, Father Jerome, who also left his mark on Cat Island, built two of the town's churches, one Catholic and the other Anglican.

Spanish Church ★

The Bight • The oldest Spanish church in the Bahamas dates from the time of an early Spanish settlement.

Conception Island ★★

Off the town of Stella Maris • This island, reached by boat, is northeast of Long Island's north tip. Some of the country's best dive sites are found in these waters. Protected by the Bahamas National Trust, it is a sanctuary for tropical and migrating birds, and for the protected green turtles of The Bahamas.

Adderley Plantation   ★

Off Cape Santa Maria, near Stella Maris Inn • The plantation stands in stately ruins, showing its thick walls of hand-hewn stone, its tall chimney and the stone fence that once defined the manor's limits. The remaining pieces of cedar window and door frames are still fragrant. The various houses are difficult to reach because of overgrown vegetation and neglect. Even more difficult to see is the old slave burial ground, which is a short distance north just off the beach. Scattered mounds can be discerned if you brave slashes and scratches to reach the area through the underbrush.

Columbus Point   ★

North of Stella Maris • A dirt road near the bridge to Newton Cay leads to Columbus Point. As you climb the rocky hill, you'll pass a small cove, opening to the ocean, that is good for **snorkeling**. A monument stands on a cliff with sweeping views of the Atlantic and the rocky coast. The inscription reads, "This monument is dedicated to the Gentle Peaceful and Happy Aboriginal People of Long Island, the Lucayans, and to the Arrival of Christopher Columbus on October 17, 1492." Be sure to wear sturdy shoes.

WHERE TO STAY

MODERATE

Stella Maris Inn

The largest of the Long Island hotels, Stella Maris offers cottages, apartments and individual rooms. The hilly, sprawling grounds provide beautiful views of the beach. Just about all watersports are available here, including fishing, boating and an exceptional diving program. Weekly cruises and bikes are complimentary. This German-owned inn is popular for its "rake-and-scrapes," when local musicians play up a storm. Guests are also invited to weekly cave parties. While they dance and dine in the torch-lit grotto, they'll feel like Cro-Magnon Man. As with many Family Island hotels, no keys are used for guest rooms, but there are safety deposit boxes for those who choose to bring the family jewels. Along the road overlooking the shore are the inn's dramatically perched luxurious villas as well as private homes owned mainly by Germans. Direct flights are available from Ft. Lauderdale, Florida.

SAN SALVADOR & RUM CAY

No, *this* San Salvador is not in Central America. Called Guanahani by its early Indian inhabitants, and Watling's Island until 1926, it sits 200 miles southeast of Nassau. Tiny Rum Cay lies just southwest. San Salvador is known worldwide as the place where Columbus first set foot in the "New" World. However, in the mid-1980s, a replotting of his voyage by a *National Geographic* team placed Columbus' landing some 65 miles to the south at Samana Cay, another Bahamian island.

This contention has sparked bitter debates. Some historians maintain that Columbus couldn't possibly have made it past the reef that surrounds Samana Cay in the time indicated in his log. In addition, they note that the Indian village he mentioned had to have been on San Salvador, not only because of the location he described, but also because of archaeological evidence. An excavation of the site in question turned up 15th-century Spanish artifacts, including belt buckles, buttons, a musket ball and a Henry IV of Spain coin from 1454. All have been carbon dated. No such items have been found on Samana Cay. Thus, many people refuse to believe that the "New" World began anywhere but San Salvador. One government official remarked, "I have no concern for the particular island, as long as it's in the Bahamas."

Dixon Hill Lighthouse offers a panoramic view of San Salvador.

By 1527, the entire population of Lucayan Indians had been wiped out by slavery, beatings and disease. However, just as in the United States, this horrifying side to the story is rarely remembered. Every year on the weekend closest to October 12, far-flung native sons and daughters return to San Salvador, and Bahamians from other islands arrive for the spirited Columbus Day celebrations. Music and food

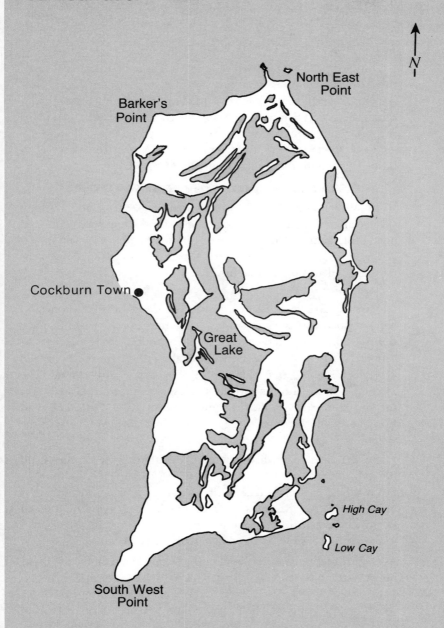

San Salvador

North East Point

Barker's Point

N

Cockburn Town

Great Lake

High Cay

Low Cay

South West Point

stands are everywhere. "You can eat your way around the island," said one veteran. In 1992, the 500th anniversary of Columbus' landing, the festivities were more extensive than ever. The most prominent Columbus monument, a tall white cross, stands in a beachfront park. Columbus Isle Village, a new Club Med, has opened at Bonefish Bay on the west coast, three-and-a-half-miles north of Cockburn Town (pronounced "Coburn").

Along with the white cross, which stands at the edge of Long Bay, three other Columbus monuments honor the disputed event. Near the cross, which is the easiest to find, another monument commemorates the 1968 Olympic Games in Mexico. A spiral walkway leads to the top of this structure, where the bowl of the dark metal sculpture held the Olympic flame that had been brought from Greece. It burned here until the games opened in Mexico City.

EXPLORING SAN SALVADOR

The waters around San Salvador, with reefs, shoals and crashing surf, teem with marine life and are ideal for fishing, snorkeling and diving. Big game fishing for blue marlin, wahoo and yellowfin tuna is very good. June and July are best for marlin. A full-fledged dive center is located at Riding Rock Inn, where you can book scuba packages.

Like most Bahamian islands, San Salvador's crust is limestone and coral, topped with a variety of low-growing tropical brush. In addition to palms, the feathery casuarinas provide a deep green background. Girding the five-by-twelve mile area of this island is the Queen's Highway, a 35-mile stretch of limestone-dusted road. The interior is laced with a network of lakes, ranging from Great Lake, the largest, to smaller ones including Granny Lake, Little Lake and Long Lake, which connects the northeast and northwest arms of the system.

The terrain is somewhat rolling and, at the northeast, the island boasts a hill crowned by gleaming white Dixon Hill Lighthouse. From the top, you can take in the network of lakes and the settlement called United Estates. Offshore, Golding Cay and Man Head Cay, their bleached limestone terrain chalky against the blue-green water, are also visible, along with verdant Green Cay.

An old-timer remembers his childhood days when oil for the lighthouse was unloaded from boats docked at Cockburn Town and transported over land and, by way of the lakes, to Dixon Hill. With other small boys his age, he helped men roll the heavy oil casks from the dock and along the primitive road to Long Lake. There, the barrels were again loaded onto small rowboats and ferried through the lake passages to the lighthouse. The boys who helped with this task were rewarded with British coins, which they quickly traded for candy and other treats.

On the way to the lighthouse, most visitors can't resist snapping photos of the nearby house hung with countless colorful buoys. Solomon Jones and his family don't mind visitors driving up their road to gawk at their creation. Every time he goes to the beach, Mr. Jones collects stray buoys. At Christmastime, he also strings lights all over the building. This house is on a side road near **Ed's First and Last Bar**, which can be seen from the main road. Here in rural U.E., as United Estates is called by locals, you might see women walking gracefully along carrying loads of firewood or other bundles on their heads. Residents say that the island's best cooks live in this town. Everyone looks forward to the periodic food sales held to raise money for various causes.

Cockburn Town, where the airstrip is located and the mailboat docks, is the administrative seat of the island. It is named for Sir Frances Cockburn, the governor of the Bahamas during the 1840s. Riding Rock Inn, the island's main hotel, is about a mile up the road from the town center. The huge waterfront almond tree, where you turn off the main road into town, is also known as the Lazy Tree, since some people enjoy loafing in its shade.

Once the nearby library is relocated to the old grammar school, the building will be turned into a straw market, which is presently beneath the almond tree. The neighboring **Ocean View Club**, which usually serves breakfast and lunch, is owned by "Snake Eyes," who also owns a few waterfront guest cottages north of town. The **San Salvador Gift Shop** sells everything from film and t-shirts to books about the Bahamas. Across from the boat-studded ocean and the dock, three-storey Holy Savior Catholic Church has a bas relief of Christopher Columbus over its entrance. Next door, in the old jail, is the San Salvador Museum.

Along the peaceful streets of Cockburn Town, weather-beaten wooden clapboard houses are mixed in with newer cinder block affairs. If you wander around in the early morning, you might see women washing clothes in metal basins in their yards. Roosters crow, birds chirp, flies buzz and foraging goats let out cries that sound like human babies. **The Harlem Square Club** is a local hangout after dark. Across the street, **Three Ships Restaurant** serves delicious cracked conch, fried grouper and peas and rice. It is owned by Faith Jones, who used to cater meals from her house next door before she built this bar and restaurant. Ms. Jones cooks breakfast upon request and she prepares a limited number of dinners, which usually run out by 6 p.m. **Jake Jones Food Store** stands near the small whitewashed, red-roofed St. Augustine of Canterbury Anglican Episcopal Church.

The remnants and ruins of former plantations remain as reminders of what used to be. The most notable, Watling's Castle, stands on a rise at Sandy Point Estate. The 18th-century plantation house was owned by George Watling, a slaveholder and reputed pirate, for whom the island was once named. Many of the stone walls, with empty window openings, still stand, including the cook house chimney and boundary fences built by slaves. Much of the site is overgrown and inaccessible.

To the east is Farquharson's plantation, another ruin. Charles Farquharson was a justice of the peace for the island and his journal covering the years 1831 and 1832 is one of the few remaining documents of plantation life at the time.

During World War II, there were both British and American installations on the island. The Royal Air Force had a submarine watching station and the United States had a naval base and a coast guard station. Later, the U.S. also maintained a missile tracking station on the island. The naval base, in U.E., now houses the mostly American students of the Bahamas Field Station, where they study marine life and the environment.

At Sandy Point, not far from Watling's Castle, a number of well-appointed private homes are owned by foreigners and built on one of the most beautiful stretches of beach on the island. Not far off, but in a less ideal area away from the beach, is a more modest development of condominiums, also housing non-Bahamians who use them as vacation homes. Near these developments, an interesting place to visit is Dripping Rock, one of the limestone caves that riddle the island.

While exploring the island's wooded areas, be careful not to touch poisonwood or manchioneel. Poisonwood can be a large bush. The glossy dark green leaves, shaped like elongated hearts, have yellow veins and outlines. The sap of the small manchioneel trees, with oval leaves, is caustic. If you're not sure what these plants look like, ask someone to point them out to you.

RUM CAY

Located between San Salvador and Long Island, Rum Cay makes a pleasant sailing destination. It is under the same jurisdiction as San

Salvador. The island boasts rolling hills, miles of empty beaches and caves with pre-Columbian drawings. Port Nelson, the small friendly town, is where you'll find **Kay's Bar**, which periodically hosts parties on weekends, and the **Ocean View Restaurant**. Both are local hangouts before, during and after sundown. The bars and boats communicate by VHF. Hike, bike or rent a jeep to get to the other (eastern) side of the island (about five miles away) to the stunning, deserted beach there. Along the way, up and down gentle rises, you'll pass old farms, salt ponds and wild cows in the distance.

WHAT TO SEE AND DO

PERSONAL FAVORITES

*Adventure: Finding all the **Columbus Monuments**. Visiting the past at crumbling **Watling's Castle**.*

Columbus Monuments   ★ ★
Various locations • A small obelisk, the Tappan Monument (also called the Heloise Marker) sits on the beach at Fernandez Bay (Mile Marker #5, south of Cockburn Town). It was put there on February 25, 1951, by the Tappan gas company, which financed the expedition of the Heloise yawl. Down the road, the tall, stark, white cross (Mile Marker #6), perhaps the most photographed monument, stands at the edge of the water. Yet another monument lies hidden here on the ocean floor. Uniformed schoolchildren often play in the waterfront park where the cross stands.

It takes determination to get to the fourth memorial, the Chicago Monument (Mile Marker #24, east coast). When you turn off the main road, drive a mile to beautiful East Beach (where sharks have been sighted). If you have a four-wheel drive, turn right and go two more miles. Otherwise, get out and walk, or your car will get stuck in the sand. Where the road ends, you'll see a cave to the left, at the water's edge. Take the jungled path to the right, and you'll pass flourishing bromeliads, orchids, frangipani, tall trees with aerial roots and other plants. Amid electric green vegetation, the crude stone structure sits on a narrow piece of land between the churning ocean and the calm bay. The marble plaque reads, "On this spot Christopher Columbus first set foot upon the soil of the New World, erected by the *Chicago Herald*, June 1891." A marble ball represents the world.

Observation Platform   ★
Near Riding Rock Inn • The view from the Observation Tower platform will give you a good idea of the island's inland lake network. Walking about two miles straight ahead from the Inn, past an abandoned military installation filled with rusted, discarded vehicles, visi-

tors can reach the wooden tower. The platform is in need of repair, so sightseers are warned to be careful.

San Salvador Museum   ★

Next to the Catholic church, Cockburn Town • In 1989, the island's former jail was transformed into this petite museum. When the jail closed in 1988, there hadn't been a local prisoner since 1967 (but a few foreign drug smugglers had spent some nights in the tiny dark cells). The exhibits in one room in this two-story building are dedicated to the Lucayan Indians. Another room honors Columbus. Upstairs you'll see old photos of island plantations. Arrange to visit the museum through Iris Fernander, the caretaker, who works in the nearby gift shop.

New World Museum   ★

North Victoria Hill • This one-room museum displays Indian pottery and beads, a prehistoric skull and whale bones, among other intriguing items. Located at palm shaded Blackwood Rock Point Beach, it is 3.5 miles north of Riding Rock Inn.   ***Admission: $1.***

Grahams Harbour   ★

Northern San Salvador • Every October 12, Discovery Day celebrations take place at this huge harbor—dinghy races, dances on the dock, kite flying, three-legged races. When Columbus saw the size of the harbor, he is said to have remarked that it could accommodate all the ships in Christendom. The best view is from the lookout point that was once a helicopter landing pad. However, the scene could do without the water tower in the distance. Swimming here is out, since sharks have been sighted in the area.

Father Schreiner's Grave   ★

Mile Marker #20, near Grahams Harbour • Walk up a rocky inland path, and you'll come to the grave of Father Chrysostomus Schreiner (1859–1928). In 1926, he helped change the name of the island from Watlings to San Salvador. He's also responsible for putting the bas relief of Columbus on the front of the Catholic church in Cockburn Town. He died in the church's upstairs bedroom. Jake Jones, whose nearby store and gas station bear his name, galloped on horseback all the way from Cockburn Town to this side of the island to tell the priest here that Schreiner had died. Next to the grave, the circular stone platform is thought to have been used as an auction block or whipping post during slavery.

Dixon Hill Lighthouse   ★

Dixon Hill, northeast San Salvador • Twice every 25 seconds, this sparkling white lighthouse, built in 1856, sends out a 400,000 candlepower beam that can be seen for 19 miles. The lighthouse is 160 feet high, still hand operated and uses oil. Visitors climbing to the top are astounded by the tiny light source and then transported by the spectacular view of surrounding cays, inland lakes and, far in the distance, the *Chicago Herald* marker on Crab Cay in memory of Columbus' landfall. The lighthouse keeper's house is next door and, if asked, he will show you the inspector's book with signatures dating back to the queen's rule. Below the lighthouse are the tombs of Mary Dixon and her husband John, the stepson of plantation owner Charles Farquharson.

East Beach   ★★

Northeast coast • Although sharks have been spotted in these waters, this scenic beach is worth a trip just for an eyeful. Reminiscent of the Hamptons in New York or Cape Cod in Massachusetts, tall sea wheat sprouts from the sand. But here the shore is pinkish in color and is stunning against the gentle aquamarine water where coral heads appear as deep turquoise patches. Snorkeling is excellent here, if you dare. Note that there's absolutely no shade along most of this nearly six-mile stretch.

Fortune Hill Plantation   ★

Mile Marker #25, eastern San Salvador • When you turn off the main road, the unpaved, bumpy path takes you to this former cotton plantation that was inhabited until 1794 by Burton Williams, who is buried here. One of the octagonal stone buildings was his study, the other, the outhouse. Look for the built-in "couch" inside the structure that has an intact outside staircase. With its tiny windows, the high-walled warehouse where cotton was stored still remains.

Watling's Castle   ★★

Mile Marker #9, Sandy Point Estate, Southern San Salvador • The forlorn remains of a group of stone plantation houses known as Watling's Castle are planted on a rise overlooking the sea. Named for George Watling, a onetime pirate whose name the island bore for a time, the crumbling walls still stand with gaping windows. You'll also see stone boundary walls and the cookhouse oven. Much of the site is inaccessible because of the surrounding overgrown vegetation. As time-worn as they are, the ruins are quite impressive, especially when the empty stone shells are seen from below.

Watling's Castle had the island's only black plantationist, Henry Storr, who came with the British Loyalists from the Carolinas after the American Revolution. He owned black slaves along with his white counterparts. Some slave huts remain, hidden by the vegetation on both sides of the road, but they are difficult to reach since access is so overgrown. This was the island's last active plantation. People lived and farmed here until 1910.

Nearby is the **Lookout Tower**, from which people once watched approaching ships. Climb it and you can see the ocean on two sides, a duck pond and Watling's Castle in the distance. You'll pass an octagonal private house next to the Tower. Be sure to respect the privacy of the home dwellers.

Farquharson's Plantation   ★

Pigeon Creek • On the eastern side of the island, this old estate is now
in ruins. It was once owned by Charles Farquharson, the island's justice of the peace. You'll see the remains of the main house, slave quarters, fireplaces and ovens.

Big Well   ★

Sandy Point Estate • Big Well is south of the Columbus monument at
Long Bay. The well is almost 150 years old and was an early source of
fresh water for locals.

Dripping Rock   ★

Sandy Point • This is one of the many limestone caverns at the southern end of the island. There are fruit trees in this fertile aea and the
cool cave encloses a fresh water well.

WHERE TO STAY

SAN SALVADOR

MODERATE TO EXPENSIVE

Club Med Columbus Isle   ★ ★ ★ ★ ★

One of Club Med's most attractive and upscale villages, Columbus
Isle made its debut in 1992. Both public areas and guest rooms are
decked out with a stunning collection of art and artifacts from the
Pacific, Asia, South America and Africa. Beautifully carved wooden
doors from Mali, bird cages from India, feathered Brazilian headdresses, colorful Turkish rugs and dramatic staues from Thailand and
the Ivory Coast are everywhere. If you'd like to know more about
what you see, take the art tour.

Guest rooms (all with TVs, refrigerators and safes) are found in two-
story gingerbread cottages, painted bright blue, pink, yellow, red and
green. Since they are ranged along a spectacular beach that goes on
and on, you may have to walk quite a distance to restaurants or the
sports center. But with such wonderful surroundings, most guests
welcome the chance for long strolls. Paths inlaid with patterns made
by stones wind through the property so that humans don't disturb the
natural beauty of the rolling grassy dunes between the cottages and
the beach.

The cheers and whistles that accompany the daily activities in and
around the "overflowing" pool by the main building may be a bit loud
for some. However, this resort is so expansive that it is easy to find a
quiet corner. Meals in the main dining room are lavish buffets. Specialized restaurants feature Italian and French cuisine. Veterans of
other Club Meds have reported that Columbus Isle serves some of the
best eats by far.

Like camp counselors for adults, the GO's are always on hand to make
sure vacationers are enjoying themselves. Pool aerobics, a variety of

watersports (including scuba), tennis and volleyball tournaments, sunset cruises, guided bike trips, and island tours are all part of the fun. At least once a week, guests are invited to join GOs on stage in the nightly entertainment at the theater. All meals, airport transfers and most activities are included in the rates.

MODERATE

Riding Rock Inn ☆☆☆

Cockburn Town • Named for offshore boulders that once rolled on the ocean floor, Riding Rock Inn was the main tourist accommodation on San Salvador until the birth of the island's Club Med. Although it is located a stone's throw from the island's only airstrip, noise is not a problem since planes fly in and out infrequently. Most guests are serious divers, and many book scuba packages. Everything from lessons to rental of wetsuits and underwater cameras is available. Film can be processed at the nearby underwater photography school, next to Riding Rock Inn's marina. Services are on hand here for boating and fishing.

Rooms are set along the rim of a rocky or sandy shore. Some look out to the ocean, and the remaining face inland with views of the swimming pool, the main road and the lush island foliage. The newer two-story building houses the nicest units, each with two double beds, a TV, a phone, a refrigerator and a balcony or patio with an ocean view. Plainly furnished, the rooms all have patios and chaises that invite sprawling. The patios on the seaside are ideal for lounging and watching the often glorious sunsets. Some 50 yards south of the inn, the rocks have been cleared away for a serviceable sandy beach with a panoramic view to the north and south. In addition to the pool, there are tennis courts, which are almost always free for playing. For sightseeing, motor bikes, bicycles and cars are available for rent just outside the office.

Bahamian specialties are served in the dining room, as well as American and Continental cuisine. Among the local dishes are conch chowder, okra soup, peas and rice and turtle steak. Especially mouthwatering when toasted and laden with butter at breakfast, homebaked bread is often served. Off the dining room and adjacent Driftwood Bar, an oceanfront deck runs the length of the building. The bar is where locals and visitors get to know each other over beer, tropical drinks and freshly made popcorn. The ceiling is panelled in—what else?—driftwood, which has been carved and scrawled with patrons' names and initials. Many people try their hand at the addictive Ring Game: they attempt to swing a ring attached to a long string so that it catches onto a hook on the wall across the room. On Wednesday nights, a live band usually plays and American students from the Bahamas Field Station in U.E. are bused in for a party. Most locals come to the bar on Friday nights.

INEXPENSIVE

Ocean View Villas

Run by Cliff "Snake Eyes" Fernander, these three cottages sit across the road from the shore, north of Cockburn Town. Individual rooms are rented in the three-bedroom/two-bath villa, and guests share the living room and kitchenette. One of the two-bedroom/one-bath cottages is air-conditioned while the other is not. All have ceiling fans. Snake Eyes can make arrangements for visitors to rent bicycles, scooters, boats, or cars.

ACCOMMODATIONS CHART

FACILITIES KEY

BT	Boating	PCF	Physically Challenged Facilities
F	Fishing	MP	Mopeds
G	Golf	S	Water-skiing
B	Beach	M/D	Marina-Dock
SC	Scuba	HC	Health Club
T	Tennis	HB	Horseback Riding
WSF	Windsurfing	CA	Casino
PS	Parasailing	DI	Disco
P	Swimming Pool	BA/B	Barber-Beauty Salon

CREDIT CARDS

A	American Express
B	Barclays

CREDIT CARDS

BA	BankAmericard
T	Texaco
C	Carte Blanche
D	Diners Club
M	MasterCard
V	Visa

MEAL PLANS

CP	Continental Plan: Light Breakfast
EP	European Plan: Room only
FB	Full American Breakfast
MAP	Modified American Plan: Breakfast and Dinner
FAP	Full American Plan: Three meals

The following approximate daily rates, which are for two people sharing a standard double room, are all EP, in-season (December through April). Unfortunately, rates for single travelers are usually not much lower than the cost of a double room for two.

For MAP, add from $30 to $70 per person, per day.

CABLE BEACH

Establishment, Mailing Address, Telephone	Meal Plans Offered	No. Rooms	Double Room (in Season)	Credit Cards	Facilities	Other
Cable Beach Manor P.O. Box N-8333 Nassau ☎ (809) 327-7785 (800) 327-7788	EP	44	$125	A, M, V, D	B, P	studios, 1 and 2 bedrooms

CABLE BEACH

Establishment, Mailing Address, Telephone	Meal Plans Offered	No. Rooms	Double Room (in Season)	Credit Cards	Facilities	Other
Carnival's Crystal Palace Resort & Casino P.O. Box N-8306 Nassau ☎ (809) 327-6200 (800) 453-5301 fax: (809) 327-4346		860	$215	A. M. V. D	B, P, T, G, HC, PDF	duplex suites available room safes, 24-hour room service
Days Inn Casuarina's of Cable Beach P.O. Box N-4016 Nassau ☎ (809) 327-8153 (800) 325-2525	EP	80	$100	A, M, V, D	P	on Cable Beach, some kitchenettes complimentary continental breakfast
Forte Nassau Beach Hotel Cable Beach Nassau ☎ (809) 327-7711 (800) 225-5843 fax: (809) 327-8829	EP, BP, CP, FAP	411	$120	A, M, V, D, C, TF	P, B, BT, F, SC, S, T, PS, PDF	shops, entertainment, complimentary tennis, all-inclusive section, children's village
Le Meridien Royal Bahamian P.O. Box N-10422 Nassau ☎ (809) 327-6400 (800) 543-4300 fax: (809) 327-6961	EP	173	$185-200	A, M, V, D	B, P, T, BT	on Cable Beach, suites and villas available, complimentary transportation to casino
Radisson Cable Beach Casino & Golf Resort P.O. Box N 4914 West Bay Street, Nassau ☎ (809) 327-6000 (800) 333-3333	EP	682	$170	A, M, V	P, PB, T, G, BT, CA, SC, S, WSF	
Wyndham Ambassador Beach Hotel P.O. Box N-3026 Nassau ☎ (809) 327-8231 fax: (809) 327-6727	EP, MAP	400	$140	A, M, D	B, P, BT, SC, WSF	health club, complimentary windsurfers, sunfish

NASSAU

Establishment, Mailing Address, Telephone	Meal Plans Offered	No. Rooms	Double Room (in Season)	Credit Cards	Facilities	Other
British Colonial Beach Resort P.O. Box N-7148 Nassau ☎ (809) 322-3301 (800) 528-1234 fax: (809) 323-8248	EP, MAP	325	$140	A, BA, B, C, D, M, V	B, P, T, BA/ B, F, S, SC, MP, DI, PDF	shops, shuffleboard, ping pong, restaurants, downtown
Buena Vista Hotel P.O. Box N-564 Nassau ☎ (809) 322-2811 fax: (809) 322-5881	EP	5	$100	A, M, V, D, C		downtown, 19th-century mansion
Dillet's Guest House Dunmore Ave. & Strachan St. Chippingham, Nassau ☎ (809) 325-1133 fax: (809) 325-7183		7	$50	V, M		afternoon tea, senior citizen discount, continental breakfast
El Greco Hotel P.O. Box N-4187 Nassau ☎ (809) 325-1121	EP	26	$100	A, M, V, D	P	close to downtown
Grand Central Hotel P.O. Box N-4084 Nassau ☎ (809) 322-8356	EP	35	$95	A, D, M, V		
Graycliff Hotel P.O. Box N-10246 Nassau ☎ (809) 322-2796	CP	21	$165 (CP)	A, M, V, D, C, B	P	good food, old mansion
Nassau Harbour Club Hotel & Marina P.O. Box SS5755 Nassau ☎ (809) 393-0771 (800) 327-0787 fax: (809) 393-5393	EP	50	$90	A, M, V	P	shopping center across street, complimentary ferry to Paradise Island

Establishment, Mailing Address, Telephone	Meal Plans Offered	No. Rooms	Double Room (in Season)	Credit Cards	Facilities	Other
NASSAU						
Ocean Spray Hotel P.O. Box N-3035 Nassau ☎ (809) 322-8032 (800) 327-0787 fax: (809) 325-5731	EP	30	$90	A, M, V, D		
Orange Hill Beach Inn P.O. Box N-8583 Nassau ☎ (809) 327-7157 (800) 327-0787 fax: (809) 325-1097	EP	21	$90	A, M, V	P, B	kitchen facilities
The Parliament Inn P.O. Box N-4138 Nassau ☎ (809)322-2836/7 (800) 327-0787 fax: (809) 326-7196	CP	10	$70 (CP)	A, M, V, D	MP, PDF	downtown Nassau, good restaurant
Parthenon Hotel P.O. Box N-4930 Nassau ☎ (809) 322-2643	EP	18	$65	A, M, V		downtown, near beach, breakfast in room or on patio
Pilot House Hotel P.O. Box N-4941 Nassau ☎ (809) 322-8431 (800) 327-0787	EP	80	$100	A, M, V, C, D	P, BA/B, BT, F, SC	
Ramada South Ocean Golf & Beach Resort 808 Adelaide Road Nassau ☎ (809) 362-4391 (800) 228-9898 fax: (809) 362-4728	MAP, EP	250	$130	A, M, V	B, P, T, G, SC, WSF, PS	

NASSAU

Establishment, Mailing Address, Telephone	Meal Plans Offered	No. Rooms	Double Room (in Season)	Credit Cards	Facilities	Other
Villas on Coral Island P.O. Box N-7797 Nassau ☎ (809) 328-1036 (800) 328-8814 fax: (809) 323-3202	CP	22	$200	A, M, V, D		each room has private pool, complimentary continental breakfast, free snorkeling, complimentary marine park, downtown transport

Paradise Island

Establishment, Mailing Address, Telephone	Meal Plans Offered	No. Rooms	Double Room (in Season)	Credit Cards	Facilities	Other
Atlantis, Paradise Island P.O. Box N-4777 Nassau ☎ (809) 363-2000 (800) 321-3000 fax: (305) 893-2866	EP, MAP	1150	$170	A, M,V, D	P, T, B, SC, WSF, HC, CA, DI, PDF	aquarium and waterscape
Bay View Village P.O. Box SS-6308 Nassau ☎ (809) 363-2555 (800) 321-3000 (800) 327-0787 fax: (809) 363-2370	EP	72	$165	A, M, V	PDF	apartments, villas, laundry room, 3 pools
Comfort Suites Paradise Island P.O. Box SS 6202 Nassau ☎ (809) 363-3680 (800) 228-5150 fax: (809) 363-2588	CP	150	$150	A, M, V, D	P, PDF	use of Paradise Is. Resort & Casino beach facilities, tennis courts, health spa, family rates
Club Med Paradise Island P.O. Box N-7137 Nassau ☎ (809) 363-2640 (800) CLUBMED fax: (809) 363-3496	FAP	620 beds	call for rates	A, M, V	P, B, T	weekly rates vary according to point of origin—airfare included
Club Land'Or P.O. Box SS-6429 Nassau ☎ (809) 363-2400 (800 321-3000	BP, MAP	72	$225 (BP)	A, M, V, D		apartments and rooms, mostly time-share

NASSAU

Establishment, Mailing Address, Telephone	Meal Plans Offered	No. Rooms	Double Room (in Season)	Credit Cards	Facilities	Other
Golden Palm Resort P.O. Box N-3881-1 Nassau ☎ (809) 363-3309 (809) 363-3312 (800) 832-2789 fax: (809) 363-3121	EP	16	$165	A, V, M	P	3-night min. stay
Harbour Cove--Paradise Island Fun Club P.O. Box SS 6249 Paradise Island ☎ (809) 363-2561 (800) 952-2426 fax: (809) 363-3803	FAP	250	$200	A, V, M	P, B, T	all inclusive, 3-night minimum
Ocean Club Golf & Tennis Resort P.O. Box N-4777 Nassau ☎ (809) 363-2501 (800) 321-3000 fax: (305) 893-2866	EP, MAP	70	$275	A, M, V, D	P, B, BT, S, SC, M/D, G, T	complimentary transportation to casino
Paradise Paradise P.O. Box SS-6259 Nassau ☎ (809) 363-3000 (800) 321-3000 fax: (305) 893-2866	EP, MAP	100	$115	M, V	B, SC, P	special sports package deals available
The Pink House P.O. Box N 1968 Nassau ☎ (809) 363-3363 (800) 363-3363 fax: (809) 393-1786	CP	4	$90	A, V, M		afternoon tea
Pirate's Cove Holiday Inn P.O. Box 6214 Nassau ☎ (809) 363-2101 (800) HOLIDAY fax: (809) 363-2206	EP, MAP, BP, FAP	535	$200	A, M, V, D	BT, DI, PB, F, S, SC, T, PDF	rents motor scooters, children's program, refrigerators, coffee makers

NASSAU

Establishment, Mailing Address, Telephone	Meal Plans Offered	No. Rooms	Double Room (in Season)	Credit Cards	Facilities	Other
Radisson Grand Resort Paradise Island P.O. Box SS-6307 Paradise Island ☎ (809) 363-3500 (800) 333-3333 fax: (809) 363-3193	EP, MAP	360	$210	A, M, V, D	B, P, BT, F, T, G, PS	all rooms ocean view, refrigerators in rooms, coffee makers, free transport on Paradise Island
Sunrise Beach Club & Villas P.O. Box SS-6519 Nassau ☎ (809) 363-2234 (809) 363-2250 (800) 451-6078 fax: (809) 363-2252	EP	35	$180		B,P	time-share units available, complimentary breakfast kit
Villas in Paradise P.O. Box 6379 SS Nassau ☎ (809) 363-2998 (800) 321-3000 fax: (809) 363-2703	EP	30	$135	A, M, V		some villas with private pools, 1 day free car for stays of 3 to 6 nights, 2 days free car for 7-night stays

FREEPORT

Establishment, Mailing Address, Telephone	Meal Plans Offered	No. Rooms	Double Room (in Season)	Credit Cards	Facilities	Other
Atlantik Beach Hotel P.O. Box F-531 Freeport ☎ (809) 373-1444 (800) 622-6770 fax: (809) 373-7481	BP	175	$140 (BP)	A, BA, M, D, M, V	PDF, P, T	situated on beach, complimentary transport to golf course

FREEPORT

Establishment, Mailing Address, Telephone	Meal Plans Offered	No. Rooms	Double Room (in Season)	Credit Cards	Facilities	Other
Bahamas Princess Resort & Casino P.O. Box F-207 Freeport ☎ (212) 582-8100 (800) 223-1818 (809) 352-6721	MAP, EP	960	$150	A, M, V, D	P, G, T, MP, PDF	free shuttle to beach
Castaways Resort P.O. Box 2629 Freeport ☎ (809) 352-6682 (800) 327-0787	EP	138	$85	A, M, V, D	P, DI	free shuttle to beach
Coral Beach Hotel P.O. Box F-2468 Freeport ☎ (809) 373-2468	EP	10	$85	A	B, P, F	golf privileges
Club Fortuna Beach Resort Freeport ☎ (809) 373-4000 Miami (305) 538-5467 (800) 847-4502 FAX (809) 373-5555	FAP	204	$280	major	B, P, T, BT, WSF	all-inclusive
Deep Water Cay Club P.O. Box 40039 Freeport ☎ (809) 359-4831 (407) 684-3958 fax: (407) 684-0959	FAP	11	$1050 (FAP)	none	F, PB	east end, own air strip, fishing skiff, guide and bait included in rates; minimum stay is 3 nights, closed Aug. and Sept., private airstrip, cottages
Lucayan Beach Resort & Casino P.O. Box F-336, Freeport/Lucaya ☎ (809) 373-7777 (800) 772-1227 fax: (809) 373-2826	EP, MAP	243	$160	A, M, V, T, G, BT, F	WSF, P, B,	

FREEPORT

Establishment, Mailing Address, Telephone	Meal Plans Offered	No. Rooms	Double Room (in Season)	Credit Cards	Facilities	Other
Port Lucaya Resort & Yacht Club Bell Channel Bay Road P.O. Box F-2452 Freeport/Lucaya ☎ (809) 373-6618 (800)LUCAYA-1 fax: (809) 373-6652	EP	160	$110	M, V, A	M/D, P	attracts cruise ship passengers, near beach, next to Port Lucaya Marketplace
Radisson Resort on Lucaya Beach P.O. Box F-2496 Freeport ☎ (809) 373-1333 (800) 333-3333 fax: (809) 373-8662	CP	500	$155	A, M, V	P, B, HC, T, BT	
Running Mon Marina & Resort P.O. Box F-2663 Freeport ☎ (809) 352-6834 fax: (809) 352-6835	EP	32	$110	A, M, V	P, F	5 min from beach
Silver Sands Sea Lodge P.O. Box F-2385 Freeport ☎ (809) 373-5700	EP, MAP	164	$105	A, M, V, D, B	B, BT, T, SC, P	apartments and suites
Xanadu Beach Resort & Marina P.O. Box F-2438 Freeport ☎ (809) 352-6782 (800) 222-3788 (804) 270-4313	EP, MAP	184	$165	A, BA, D, M, V	T, BT, P	marina on premises and villas

THE ABACOS

Establishment, Mailing Address, Telephone	Meal Plans Offered	No. Rooms	Double Room (in Season)	Credit Cards	Facilities	Other
Walkers Cay						
Walker's Cay Hotel & Marina 700 S.W. 34 St. Ft. Lauderdale, FL. ☎ (809) 352-5252 (800) 432-2092 fax: (809) 352-3301	EP, MAP	62	$125	A, D	P, DI, M/ D, BT, F, S,SC, T	villas and suites
Spanish Cay						
The Inn at Spanish Cay P.O. Box 882 Coopers Town, Abaco (809) 365-0083 fax: (809) 365-0466	EP	12	$180-$275	M, V	T, B	
Green Turtle Cay						
Bluff House Club & Marina Green Turtle Cay ☎ (809) 365-4247 fax: (809) 365-4248	EP, MAP	25	$100	M, V	BT, SC, F	closed Sept.-Oct., all rooms have ocean views
Green Turtle Club P.O. Box 270 Green Turtle Cay ☎ (809) 365-4271 fax: (809) 365-4272	EP, MAP	30	$150	A, M, V	P, B, M/D, BT, F, WSF, T	closed Sept-Oct., hosts annual fishing tournament and annual regatta, units available with kitchens, boat rentals
New Plymouth Club & Inn Green Turtle Cay ☎ (809) 365-4161 fax: (809) 365-4138	MAP	9	$110 MAP)	none	BT, F	pets allowed

THE ABACOS

Establishment, Mailing Address, Telephone	Meal Plans Offered	No. Rooms	Double Room (in Season)	Credit Cards	Facilities	Other
Sea Star Beach Cottages P.O. Box 282 Gilam Bay Green Turtle Cay ☎ (809) 359-6592 (800) 752-0166	EP	12	$75	none	BT, SC, F	
Great Guana Cay						
Guana Beach Resort & Marina P.O. Box 474, Marsh Harbour Great Guana Cay ☎ (809) 367-3590 800-BAREFOOT fax: (809) 367-3590	EP, MAP	15	$130	M, V	B, M/D, BT, S, F	7 miles of beach
Pinder's Cottages Great Guana Cay Abaco ☎ (809) 367-2207	EP	4 cottages	rates on request	none	BT, F, SC	
Elbow Cay						
Abaco Inn Hope Town, Abaco ☎ (809) 366-0133 (800) 468-8799 fax: (809) 366-0113	EP, MAP	12	$130	M, V	P, B, M/D, SC, F, S, WSF	complimentary bicycles, boats rented, pets allowed, closed Sept. and Oct.
Hope Town Harbour Lodge Hope Town, Abaco ☎ (809) 366-0095 (800) 626-5690	EP	21	$165	A, M, V	P, M/D, BT, SC, F, WSF	closed Sept-Oct.
Sea Spray Resort & Villas White Sound Elbow Cay, Abaco ☎ (800) 327-0787 fax: (809) 366-0065	EP	9	$500-$850 per week		BT, F, B,WSF	1 and 2 bedroom villas, boat rentals, complimentary use of windsurfers and sunfish, bakery on premises, catered meals available

THE ABACOS

Establishment, Mailing Address, Telephone	Meal Plans Offered	No. Rooms	Double Room (in Season)	Credit Cards	Facilities	Other
Hope Town Hideaways Hope Town, Elbow Cay, Abaco ☎ (809) 366-0224 fax: (809) 367-2954	EP, MAP	4 villas	$200	M, V	BT	on harbor, with dock, monthly rates available
Tangelo Hotel P.O. Box 830 Coopers Town, Abaco ☎ (800) 688-4752 (809) 365-2222 fax: (809) 365-2200		12	$66	none		
Club Soleil Resort Hope Town, Elbow Cay Abaco	EP	6	$100		BT, F, M/D, P	boat rentals
Marsh Harbour						
Conch Inn P.O. Box 469, Marsh Harbour ☎ (809) 367-2800 fax: (809) 367-2980	EP	9	$90	A, M, V	P, M/D, BT, SC, S	bicycles rented, good scuba operation
Great Abaco Beach Hotel P.O. Box 511 Marsh Harbour ☎ (809) 367-2158 (800) 468-4799 fax: (809) 367-2819	EP	20	$170	A, M, V	B, P, T	on waterfront, adjoins a marina, villas available, building additional rooms
Island Breezes Motel P.O. Box 20030 Marsh Harbour ☎ (809) 367-3776 fax: (809) 367-4179		8	$82	M, V		
The Lofty Fig Villas Box 437 Marsh Harbour Abaco ☎ (809) 367-2681	EP	6	$80			no pets

THE ABACOS

Establishment, Mailing Address, Telephone	Meal Plans Offered	No. Rooms	Double Room (in Season)	Credit Cards	Facilities	Other
Pelican Beach Villas P.O. Box AB 20304 Marsh Harbour, Abaco ☎ (809) 367-3600 (800) 642-7268		5 villas	$150 dbl rm $950-$1000 per wk	A, M, V		hammocks, boat rentals

Man-O-War Cay

Establishment, Mailing Address, Telephone	Meal Plans Offered	No. Rooms	Double Room (in Season)	Credit Cards	Facilities	Other
Schooner's Landing Resort Man-O-War Cay ☎ (809) 365-6072 fax: (809) 365-6285			$175		B, F, BT	2-bedroom units, 1-1/2 baths

ACKLINS/CROOKED ISLAND

Establishment, Mailing Address, Telephone	Meal Plans Offered	No. Rooms	Double Room (in Season)	Credit Cards	Facilities	Other
Crooked Island Beach Inn Colonel Hill ☎ (809) 336-2096	EP	11	$50	none	B, F, BT	transport provided to and from airport
Pittstown Point Landing Bahamas Caribbean International P.O. Box 9831 Mobile, Alabama 36691 (205) 666-4482	EP, FAP	12	$100	A, M, V	B, BT, F, WSF, SC	closed Sept., Oct., bicycles rented, airstrip nearby
T & S Guest House Church Grove ☎ Church Grove	EP	10	$60	none	BP, F	

ANDROS

Establishment, Mailing Address, Telephone	Meal Plans Offered	No. Rooms	Double Room (in Season)	Credit Cards	Facilities	Other
Cargill Creek						
Andros Island Bonefish Camp Cargill Creek Andros ☎ (809) 329-5167	EP	16				
Cargill Creek Fishing Lodge Cargill Creek , Andros P.O. Box 21668 Ft. Lauderdale, FL 33335 ☎ (809) 329-5129 fax: (809) 329-5046	FAP	15	$270 (FAP)	A, M	F,SC	game room, daily movies, diving
Behring Point						
Behring Point Charlie's Haven Behring Pt. Andros ☎ (809) 329-5261	EP					
Andros Town Area						
Small Hope Bay Lodge Andros Town Area P.O. Box 21667 Ft. Lauderdale, FL 33335-1667 ☎ (809) 368-2014 (800) 223-6961 fax: (809) 368-2015	FAP	20 plus 3-bed-room, 3 bath villa	$285 (FAP)	A, V, M	B, BT, F, SC, WSF	complimentary bicycles, closed Sept.-Oct., Androsia works nearby
Chickcharnie Hotel Fresh Creek Andros Town ☎ (809) 368-2025	EP	8	$45	none	BT	game room, daily movies, diving

ANDROS

Establishment, Mailing Address, Telephone	Meal Plans Offered	No. Rooms	Double Room (in Season)	Credit Cards	Facilities	Other
Lighthouse Yacht Club & Marina P.O. Box Andros Town ☎ (809) 368-2305 (800) 825-5255 fax: (809) 368-2300	EP	20	$135		P, BT, M/D, F	

Mangrove Cay

Mangrove Cay Bannister's Cottages Lisbon Creek, Mangrove Cay ☎ (809) 369-0188	EP, MAP	6	$75 (MAP)	none	BT, F, WSF	bicycles rented, shared baths, adjacent club with fish and turtle pool
Longley's Guest House Lisbon Creek Mangrove Cay ☎ (809) 325-1581	EP	5	$55	none	PB, BT, F, SC	
Moxey's Guest House Mangrove Cay ☎ (809) 329-4159	EP, FAP	6	$55	A	B, F	pool room, dancing club, some private baths

Congo Town

Emerald Palms by the Sea P.O. Box 800 Driggs Hill ☎ (809) 369-2661 (800) 325-5099 fax: (809) 369-2667	MAP	20	$155	A, M, V	P, T, BT, SC, B, F, WSF, HB	superb food and ambience

THE BERRY ISLANDS

Establishment, Mailing Address, Telephone	Meal Plans Offered	No. Rooms	Double Room (in Season)	Credit Cards	Facilities	Other
The Chub Cay Club P.O. Box 661067 Miami Springs, FL 33266 ☎ (305) 445-7830 (809) 325-1490 (800) 662-8555 fax: (809) 322-5199	EP, MAP	17	$90	A, M, V	M/D, B, F, P, T, BT	permanently docked houseboat
Great Harbour Cay Berry islands, Bahamas 3512 N. Ocean Drive Hollywood, FL 33019 (305) 921-9084 fax: (305) 921-1044 (800) 343-7256 (809) 367-8838		villas and townhouses	$175-$250	major		private yacht club, boat rentals, 81-slip marina

BIMINI

Establishment, Mailing Address, Telephone	Meal Plans Offered	No. Rooms	Double Room (in Season)	Credit Cards	Facilities	Other
Bimini Big Game Fishing Club P.O. Box 523238 Miami, FL 33152 ☎ (809) 347-2391 (800) 327-4149 fax: (809) 347-3392	EP	50	$150	A, M, V	M/D, P, BT, F, S, SC	owned by Bacardi Rum
Bimini Blue Waters Resort P.O. Box 627 Alice Town ☎ (809) 347-2166 fax: (809) 347-2293	EP	12	$100	A, M, V	P, B, M/D, BT	water view on each side of hilltop building
Compleat Angler Hotel P.O. Box 601 Alice Town ☎ (809) 347-3122	EP	12	$85	A	SC	Hemingway memorabilia

BIMINI

Establishment, Mailing Address, Telephone	Meal Plans Offered	No. Rooms	Double Room (in Season)	Credit Cards	Facilities	Other
Sea Crest Hotel P.O. Box 654 Alice Town ☎ (809) 347-2071	EP	14	$90	none		
Admiral Hotel Bailey Town ☎ (809) 347-2347	EP	27	$85	none		

CAT ISLAND

Establishment, Mailing Address, Telephone	Meal Plans Offered	No. Rooms	Double Room (in Season)	Credit Cards	Facilities	Other
Fernandez Bay Village P.O. Box 2126 Ft. Lauderdale, FL 33303 ☎ (305) 792-1905 (809) 342-3043 (800) 940-1905 fax: (809) 342-3051	EP, MAP	5 cottages	$170	A	B, BT	1-2 person and 1-8 person cottages, airstrip

ELEUTHERA

Establishment, Mailing Address, Telephone	Meal Plans Offered	No. Rooms	Double Room (in Season)	Credit Cards	Facilities	Other
Harbour Island						
Coral Sands Hotel Coral Sands Harbour Island ☎ (809) 333-2350 (800) 327-0787 fax: (809) 333-2368	MAP, EP	33	$160	A, M, D, V	B, T, F, SC	3-mile beach, closed Sept.-Nov., night tennis, extensive wine cellar
Dunmore Beach Club P.O. Box 122 Harbour Island ☎ (809) 333-2200 fax: (809) 333-2429	FAP	12	$325 (FAP)	none	B, T, F, BT	closed May-July

ELEUTHERA

Establishment, Mailing Address, Telephone	Meal Plans Offered	No. Rooms	Double Room (in Season)	Credit Cards	Facilities	Other
Ocean View Club P.O. Box 134 Harbour Island ☎ (809) 333-2276	FAP	10	$125 (FAP)	M, V, C	F, SC, P, B, T, BT	
Rock House General Delivery, Harbour Island Overseas Operator ☎ (809) 333-2053	FAP	7	$100	A, M, V	T, WSF	closed Sept.-Oct., 2-night minimum stay
Romora Bay Club P.O. Box 146 Harbour Island ☎ (809) 333-2325 (800) 327-8286 fax: (305) 427-2746	EP, MAP	38	$158	A, M, V	T, M/D, F, SC	closed Sept.-Nov., dive packages available, rooms and suites
Runaway Hill Club P.O. Box 31 Harbour Island ☎ (809) 333-2150 fax: (809) 333-2420	EP, MAP	10	$172	A, M, V	P, B	homelike atmosphere, closed day after Labor Day to mid-Oct.
Tingum Village P.O. Box 61 Harbour Island ☎ (809) 333-2161	EP, MAP, CP, BP, FAP	12	$85	A, M, V		good food and parties
Valentine's Inn & Yacht Club P.O. Box 1 Harbour Island ☎ (809) 333-2080 (809) 333-2142 Florida (305) 491-1010	EP, MAP	21	$125	M, V	P, B, M/D, WSF, BA/B	closed Sept., hot tub, X-rated island
Gregory Town						
Caridon Cottages P.O. Box 5206 Gregory Town ☎ (809) 332-2690 Ext. 230	EP, MAP	14 cottages	$30	none	T, BT, F, SC	open year round, add $10 MAP, scooter rental

ELEUTHERA

Establishment, Mailing Address, Telephone	Meal Plans Offered	No. Rooms	Double Room (in Season)	Credit Cards	Facilities	Other
The Cove Eleuthera P.O. Box 1548 Gregory Town ☎ (809) 332-0142 (800)552-5960 fax: (201) 835-5783	EP, MAP, FAP	28	$110	A, M, V	P, B	good snorkeling
Oleander Gardens P.O. Box 5165 Gregory Town ☎ (809) 333-2058	EP					
Governer's Harbour						
Cigatoo Inn P.O. Box 86 Governor's Harbour ☎ (809) 332-2343 fax: (809) 332-2159	EP, MAP	28	$100	A, V, M	P, T, F, BT	refrigerators
Laughing Bird Apartments P.O. Box 76 Governor's Harbour ☎ (809) 322-2012 fax: (809) 332-2358	EP	8	$75	V, M		children under 4 free, 4-12 half price, weekly rates available, free tour of town and nearby beaches
Club Med Eleuthera P.O. Box 80 ☎ (809) 332-2270 (800) CLUBMED fax: (809) 332-2691	FAP	600 beds	call for rates	A, M, V	B, S, BT, T, G	rates vary according to point of origin—airfare included
Tuckaway Motel P.O. Box 45 Governor's Harbour ☎ (809) 332-2005 (809) 332-2013 (809) 332-2591	EP	10	$60	none		in town, fruit trees

ELEUTHERA

Establishment, Mailing Address, Telephone	Meal Plans Offered	No. Rooms	Double Room (in Season)	Credit Cards	Facilities	Other
Rainbow Inn P.O. Box 53 Governor's Harbour Hatchet Bay ☎ (809) 335-0294 (800) 327-0787 fax: (809) 335-0294	EP, MAP	10	$100	A	B, T, P	good restaurant (closed May–June and Sept.–Nov.), hotel open year-round
Scriven's Villas P.O. Box 35 Governor's Harbour ☎ (809) 322-2503	EP	4	$45	none	B, M/D, T, G, SC	

Rock Sound

Establishment, Mailing Address, Telephone	Meal Plans Offered	No. Rooms	Double Room (in Season)	Credit Cards	Facilities	Other
Cartwright's Ocean View Cottages Tarpum Bay ☎ (809) 334-4215	EP	5	$80	none	B	bike and moped rentals
Cotton Bay Club P.O. Box 28 Rock Sound Eleuthera ☎ (809) 334-6101 (800) 221-4542 fax: (809) 334-6082	MAP, EP	75	$260	A, M, V	P, B, F, T, G	7 miles of beach, 18-hole golf course, bike rentals
Edwina's Place P.O. Box 30 Rock Sound ☎ (809) 334-2094	EP	9	$75	none	P	closed Sept.
Ethel's Cottages P.O. Box 27 Tarpum Bay ☎ (809) 334-4233	EP	18	$70	A, B	F	
Hilton's Haven Tarpum Bay ☎ (809) 334-4281 (800) 327-0787	EP, MAP	10	$53 (EP)	none	BT, F	

ELEUTHERA

Establishment, Mailing Address, Telephone	Meal Plans Offered	No. Rooms	Double Room (in Season)	Credit Cards	Facilities	Other
Ingraham's Beach Inn P.O. Box 7 Tarpum Bay ☎ (809) 334-4263 (809) 334-4285	EP	12 (apts.)	$130		B	10 percent discount for 10-day stay or longer

THE EXUMAS

Establishment, Mailing Address, Telephone	Meal Plans Offered	No. Rooms	Double Room (in Season)	Credit Cards	Facilities	Other
Happy People Marina Staniel Cay Exuma ☎ (809) 355-2008	EP	8	$90	none	B, BT, F, SC	
Peace and Plenty Beach Inn P.O. Box 29055 George Town ☎ (809) 336-2551 fax: (809) 336-2253	EP, MAP	16	$120	A, M, V	B, P	
Peace & Plenty Bonefish Lodge P.O. Box 29173 George Town (809) 345-5556	FAP	8	$		F, BT	fishing guides, fly-tying facilities
Club Peace and Plenty P.O. Box 55 George Town ☎ (809) 336-2551 (800) 525-2210 fax: (809) 336-2093	MAP, EP	35	$110	A, M, V	P, BT, F, SC,M/D	free bikes, free ferry to Stocking Island, no children under 6 years, club on own beach
Marshall's Guest House P.O. Box 27 George Town ☎ (809) 336-2571	EP	12	$75	M	F	

THE EXUMAS

Establishment, Mailing Address, Telephone	Meal Plans Offered	No. Rooms	Double Room (in Season)	Credit Cards	Facilities	Other
Regatta Point P.O. Box 6 George Town ☎ (809) 336-2206 (800) 327-0787 fax: (809) 336-2046	EP	5	$105	V, M	B	all units have kitchens, good view for regatta
Coconut Cove Hotel P.O. Box 29299 George Town ☎ (809) 336-2659		11	$153	V, M		fresh water pool, bath robes
Staniel Cay Yacht Club c/o Island Services 1100 Lee Wagener Blvd. #309 Ft. Lauderdale, FL. 33315 ☎ (809) 355-2024 or (809) 355-2011 fax: (809) 355-2044	FAP	6	$195 (FAP)	A, M, V	BT, F, SC, WS, B	free sailboats, wind-surfing for guests 3 nights and more
Two Turtles Inn P.O. Box 51 George Town ☎ (809) 336-2545 fax: (809) 336-2528	EP	12	$90	A, M, V		bicycles, some kitchens

INAGUA

Establishment, Mailing Address, Telephone	Meal Plans Offered	No. Rooms	Double Room (in Season)	Credit Cards	Facilities	Other
Ford's Inagua Inn Matthew Town Inagua ☎ 277	EP, MAP	5	$50	none	F, M/D, PDF	
Kirk & Eleanor's Walk-Inn Gregory Street Matthew Town Inagua	EP		$80			

INAGUA

Establishment, Mailing Address, Telephone	Meal Plans Offered	No. Rooms	Double Room (in Season)	Credit Cards	Facilities	Other
Main House Matthew Town, Inagua ☎ 267	EP	5	$50	none		

LONG ISLAND

Establishment, Mailing Address, Telephone	Meal Plans Offered	No. Rooms	Double Room (in Season)	Credit Cards	Facilities	Other
Stella Maris Inn P.O. Box 105 Stella Maris ☎ (809) 336-2106 (305) 359-8236 (800) 426-0466 fax: (305) 359-8238	EP, MAP	50	$125	A, M, V	B, P, BT, F, SC, T, S, PDF	exceptional diving program, 3 pools, pets allowed
Thompson Bay Inn P.O. Box SM 30-123 Stella Maris ☎ Salt Pond Operator	EP	8	$60	none		some apartments, good food

SAN SALVADOR/RUM CAY

Establishment, Mailing Address, Telephone	Meal Plans Offered	No. Rooms	Double Room (in Season)	Credit Cards	Facilities	Other
Club Med Columbus Isle San Salvador ☎ (809) 331-2000 (800) CLUB MED fax: (809) 331-2222	FAP	432 beds	call for rates	A, M, V	WSF, S, BT, T, B	rates vary according to place of origin—airfare included
Riding Rock Inn 701 Southwest 48th St. Ft. Lauderdale, FL 33315 ☎ (809) 332-2631	EP, MAP, FAP	24	$100	V	P, T, B	dive packages available, on rocky beach (sandy beach nearby)

SAN SALVADOR/RUM CAY

Establishment, Mailing Address, Telephone	Meal Plans Offered	No. Rooms	Double Room (in Season)	Credit Cards	Facilities	Other
Ocean View Villas North Victoria San Salvador Bahamas ☎ (809) 331-2694 fax: (809) 322-5080	EP	3	$55	none		
Rum Cay Club P.O. Box 22396 Ft. Lauderdale, FL 33335 ☎ (305) 467-8355 (800) 334-6869		closed inde- finitely				B, SC, F

INDEX

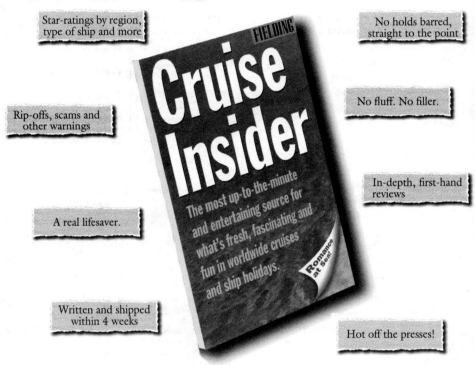

Order Your Fielding Travel Guides Today

BOOKS	$ EA.
Amazon	$16.95
Australia	$12.95
Bahamas	$12.95
Belgium	$16.95
Bermuda	$12.95
Borneo	$16.95
Brazil	$16.95
Britain	$16.95
Budget Europe	$16.95
Caribbean	$18.95
Europe	$16.95
Far East	$19.95
France	$16.95
Hawaii	$15.95
Holland	$15.95
Italy	$16.95
Kenya's Best Hotels, Lodges & Homestays	$16.95
London Agenda	$12.95
Los Angeles Agenda	$12.95
Malaysia and Singapore	$16.95
Mexico	$16.95
New York Agenda	$12.95
New Zealand	$12.95
Paris Agenda	$12.95
Portugal	$16.95
Scandinavia	$16.95
Seychelles	$12.95
Southeast Asia	$16.95
Spain	$16.95
The World's Great Voyages	$16.95
The World's Most Dangerous Places	$19.95
The World's Most Romantic Places	$16.95
Vacation Places Rated	$19.95
Vietnam	$16.95
Worldwide Cruises	$17.95

To order by phone call toll-free 1-800-FW-2-GUIDE

(VISA, MasterCard and American Express accepted.)

To order by mail send your check or money order,
including $2.00 per book for shipping and handling (sorry, no COD's) to:
Fielding Worldwide, Inc. 308 S. Catalina Avenue, Redondo Beach, CA 90277 U.S.A.

Get 10% off your order by saying "Fielding Discount"
or send in this page with your order

Favorite People, Places & Experiences

ADDRESS:	NOTES:

Name

Address

Telephone

Name

Address

Telephone

Name

Address

Telephone

Name

Address

Telephone

Name

Address

Telephone

Name

Address

Telephone

Name

Address

Telephone

Favorite People, Places & Experiences

ADDRESS:	NOTES:

Name

Address

Telephone

Name

Address

Telephone

Name

Address

Telephone

Name

Address

Telephone

Name

Address

Telephone

Name

Address

Telephone

Name

Address

Telephone

Favorite People, Places & Experiences

ADDRESS:	NOTES:

Name

Address

Telephone

Name

Address

Telephone

Name

Address

Telephone

Name

Address

Telephone

Name

Address

Telephone

Name

Address

Telephone

Name

Address

Telephone

Favorite People, Places & Experiences

ADDRESS:	NOTES:

Name

Address

Telephone

Name

Address

Telephone

Name

Address

Telephone

Name

Address

Telephone

Name

Address

Telephone

Name

Address

Telephone

Name

Address

Telephone

Favorite People, Places & Experiences

ADDRESS:	NOTES:

Name

Address

Telephone

Name

Address

Telephone

Name

Address

Telephone

Name

Address

Telephone

Name

Address

Telephone

Name

Address

Telephone

Name

Address

Telephone

Favorite People, Places & Experiences

ADDRESS:	NOTES:

Name

Address

Telephone

Name

Address

Telephone

Name

Address

Telephone

Name

Address

Telephone

Name

Address

Telephone

Name

Address

Telephone

Name

Address

Telephone